A Political Theology for the US–Mexico Borderlands

I0084283

Political and Public Theologies

COMPARISONS – COALITIONS – CRITIQUES

VOLUME 6

The titles published in this series are listed at *brill.com/ppt*

A Political Theology for the US–Mexico Borderlands

"Can These Bones Live?"

By

Bryan M. Ellrod

BRILL

LEIDEN | BOSTON

Ellrod, Bryan. "The Remembrance of Dismembered Bodies: The Promise and Challenge of Mourning in the Southwestern Borderlands." Body and Religion 5, no. 2 (2021): 204-21. doi:10.1558/bar.22145.

Cover illustration: Airport Mesa. Used with permission of the photographer, Travis William Clark.

Library of Congress Cataloging-in-Publication Data

Names: Ellrod, Bryan M., editor.
Title: A political theology for the US-Mexico borderlands / edited by Bryan M. Ellrod.
Description: Boston, Massachusetts : Brill, [2025] | Series: Political and public theologies, 2666-9218 ; volume 6 | Includes bibliographical references and index.
Identifiers: LCCN 2024057527 (print) | LCCN 2024057528 (ebook) | ISBN 9789004721517 (paperback) | ISBN 9789004721524 (ebook)
Subjects: LCSH: United States–Emigration and immigration–Government policy. | United States–Emigration and immigration–Religious aspects. | Mexico–Emigration and immigration–Religious aspects | Emigration and immigration–Religious aspects–Christianity. | Emigration and immigration–Moral and ethical aspects. | Christian ethics–United States. | Political theology–United States. | Mexican-American Border Region–Social conditions
Classification: LCC JV6483 .P655 2025 (print) | LCC JV6483 (ebook) | DDC 320.55/30973–dc23/eng/20250208
LC record available at https://lccn.loc.gov/2024057527
LC ebook record available at https://lccn.loc.gov/2024057528

Typeface for the Latin, Greek, and Cyrillic scripts: "Brill". See and download: brill.com/brill-typeface.

ISSN 2666-9218
ISBN 978-90-04-72151-7 (paperback)
ISBN 978-90-04-72152-4 (e-book)
DOI 10.1163/9789004721524

This book is printed on acid-free paper and produced in a sustainable manner.

Contents

Preface: Besetting Danger

Philosophy does not begin in an experience of wonder, as ancient tradition contends, ... but rather in the indeterminate but palpable sense that something desired has not been fulfilled, that a fantastic effort has failed. Philosophy begins in disappointment.

　　—SIMON CRITCHLEY, *Infinitely Demanding*

• • •

The hand of the Lord came upon me, and he brought me out by the spirit of the Lord and set me down in the middle of a valley; it was full of bones. He led me all around them; there were very many lying in the valley, and they were very dry. He said to me, "Mortal, can these bones live?"

　　—EZEKIEL 37.1–3

• •
•

"Mortal, can these bones live?" God addresses this question to Ezekiel in a moment of profound disappointment as he stands in a bleak landscape surrounded by dry bones. No breath disturbs the air. No word breaks the silence. No sign of life makes itself known amid the desolation. However, even if the prophet finds himself transported to a strange place, these are not the bones of strangers. They are the bones of his own people laid waste. Moreover, the question posed by the divine is not an abstract question about bodily resurrection in some heavenly hereafter.[1] It is an immanent question of concrete, corporate redemption amid material history.

"Your house and your kingdom shall be made sure forever before me; your throne shall be established forever." (2 Sam. 7.16) This was God's promise to David. His kingdom was to be God's covenant community on Earth.[2] David swore

---

1　See Kathryn Pfisterer Darr, "The Book of Ezekiel," in *New Interpreters Bible Commentary*, vol. 6, 12 vols. (Nashville: Abingdon Press, 1994), 1497–1500.

2　For more extended treatments of Ezekiel's theological response to the Davidic Covenant, see Pfisterer Darr, "The Book of Ezekiel," 1073–1107; & Roseanne Liebermann, "Justice, Righteousness, and the Davidic Dispute in Jeremiah and Ezekiel," *Vetus Testament* 73 (2022): 62–81.

that, under his rule and that of his heirs, the kingdom would bear witness to God's power, justice, and steadfast love. They would not accomplish this task by their word but by their distinctive form of life. Theirs would be a life dedicated to the praise of the Most High and the care of the lowly—those with whom their God most closely identified. Guided by the statutes and judgments condensed in the Levitical Holiness Code, the nation's 'shepherd kings' would be first among these witnesses.[3] Both domestically and before the nations, they would model a life faithful to the divine sovereign that had elevated them from the pastures to the palace.

Yet, none of this came to pass. Ezekiel's thirty-seventh chapter finds the prophet in the wake of this fantastic effort's failure. War and strife tore the Davidic Monarchy apart. Yet, David's afflictions had not assailed him from without. They came from within his own household. Even before his death, his children's desires for the throne sewed bloody enmities between them.[4] After David's death, civil war fractured the united monarchy, and competing princes set the north of the kingdom against the south. Ultimately, neither side would hold to the covenant God made with David. Neither would practice fidelity to the statutes and judgments of the Holiness Code. Neither would live. With time, the northern and the southern kings learned to prefer avarice and dominion to care for the lowly. Only after corruption had rotted their kingdoms from within, did judgment come in the guise of foreign conquerors. In 721 BCE, the Northern Kingdom of Israel fell to an invading Assyrian Force. The Southern Kingdom of Judea would linger on a little longer. However, in 597 BCE, Nebuchadrezzar II and the Babylonian Empire sacked Jerusalem, destroyed its temple, captured its king, and sent its elites into exile.

Ezekiel was among the exiles at Tel Abib in Babylon. He minced no words when he attributed the catastrophe to the moral depravity of Israel's kings:

> Woe, you shepherds of Israel who have been feeding yourselves! Should not shepherds feed the sheep? You eat the fat; you clothe yourselves with the wool; you slaughter the fatted calves, but you do not feed the sheep.

---

3 On the Levitical Law's significance to the structure and themes in Ezekiel, including Ezek. 37, see Preston Sprinkle, "Law and Life: Leviticus 18.5 and the Literary Framework of Ezekiel," *Journal for the Study of the Old Testament* 31 (2007): 275–93.

4 2 Sam. 13–15 depicts a struggle between his sons Amnon and Absalom following Amnon's rape of Absalom's sister Tamar. After sheltering his sister in his house for two years, Absalom would murder his half-brother Amnon and flee his father David. Although Absalom would eventually be reconciled to his father, this would not stop him from attempting to usurp the throne. Likewise, 1 Kgs 1–2 recounts a struggle of succession at the end of David's life. This struggle included his son Adonijah's effort to usurp the throne, Solomon's appointment as heir, and Adonijah's execution.

You have not strengthened the weak; you have not healed the sick; you have not bound up the injured; you have not brought back the strays; you have not sought the lost, but with force and harshness you have ruled them. (Ezek. 34.2–4)

Derelict of their responsibilities, Israel's rulers had abandoned the form of life that was to be the content of their witness.[5] In so doing, they had alienated themselves from the very source of their life: the God that had brought them out of captivity in Egypt, the God that placed a lowly shepherd on the throne, the God that dwelt with the least and the marginalized. Thus, the nation that was to endure forever and manifest God's presence to all the Earth was scattered across its face instead. With their throne and temple consigned to the ash heap, Ezekiel's fellow exiles believed themselves to be living after the end of their history. "Our bones are dried up, and our hope is lost," the lament went out, "we are cut off completely." (Ezek. 37.11) Ezekiel's commentators have noted that to be 'cut off' connotes more than bodily death. It connotes more than a kind of symbolic ritual death as well. As Saul M Olyan observes, in the Hebrew Bible, to be 'cut off' from the hand of God means to have passed from the divine memory and, by consequence, to inhabit a place of utter oblivion where even God cannot intervene.[6] For Israel's diasporic community in Tel Abib, the Babylonian conquest signaled the Davidic Covenant's total revocation and the collapse not only of their political system but also the nihilation of the religious order of meaning that grounded their self-understanding. Dry bones

---

5   Although most commentators agree that Ezekiel's criticisms are principally focused on the kingdom's ritual transgressions and its failures in international politics, commentators like Robert Jenson and Margaret Odell note that these concerns are not mutually exclusive of the concerns with social justice that occupy other exilic prophets. Attending to the rhetorical significance of Ezekiel's depictions of the kings' 'harsh rule,' Jenson notes that this language was typically reserved to juxtapose foreign rulers, who oppressed their people, to Israel's princes, whose charge was to care for the people. In effect, this passage proposes that the kings had forgotten their purpose and become indistinguishable from their foreign rivals. Noting references to the consumption of the fatted portions of the sheep, Odell identifies in Ezek. 34 an overlap between ritual orthopraxis and social justice. To eat the fat of an animal was prohibited, since this portion was to be God's part. Transposed into the political, this imagery suggests that the leaders' avaricious consumption of their people was at once an abuse of power that transgressed both the people and the sovereignty of the divine. See Robert Jenson, *Ezekiel*, The Brazos Theological Commentary on the Bible (Grand Rapids: Brazos Press, 2009); & Margaret Odell, *Ezekiel*. Vol. 16. Smyth & Helwys Bible Commentary (Macon: Smyth & Helwys Publishing, 2005); c.f. Andrew Mein, *Ezekiel and the Ethics of Exile* (New York: Oxford University Press, 2001).

6   See Saul M. Olyan, "'We Are Utterly Cut Off': Some Possible Nuances in Ezek 37:11," *The Catholic Biblical Quarterly* 65 (2003): 43–51.

without hope, the exiles were a people without a future, already consigned to the afterlife.

Critics have noted similarities between Ezekiel's valley of dry bones and Ancient Near Eastern treaty curses for defeated armies.[7] Nevertheless, the text makes clear that the imagery of a military host laid waste functions as a synecdoche for the larger calamity that began with the kingdom's moral decay and culminated with the Babylonian conquest and exile. God's question regards the possibility of redemption for the whole house of Israel. Can these people be reconciled with the ideals that once constituted their distinctive form of life? Can their polity recover its purpose even after its downfall? Do they yet retain a future, or are they the last vestiges of a people all but forgotten from the world's (and from God's) memory? "Mortal, can these bones live?" As the words hang in the silence, Ezekiel does not know how to answer. If the lament is true, and if to be 'cut off' from God's hand is to be beyond the hope even of divine intervention, then the answer, it seems, must be 'no.' From the valley's floor, he can only sound the question back to heaven: "Oh Lord God, you alone know." (37.3)

Though the war with Babylon had ended, Ezekiel undertook his prophetic mission amid besetting danger. As far as the exiles could see, whatever hope there might have been for any form of reconciliation, whether with themselves or with their God, was razed with the city from which they had been dispersed. To be without hope was to be without a future. It was to be stranded in a time after history when the possibility of all meaningful action had evaporated.[8] The exiles could live in relative peace in Tel Abib. They could work, eat, sleep, and carry on the routines necessary to maintain biological life. No one would disturb them now. They posed no threat to the Babylonian Empire. However, this existence would be a form of life unrecognizable under the old rubrics that once organized their self-understanding.[9] It would be no life at all, really, but

---

7 See Andrew R. Davis, "A Near Eastern Treaty Parallel to Ezekiel's Dry Bones," *Vetus Testamentum* 68 (2018): 337–345.

8 For a compelling account of the problem of discerning moral meaning in the wake of social collapse, see Jonathan Lear, *Radical Hope: Ethics in the Face of Cultural Devastation* (Cambridge: Harvard University Press, 2006).

9 See Andrew Mein, *Ezekiel and the Ethics of Exile*. Attending to the sociological context of Ezekiel's ethics, Mein proposes that the exiles must be understood as a people positioned between two different moral worlds, one defined by the concerns and possibilities posited by their former elite status, and the other by their new status as exiles. In a brief review of Mein's book, Thomas Renz raises an important question as to whether these two social-moral horizons could reasonably be expected to add up to a single coherent moral vision. See Thomas Renz, "Ezekiel and the Ethics of Exile by Andrew Mein," *The Journal of Theological Studies* 54 (2003): 180–182.

rather an afterlife. In this situation, with violence abated, they would face the besetting danger of nihilism.

This book contends that the same question God posed to Ezekiel in the sixth century bce and the same danger by which it was accompanied find us again today in the twenty-first century CE. Like Ezekiel, we, too, find ourselves on the knife's edge between hope and despair at a historical threshold between what was to be, what is, and what may yet be. In the pages that follow, I transpose Ezekiel's question to another valley—another valley of dry bones—one that spans the United States-Mexico borderline. In the valleys of the Sonoran Desert, where thousands of migrants have lost their lives in the effort to enter the United States, we are faced with the challenge of realizing justice in a violently unjust world. To consign these migrants to a lonely and anonymous demise in the desert, on the one hand, seems to amount to an ethical failure that brutalizes not only their humanity but also our own. On the other hand, to surrender the political association's right to secure its borders and determine its membership also seems to confront us with a fundamental loss of liberty and capacity for collective self-determination.[10] In the borderlands, that is, the crisis of migrant mortalities reveals a discontinuity between our ethical and political self-understandings, between our conditions as vulnerable interdependent creatures and as free actors. This discontinuity has been rendered particularly painful by border enforcement strategies that have sought to purchase political stability at the expense of migrants' lives and freedom with contempt for interdependence.

Lest the focus on the United States context make this problem appear too idiosyncratic, I hasten to note that, for well over a decade, a rising tide of ethno-nationalism and xenophobia has been making its way through Europe and the United Kingdom. Moreover, like the United States, which has leveraged the Sonoran Desert to halt migrants' advance, the European Union has relied on the Mediterranean Sea, going so far as to criminalize sailors and organizations who would pull migrants from the waves.[11] The bones in the valleys of the

---

10   This point finds its clearest articulation in Michael Walzer's *Spheres of Justice*, to which I will return in due time, but it has also found recent expression in Michael Blake, *Justice, Migration, and Mercy* (New York: Oxford University Press, 2022).

11   See, for instance, the legal travails of the Germany-based humanitarian organization Sea Watch. Sea Watch uses its ships to carry out systematic search and rescue operations designed to mitigate drowning deaths in the Mediterranean Sea. In August of 2022, an EU Court of Justice took up a suit between Sea Watch and the Italian government after two of the aid group's ships allowed rescued persons to disembark in Palermo and Porto Empedocle. Although the court's 2022

Sonoran, therefore, find their counterpart in the bodies of the drowned that are washed up on European shores. I fix this book's attention on the US–Mexico borderlands not because I believe them to be wholly unique but because I believe that here, on this ground, we see playing out the same forms of identarian boundary maintenance that have inspired violence and cost lives at international lines, in the American interior, and abroad.

"Can these bones live?" As for Ezekiel, this question is for us at once ethical, political, and theological. As ethical subjects, can we be reconciled to those who have already lost their lives in the crossing? Can our efforts to mourn these lives inspire positive action for those who remain among the living? What about the polity in whose name these lives are denied? Can it be justified to those it excludes? Finally, if, as Knud Ejler Løgstrup put it, the individual's relation to God is determined nowhere else than in their relationships with other human beings, then to what extent does the possibility of reconciliation between human beings and God yet endure in the Sonoran?[12] Have we cut ourselves off entirely? Each of these questions is exceedingly complex, and none permits a simple answer. Nevertheless, this book demands hope and refuses to despair over the impasses that, for decades, have stifled reforms to United States immigration and border enforcement policies. To succumb to the besetting danger, to acquiesce to nihilism, is not merely to withdraw ourselves from the public square but to abandon our responsibility for the thousands who continue to undertake perilous crossings on hostile terrain.

---

ruling underscored seafarers' "fundamental duty to render assistance to persons in danger or distress at sea," it nevertheless acknowledged that humanitarian vessels, after disembarking their passengers, may be subject to safety inspections by port State authorities. (Court of Justice of the European Union. "Ships of Humanitarian Organizations Systematically Carrying out Activities Relating to the Search for and Rescue of Persons at Sea May Be Subject to Controls by the Port State," Press Release [Luxembourg: Court of Justice of the European Union, August 1, 2022]) In the years since the ruling, conflicts have continued as port State authorities have, on multiple occasions, seized vessels belonging to Sea Watch and other humanitarian organizations. (See Crispian Balmer, "Italy Impounds Three Rescue Ships as Migrant Numbers Soar," *Reuters*, August 23, 2023, sec. Europe. https://www.reuters.com/world/europe/italy-impounds-three-rescue-ships-migrant-numbers-soar-2023-08-23/.)

12   Knud Ejler Løgstrup, *The Ethical Demand* (Notre Dame: University of Notre Dame Press, 1997), 4.

Acknowledgments

I owe a great many thanks to a great number of people. Professors, mentors, colleagues, family, and friends, who helped nurture this project, from its inception as a half-formed idea, to its time as a tottering prospectus, then as a babbling dissertation, and now as a book that attempts to speak with clarity and confidence as if come of age. No effort to name the sum of them would be complete. No accounting will do them justice. I offer only the following brief remarks, for whatever they may be worth.

Timothy P Jackson and Ted A Smith directed this project from prospectus to defense. They challenged my understanding of love, justice, law, politics, sanctity, dignity, and eschatology. In this way, they nurtured a theological analysis that would treat its subject matter with rigor and care. They spent hundreds of hours reading drafts, writing feedback, and answering questions. They endeavored to teach me to articulate my arguments clearly while attending to my interlocutors with critical charity. Ellen Ott Marshall and Vincent Lloyd's thoughtful comments at the defense encouraged me to carry these arguments further and to consider their bearing on the intersections of care and justice, ethics and aesthetics.

I owe further thanks to Elizabeth Bounds, Pamela Hall, and the faculty of Emory University's Graduate Division of Religion, who directed the education of an eager (if, at times, confused and slow-learning) student. Throughout my education, I had the privilege of learning alongside brilliant colleagues like Nicole Symmonds, Jared Jones, Joi Orr, Emmy Corey, Shari Mackinson, Cara Curtis, Scott Schnur, Silas Allard, and Nelly Wamaitha, to name only a few. They have not only been indispensable partners in learning but also cherished friends.

In the transition from dissertation to book, Ulrich Schmiedel and the editorial team for Political and Public Theologies have helped me further refine my thinking about vulnerability, political theology's relationship to realism, and its potency for envisioning that world which is already casting its light on our own.

I am grateful to my parents, Louise and Matthew Ellrod, who, from the outset, have encouraged their children to pursue the beautiful, the true, and the good and, with peace and good humor, have given them the security to do so. There are others still. Jon and Emily Motta, Seth Spencer, Bradley Burroughs, Elizabeth Whiting, John Carter, Nisrine Rahal, and my brothers, Stephen and Tim. However, I would close with a word of thanks to my wife, Courtney, for her support, passion, and levity. She has been a sounding board, a critic, and, more importantly, a steadfast life partner.

To these people and so many others, I owe a debt of gratitude that I will not soon repay. Whatever insights this book has captured would not have been possible without them. Whatever errors and obscurities endure in its pages, do so despite them.

Figures

Introduction

The border is a line that birds cannot see.
The border is a beautiful piece of paper folded carelessly in half.
The border is where flint first met steel, starting a century of fires.
> —ALBERTO RÍOS, "The Border: A Double Sonnet"

∙ ∙ ∙

A border is a dividing line, a narrow strip along a steep edge. A borderland is a vague and undetermined place created by the emo-
tional residue of an unnatural boundary. It is in a constant state of
transition. The prohibited and forbidden are its inhabitants.
> —GLORIA ANZALDÚA, *Borderlands / La Frontera*

∙∙
∙∙

1 The Bones in the Valley

There are bones in the valleys. There are thousands of them. For all its beauty,
the Sonoran Desert is an extreme environment. It stretches north, from
Sonora, Mexico, into Arizona and west into California, claiming roughly one
hundred thousand square miles in its expanse. In the northern desert, rugged
mountain ranges carve the terrain into a maze of jagged peaks and sweltering
valleys. Migrants crossing from Mexico into the United States face the challenge of navigating this maze. Some take their chances on the mountain paths.
Most make their way through the valleys. Here, daytime temperatures regu-
larly exceed one hundred degrees Fahrenheit and soar as high as 118° F.[1] To
cope with this heat, travelers need to consume at least two gallons of water
each day.[2] However, water sufficient for a days-long journey is too heavy to

---

1   National Park Service, "Sonoran Desert Network Ecosystems," Sonoran Desert Inventory &
    Monitoring Network, accessed July 10, 2021, https://nps.gov/im/sodn/ecosystems.htm.
2   Even after they have crossed over the U.S.-Mexico line, many migrants will spend 3–5 days
    in the wilderness before reaching civilization. On the dangers posed by the desert heat, see
    Associated Press, "Border Officials Warn of Heat Dangers in South Arizona," AP News, June 11,
    2021, https://apnews.com/article/az-state-wire-arizona-immigration-environment-and-na-
    ture-cda9efe39c45b1f5cdd2187390c2d730.

carry, and naturally occurring water is scarce. In the Sonoran, some years see no more than three inches of rain.[3] The desert's flora and fauna have adapted to this arid setting but are indifferent to human needs. Saguaros, ironwoods, and acacias offer sparse respite from the sun's beating rays. Coyotes, vultures, and hoverflies are not picky about the carrion they consume.

Many never find their way through the maze. Hundreds of human remains are recovered from the Sonoran each year.[4] The desert takes its share. In many cases, it leaves behind little more than disarticulated bones. Sometimes, it permits them the company of the last mementos too precious to abandon: family photographs, bibles, letters from loved ones.[5] Other times, it intermingles them with refuse: empty water bottles, backpacks, scraps of clothing. Be they precious or otherwise, the desert has no taste for these things. Together with the bones, they bear witness to a life consigned to the dust. But it is a witness of fragments. The details of the life no longer hang together in any narrative unity. The ligature of intention and circumstance that once connected them is mortified and swept away by the desert winds. They are like scraps of pages, torn from different chapters of a biography and tossed haphazardly onto the earth.

The Sonoran claims not only victims, then, but their memories as well. Their biographies held under erasure, the bones in the valleys do not so much tell a story as demand one.[6] However, a gulf of uncertainty separates the fragments and those who encounter them. In this gap, new narratives propose themselves. Here lies an unlucky gambler. They knew the risks. Nevertheless, they

3   National Park Service, "Sonoran Desert Network Ecosystems."
4   2021 proved one of the deadliest, with 728 migrant deaths and disappearances along the US–Mexico border. See Melissa Bock, "Strict Border Policies Contribute to Rising Immigrant Deaths," National Public Radio, July 2, 2022, https://www.npr.org/2022/07/02/1109557989/strict-border-policies-contribute-to-rising-immigrant-deaths#:~:text=Immigration%20advocates%20warn%20that%20strict,immigration%20for%20the%20Houston%20Chronicle.
5   Jason De León, *The Land of Open Graves: Living and Dying on the Migrant Trail* (Oakland: University of California Press, 2015), 170ff.
6   Arizona-based Humanitarian aid organization Humane Borders has partnered with the Pima County Medical Examiners Office to create a map of migrant mortalities. This map records each of the locations at which human remains have been discovered over the last thirty years. Wherever possible, it also lists the decedent's identity and cause of death. However, in more than a third of all cases, the remains cannot be identified. Of the 448 decedents logged in Humane Borders' database over the last two years, 238 remain unidentified. In an effort to overcome this erasure, another partnered organization, the Colibrí Center, works tirelessly to match unidentified remains with missing persons reports. See Humane Borders, "Map of Migrant Mortality," Humane Borders, accessed July 10, 2021, https://humaneborders.org/migrant-death-mapping/; & The Colibrí Center for Human Rights, "About Us," accessed July 10, 2021, https://colibricenter.org.

wagered that if they could beat the odds and escape the maze, they would become wealthy in the North. They misplayed the odds ... These are the bones of a weary and frightened asylum-seeker. She fled persecution at home in hopes of finding refuge in the north. But in her flight from one danger, she lost her bearings and stumbled into another ... These are the remains of a smuggler. He made his fortune trafficking narcotics and firearms. He might have done great harm had the Sonoran not stopped him ... Fictions such as these attempt to fill out the chapters of the biographies from which the scattered scraps are torn. These stories work feverishly to piece together identities for unknown sojourners. They attempt to explain how human bones came to reside in this desolate place. Of course, the bones rarely offer final confirmation for one narrative or another.

Nevertheless, at stake in these narratives is our understanding of the ethical relationships that persist between the living and those who have died. The narrative process advances by naming familiar character types and laying out conventional plots. Ostensibly, what we owe to a gambler differs from what we owe to a smuggler or an asylum-seeker. The gambler knowingly assumes her risks, and whatever results from her wager is hers and hers alone. We might regret the gambler's loss, but we bear no responsibility for it. No moral relationship, it would seem, persists between us and them. Not so with the asylum-seeker or the smuggler. The asylum-seeker does not choose risk. Instead, she is exposed to it. Sympathetic to her plight, if we have a refuge to offer, we might feel obliged to provide it. Her death is not only regrettable but bespeaks a possible failure of responsibility. The smuggler trafficking in narcotics or firearms, on the other hand, creates risk for others that they do not choose for themselves. His death might be regrettable, but we might also see it as justice served. Of course, these are highly simplified cases of moral reasoning. Even so, these fictions illustrate our judgments' dependence on a blend of relationships and identities, chosen and unchosen, and distributed in the narrative contexts that bind actors together.[7]

---

7 On the relationship between justice and narrative, particularly as it bears on the Christian ethics of migration, see Tisha Rajendra, *Migrants and Citizens: Justice and Responsibility in the Ethics of Immigration* (Grand Rapids: William B. Eerdmans Publishing Company, 2017). Rajendra not only advances the role narrative plays in identifying the specific rights and corresponding duties that persist between actors typically considered 'strangers' to one another, she also shows how a more accurate understanding of migration systems requires us to seek out better, more detailed narratives than those on offer in popular American discourse. Even the 'gambler,' or 'economic migrant,' is never simply an atomized actor making their decisions in isolation. Rather, they make their decisions within a complex constellation of mitigating factors to which US economic and military policies have contributed.

Nevertheless, narrative only attempts to construe the ethical relationship. It does not form its basis.[8] Even where narrative fails or proves undecidable, the dead and their behests remain before the living. With their names and stories effaced, their demand is at once interminably strange and intimately familiar. Strange because we do not really know by whom we are being addressed. We cannot narrate with confidence the events and decisions that brought us together, nor can we determine the specific relationships and obligations these stories might distribute. Yet, intimately familiar because they address in us that which is exhausted neither in name nor in story. They address a more immediate relationship, no less undeniable for all its indeterminacy. They confront us with the interdependence and vulnerability common to each human animal. Regardless of our story, we are all subject to the dangers of thirst, fatigue, exposure, isolation, and exile. Lest these vulnerabilities would be our undoing, the living must hold one another in common trust.[9] Lingering at the crossing between life and death, the bones confront us with that choice which is the first condition of our ethical subjectivity: to affirm the good of the life denied and accept the human relationship as a responsibility, or deny the relationship, break trust, and attempt to leave the bones in the field.[10]

2   Politics as a Project of Redemption

Politics, in its loftiest aims, is a fantastic effort, a project of redemption, a means for reconciling ourselves with our humanity. For those engaged in this project, few ideals enjoy such widespread approval as that of the collective

---

8   Put another way, a narrative proposes 'justifying reasons' for the specific rights and duties accruing to different characters by virtue of their specific relationships. However, most of us live in the midst of multiple, overlapping narrative contexts. Where these narratives enter into contest, the rights and duties they propose take the form of hypothetical imperatives. When both contesting narratives enjoy relative internal coherence, the presence of justifying reasons does not yet determine either narrative's normativity for the actor. The transition from justifying reasons to convicting reasons, from hypothetical imperatives to categorical imperatives, requires an additional account of moral motivation. Following theorists like Knud Ejler Løgstrup and Simon Critchley, I contend that this motivation arises from a form of 'moral experience,' which narrative may articulate and mediate, but does not originate.
9   For a phenomenology of the 'trust' that persists between persons, see Knud Ejler Løgstrop, *The Ethical Demand* (Notre Dame: University of Notre Dame Press, 1997).
10   For more on the relationship between 'ethical demands' and the structures of 'ethical subjectivity,' see Simon Critchley, *Infinitely Demanding: Ethics of Commitment, Politics of Resistance* (New York: Verso, 2012).

self-determination of peoples. In the twentieth century, it found champions as far removed from one another on the ideological spectrum as Woodrow Wilson and Vladimir Lenin. Today, it encompasses commitments to popular sovereignty, territorial integrity, and decolonization. Standing as a peremptory norm of international law, the idea of collective self-determination asserts that politics is concerned not merely with the exercise of power but with power's alignment to the social meanings that a people hold in common. As political philosopher Michael Walzer explains, humans are "culture-producing creatures" that "create and inhabit worlds of shared meaning."[11] As legal scholar Robert Cover puts it, we constantly create, maintain, and inhabit a 'nomos,' a "normative universe ... of right and wrong, of lawful and unlawful, of valid and void."[12] This 'nomos,' Cover adds, "is as much 'our world' as is the physical universe of mass, energy, and momentum."[13] As they come to reflect our creative capacity for meaning-making, our political projects—our laws and institutions of governance—show themselves to be instruments for the creation of the world we long to inhabit, instruments of our collective self-becoming. The politics of self-determination, then, promises to reconcile us to our humanity by delivering us from bare nihilistic exercises of power and by empowering our defining creativity.

However, the predominating vision of a world of collectively self-determining peoples is also a vision of a world where boundaries and borders are necessary and just. This necessity arises from the fact of human plurality. Ensuring the coincidence of power and meaning requires the provision of jurisdictions. Only when such jurisdictional boundaries are set may peoples enjoy the freedom to determine their political status and pursue their economic, social, and cultural development unconstrained by interference from other states. However, the need for boundaries goes further than this. At its most basic level, self-determination entails the autonomous constitution of the very subject that is to exercise this freedom. In a word, the syntagm 'self-determination' regards both the political subject's freedom in *what* it determines *to do* and in *whom* it determines itself *to be*. If the latter is decided by the members who make up this collective subject, then the realization of self-determination requires some form of identity maintenance, which must inevitably include practices of admission and exclusion. Moreover, where a 'people' is understood as a landed group occupying a territory, the national character's

---

11   Michael Walzer, *Spheres of Justice: A Defense of Pluralism and Equality* (New York: Basic Books, 1983), 3.
12   Robert Cover, "Nomos and Narrative," *Harvard Law Review* 97 (Nov 1983): 4
13   Ibid, 5.

boundaries appear to coincide with the boundaries of their territory.[14] Thus, borders present themselves as natural sites of exclusion, and border policing as a necessary and just precondition of the international order. In the valleys of the Sonoran, however, the actual means by which exclusions are achieved complicate this vision's connection to material history.

It is not strictly by accident that the Sonoran has become a valley of dry bones. Rather, it is the consequence of a long-standing border enforcement strategy premised on a logic of 'prevention through deterrence' (hereafter, PTD).[15] Before PTD, most migrants could cross the international line with relative ease in populous, urban centers. Migrant mortalities were rare and, when they did occur, typically resulted from automobile accidents.[16] However, in the early 1990s, as Anglo-American resentment of Mexican and Latin American migrants swelled, so too did fears of a border out of control. Determined to combat impressions that the federal government was unwilling (or incapable) of securing the border, strategists with the Border Patrol adopted a more pro-active enforcement strategy, one already pioneered in El Paso and San Diego. This strategy began with the accumulation of enforcement officials at the international line in urban ports of entry. Faced with an increased risk of apprehension in populous areas, migrants would no longer see the old routes into the United States as viable avenues of entry. Avoiding apprehension would mean making their crossings in the wilderness.

At the strategy's core was a wager that if the costs of crossing could be raised to an unbearable degree, migrants would be deterred ever from undertaking the journey in the first place. In their *Strategic Plan* for 1994 and beyond, planners observed that "illegal entrants crossing through remote, uninhabited

---

14   The frequent coincidence of territorial borders and national identities is well observed in migration studies. For a concise summary of this logic, see Bastian A. Vollmer, "Border: Meanings, practices and fields in academia, politics, and public domains," in *Contested Concepts in Migration Studies*, ed. Ricard Zapata-Barrero, Dirk Jacobs, and Riva Kastory-ano, (New York: Routledge, 2021), 12–30.

15   It is not my aim in the present analysis to recount the history leading up to this policy's implementation. However, readers can find detailed descriptions of the policy and its history in Peter Andreas, *Border Games: Policing the U.S.-Mexico Divide* (Ithaca: Cornell University Press, 2009); De León, *The Land of Open Graves*; Timothy J. Dunn, *The Militarization of the U.S.-Mexico Border, 1978–1992: Low Intensity Conflict Doctrine Comes Home* (Austin: CMAS Books, 1996); Patrick W. Ettinger, *Imaginary Lines: Border Enforcement and the Origins of Undocumented Immigration, 1882–1930* (Austin: University of Texas Press, 2009); Joseph Nevins, *Operation Gatekeeper and Beyond: The War on "Illegals" and the Remaking of the U.S.-Mexico Boundary* (New York: Routledge, 2010).

16   See Wayne A. Cornelius, "Death at the Border: Efficacy and Unintended Consequences of US Immigration Control Policy," *Population and Development Review* 27 (2001): 669ff.

expanses of land ... can find themselves in mortal danger."[17] Leveraging this reality, the Border Patrol made efforts to divert migrant traffic "over more hostile terrain, less suited for crossing and more suited for enforcement."[18] In the years that followed, a complex array of surveillance technologies and physical barriers snaked out into the desert, pressing migrant trails ever deeper into remote wilderness. It is by state design, then, that migrants find themselves navigating the Sonoran's maze under the debilitating heat of a burning sun. For nearly three decades, border enforcement has deputized the desert as the primary agent for raising and extracting the cost of the crossing. At least 6,000 migrants have paid with their lives.[19] Yet, whether the wager has succeeded, whether the extreme cost of crossing has had the intended deterrent effect, is a matter of considerable doubt. Migrant apprehensions at the US–Mexico border continue to ebb and flow, and thousands of individuals and families continue to take their chances in the Sonoran's deadly maze.[20]

---

17   Doris Meissner, *Border Patrol Strategic Plan: 1994 and Beyond* (Washington, D.C.: United States Border Patrol, 1994), 2.

18   Ibid, 7.

19   Thomas E Sheridan & Randall H McGuire, *The Border and its Bodies: The Embodiment of Risk along the US–México Line* (Tucson: University of Arizona Press, 2022), 3. This number represents a *very* conservative estimate. In FY 2021, United States Customs and Border Patrol reported approximately 600 migrant deaths in that year alone. See Government Accountability Office, Committee on Homeland Security and Government Affairs, *Southwest Border: Border Patrol's Missing Migrant Program*, 2022.

20   In the years following PTD's implementation, there has been little evidence to confirm that the strategy has achieved its deterrent effect. From 1990 to 2000, the number of migrant encounters reported by the Border Patrol nearly doubled, rising from 852,506 to 1,643,679. Though the number of reported encounters fell between 2000 and 2017, with a low of 303,916, they have since rebounded to early levels, totaling 1,659,206 in 2021. See "What's Happening at the US–Mexico Border in 7 Charts," Pew Research Center, last modified November 9, 2021, https://www.pewresearch.org/short-reads/2021/11/09/whats-happening-at-the-u-s-mexico-border-in-7-charts/) The strategy's apparent ineffectiveness is not without theoretical explanation. PTD is premised on an economic theory of migration. According to this theory, migrants make their decisions to cross the border (lawfully or unlawfully) according to a form of cost-benefit analysis. If one accepts this rational actor theory, then the strategy's failure is difficult to explain. However, the rational actor theory is now widely discredited by migration theorists for its failure to account for the larger structural and systemic factors that shape migration between sending and receiving countries. With this in mind, we may reasonably surmise that PTD has failed to deliver its intended deterrent effect, because it presupposes a theory of action ill-adapted to its context. For a concise restatement of this theory and its criticisms, see Tisha Rajendra, "The Rational Agent or the Relational Agent: Moving from Freedom to Justice in Migration Systems Ethics," *Ethical Theory and Moral Practice* 18 (2015): 355–369.

In the years since PTD's implementation, non-government organizations like Humane Borders, along with county offices like the Pima Medical Examiners Office, have endeavored to track migrant mortalities. The images below are taken from the Arizona OpenGIS Initiative for Deceased Migrants.[21] These maps of migrant mortality are marked with a red dot at each site where migrant remains have been recovered. These markings are then supplemented with data on the identity, sex, age, reporting date, location, and cause of death for each set of remains. This data not only demonstrates the sharp rise in migrant mortalities that has followed PTD's implementation, but it also reveals a shift in the leading causes of migrant mortality. Whereas, before 1994, automobile accidents were the leading cause of death, since then, the most prevalent causes of death stem from exposure and dehydration. This shift reflects the 'hostility' of the desert environment.

Figures 1–3 below are the maps for 1993, the year before PTD's formal implementation; 2004, the tenth year following implementation; and 2022, the most recent complete year at the time of this writing.

FIGURE 1   Locations of 17 human remains recovered in 1993
SOURCE: CUSTOM MAP OF MIGRANT MORTALITIES [MAP], HUMANE BORDERS,
ACCESSED JULY 7, 2024, HTTPS://HUMANEBORDERS.INFO/APP/MAP.ASP

---

21   Map of Migrant Mortality, Humane Borders, accessed July 7, 2024, https://humaneborders.info/app/map.asp (accessed July 25, 2023)

FIGURE 2   Locations of 186 human remains recovered in 2004
SOURCE: CUSTOM MAP OF MIGRANT MORTALITIES [MAP], HUMANE
BORDERS, ACCESSED JULY 7, 2024, HTTPS://HUMANEBORDERS.INFO/APP/MAP.ASP

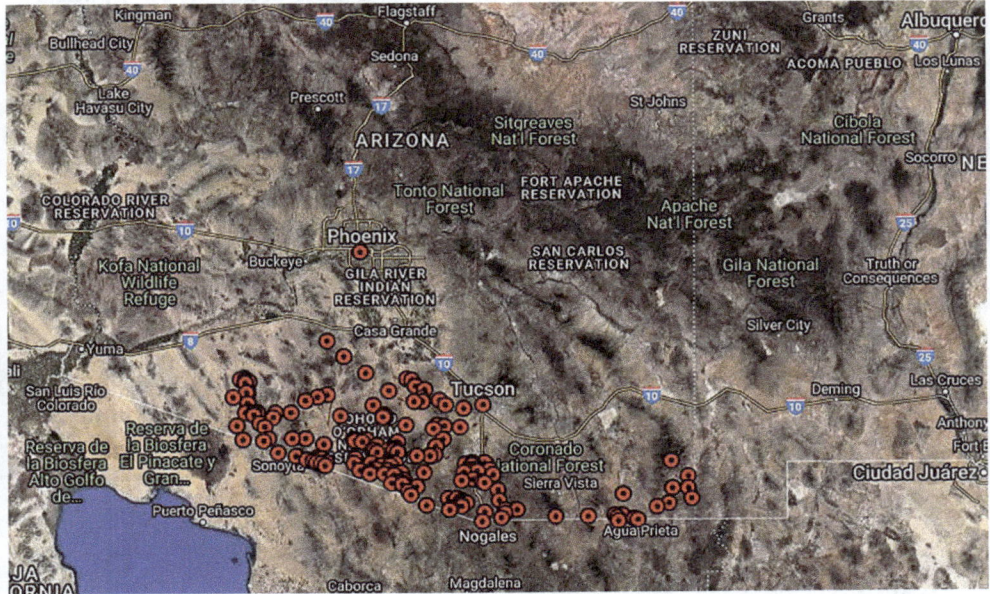

FIGURE 3   Locations of 174 human remains recovered in 2022
SOURCE: CUSTOM MAP OF MIGRANT MORTALITIES [MAP], HUMANE
BORDERS, ACCESSED JULY 7, 2024, HTTPS://HUMANEBORDERS.INFO/APP/MAP.ASP

Although PTD's deterrent effectiveness is uncertain, the strategy's lethality cannot be doubted. PTD's tactics derive their efficacy from the weaponization of our interdependence and vulnerability. However, this interdependence and vulnerability, no less than our creativity, constitute what it means to be human. Thus, PTD reveals a fundamental tension in our visions of political redemption. In the United States borderlands, the embrace of human creativity is married with contempt for our contingent creatureliness. Our status as political animals is secured by scorning our condition as embodied animals. If politics' redemptive potentials lie in its ability to reconcile us with our humanity, then PTD calls into question the possibility of such a reconciliation. In it, political power simultaneously vindicates and nihilates our humanity, alienating just as it reconciles. The bones in the valleys of the Sonoran, no less than those that lay before the prophet Ezekiel, indicate that a fantastic effort has failed or, at the very least, is failing.

Moreover, I will endeavor to argue in the pages that follow that, as for Ezekiel, the bones in the valleys of the Sonoran are not the bones of people who are strangers to us. *Our* redemption and *their* redemption are inextricably linked together. Thus, the very same question that God posed to Ezekiel is posed to us still today. "Mortal, can these bones live?"

In the US–Mexico borderlands, this question casts doubt on our political endeavors' ability to deliver us to our redemption. That is, now, no less than in the sixth century BCE, it is a question of ethical, political, and theological import. Can the excluded other's ethical demand be reconciled with the autonomous freedom that lies at the heart of the politics of self-determination? Do the structures of our ethical subjectivity and political subjectivity, at last, reveal our humanity to resolve in some essential unity, or, rather, do they reveal it to be a condition riven by irresolvable contradiction? What of the law that was to be the instrument of this reconciliation? Does the ethical demand sanctify our positive law by referring it to some higher law? Or, rather, does it reveal a fundamental limit in the law's redemptive potential, haunting it with the presence of a good it can neither refuse nor embrace? Finally, what becomes of the dead? Is there any redemption for them? Can those whom the Sonoran has claimed—can those whose memories are already lost to us—be made present to the polity and ushered into its streets?

3   Pernicious Messianism in the Borderlands

In the southwestern borderlands, theology has played a historic role in mediating the ethical and political relationships. In the nineteenth century, the fledgling United States sought to expand its territorial footprint. However, to realize these ambitions, it would first have to displace the Mexicanx, Chicanx, and Indigenous populations who already called this land their home. In the doctrine of Manifest Destiny, Anglo-Americans struck upon a distinctively American messianism that allowed them to envision their territorial acquisitions as vehicles of historical redemption. First with the annexation of Texas and, later, in the Mexican-American War, popular American intellectuals defended land grabs as "the fulfillment of [the United States'] manifest destiny to overspread the continent allotted by providence for the free development of [their] yearly multiplying millions."[22] Strikingly, 'manifest destiny' did not simply christen the United States' actions for this particular historical moment but situated them in a narrative frame that equated American political progress with history's apotheosis.

This equation finds early expression in John L. O'Sullivan's 1839 essay, "The Great Nation of Futurity."[23] O'Sullivan premised the United States' future greatness on the break it achieved from the past and the 'new history' that began with its 'birth':

> It is our unparalleled glory that we have no reminiscences of battlefields, but in defense of humanity, of the oppressed of all nations, of the rights of conscience, the rights of personal enfranchisement. Our annals describe no scenes of horrid carnage, where men were led on by hundreds of thousands to slay one another, dupes and victims of emperors, kings, nobles, demons in the human form called heroes. We have had patriots to defend our homes, our liberties, but no aspirants to crowns or thrones; nor have the American people ever suffered themselves to be led on by wicked ambition to depopulate the land, to spread desolation far and wide, that a human being might be placed on a seat of supremacy.[24]

---

22   John L. O'Sullivan, "Annexation," *United States Magazine and Democratic Review* 17 (1845): 2.

23   While O'Sullivan is credited with coining the term 'Manifest Destiny' and articulating its theology, he was by no means its only champion. As Gregory Cuéllar has demonstrated, this idea was championed by United States senators, congressional representatives, and religious leaders. Cuéllar gives particular attention to the role that Rev. John McCarty played in interpreting the United States' role in the Mexican American War as an instrument of divine justice framed by a cosmic conflict between good and evil. See Gregory Cuéllar, "Contesting State Violence: The Bible, The Public Good, and Divinely Sanctioned Violence in the Borderlands," in *La Violencia and the Hebrew Bible: The Politics and Histories of Biblical Hermeneutics on the American Continent,* ed. Pablo R. Andiñach & Susanne Scholz (Atlanta: Society of Biblical Literature, 2016), 39–58.

24   John L. O'Sullivan, "The Great Nation of Futurity," *The United States Democratic Review* 6 (1839): 426.

Juxtaposing them against their European counterparts, O'Sullivan depicts the Americans as a people without a history. The War of American Independence had achieved a clean break with the 'old world' and given rise to a new one. By virtue of this break, Americans had no share of the hereditary sins that had corrupted the politics of their European predecessors.[25] Never had they nor would they be seduced by demonic aspirations to monarchy. Theirs was an aspiration to defend humanity and not to dominate it, to liberate the oppressed and not to impose oppression.

Like the messiah, born from heaven, this people's immaculate birth was also accompanied by a task of historic importance. The young republic would represent an unflinching embodiment of 'the democratic principle'; an idea to which O'Sullivan gave poetic expression in the opening article of his *Democratic Review*: "Let man be fettered by no duty, save his brother's right—like his, inviolable."[26] Guided by this principle, the destiny manifest in the American political project would represent not only the fulfillment of this people but the culmination of all peoples' historical endeavors:

> The far-reaching, the boundless future will be the era of American Greatness. In its magnificent domains of space and time, the nation of many nations is destined to manifest to mankind the excellence of divine principles; to establish on earth the noblest temple ever dedicated to the worship of the Most High—the Sacred and the True. Its floor shall be a hemisphere—its roof the firmament of the star-studded heavens, and its congregation a Union of many republics, comprising hundreds of happy millions, calling owning no man master, but governed by God's natural and moral law of equality, the law of brotherhood—of 'peace and good-will amongst men.'[27]

---

25   Ibid. Adam Gomez cites this rejection of the doctrine of original sin as a distinct sign of O'Sullivan's departure from Orthodox Christianity. While the theology of Manifest destiny borrows considerably from Protestant theology, the former, nevertheless, cannot be reduced to the latter. Rather, as Gomez (and Edward Widmer) describe it, the political theology of Manifest Destiny is a kind of 'militant, quasi-secular religiosity' or, to use John Wilsey's classification, a distinctive form of 'civil religion' contrary to the tradition described by Robert Bellah. See Adam Gomez, "Deus Vult: John L. O'Sullivan, Manifest Destiny, and American Democratic Messianism," *American Political Thought* 1 (September 2012): 236–262; & John D. Wilsey, "'Our Country is Destined to be the Great Nation of Futurity': John L. O'Sullivan's Manifest Destiny and Christian Nationalism, 1837–1846," *Religions* 8 (2017).

26   John L. O'Sullivan, "Introduction" *United States Democratic Review* 1 (1837), 6–7.

27   O'Sullivan, "The Great Nation of Futurity," 427.

In this eschatological vision, the American people, by the expansion of United States territory, appear to outbid the people Israel as God's witnesses before all history. Left to complete the task assigned to them by providence, the United States would become the 'New Jerusalem.' Their westward march would facilitate the construction of the 'noblest temple ever dedicated to the worship of the Most High' and usher in the era of 'peace and goodwill' promised but left unfulfilled at Jesus' birth.

Moreover, typifying the divine manifest in American progress is the law that structures their political associations—'the natural and moral law of equality, the law of brotherhood.' By this characterization, O'Sullivan blurs the line between the actual body of laws posited by the young republic and those bestowed by God upon creation. Thus, he invests the promulgation of United States law with the divine imprimatur, identifying the history of its expansion with a kind of salvation history. The ethical and political implications of this identification were profound. "Democrats such as O'Sullivan," Adam Gomez asserts, "were the first to suggest that leading by moral example was not enough and that the United States should fulfill its destiny to democratize the world by any means necessary."[28] Moreover, Gomez contends, the United States' "special status as divine agent and vanguard ... [effected] what Kierkegaard [called] the teleological suspension of the ethical, exempting America from the ethical and legal standards that bind other nations[.]"[29] Consequently, the dispossession of those who had long inhabited the American southwest did not present an ethical challenge of sufficient concern to tarnish the polity's sinlessness. If the peoples who already occupied the territory could not be assimilated, if they had to be displaced or destroyed, then it must be because they opposed God's natural, moral law. It must be because they neither possessed nor desired any share of 'brotherhood' in humankind.

Several decades later, John Gast would memorialize this theology in his painting *American Progress*.

Gast portrays American westward expansion as breaking dawn, shining from the east, and beating back the darkness covering the west. Wagon trains, the Pony Express, and locomotives set out from a coastal city toward herds of buffalo untamed. Farmers and ranchers stride west, cultivating the earth beneath their feet as they go. Leading them all is Columbia, the embodiment of American virtue and ingenuity. She floats above the action, guiding it like some angelic being. Her dazzling Roman garb suggests the purity of republican governance, and the book in her right-hand underscores the enlightenment of

28   Gomez, "Deus Volt," 243.
29   Ibid.

FIGURE 4   John Gast, *American Progress*
            SOURCE: JOHN GAST, *AMERICAN PROGRESS*, 1872, OIL ON CANVAS, AUTRY
            MUSEUM OF THE AMERICAN WEST, LOS ANGELES

its laws. Moving on the heels of the dawn, American progress appears no less natural nor inevitable than the rotation of the Earth or the passage of time.

However, Gast's painting also depicts the damning conceit harbored in Manifest Destiny's messianic theology. O'Sullivan praised Americans' reverence for human equality and their fight on behalf of the 'oppressed of all nations,' even as they held in bondage millions of enslaved Africans and their children. He repudiated the 'wicked ambition to depopulate the land,' even as the US army joined settlers in displacing and massacring indigenous populations. Overcoming these contradictions and preserving the equation of the ethical and political required excepting from 'all humanity' those whom Anglo-Americans killed or kept as chattel. Gast inadvertently captures this irony in the imagery of *American Progress*. He portrays the indigenous peoples of the West alongside the buffalo and bear. Those who do not share Columbia's fair skin are cast as more animal than human. Thus, to the indigenous persons pictured fleeing with the darkness, she is a terrible sight.[30] American enlightenment fails to cast

---

30   C.f. William H. Wharton, "Texas Address of the Honorable Wm. H. Wharton," (speech, New York, April 26, 1836), Internet Archive, https://archive.org/details/texasaddress-

light on the humanity of those whose demise the nation's inevitable advance requires. Where they are concerned, the light blinds. It does not reveal.

In the shadows of desert mountains, PTD continues to perpetrate this violence, and the death it produces continues to challenge the presumption of American virtue's 'unparalleled glory.' Today, at the end of 'the era of American Greatness,' the explicit language of Manifest Destiny has receded from our political discourse. Having completed the march that Gast depicted in 1872, the American frontier has traded the language of 'progress' for the language of 'defense.' Nevertheless, Americans continue to identify border security with the defense of democracy, US sovereignty, the rule of law, liberty, equality, and the 'brotherhood' of all humankind. Furthermore, as Gregory Cuéllar observes, "the Mexican body continues to be a locus for state-sanctioned violence," and this violence bears a genealogy that can be traced to the 'civilizing mission' of Manifest Destiny.[31] The oppositions that Gast and O'Sullivan prefigure between civilization and nature, law and tyranny, and divine and demonic, reiterate themselves on the borderline. In the United States Customs and Border Protection's diction, the border is the 'frontline,' where brave men and women defend the law from the forces of anarchy, criminality, terror, and violence.[32] No longer does the light emanate from the east to dispel darkness in the west. Now, it turns to shine from the north against the south. However, the constitutive oppositions remain. Within this conflict, the divinization of the American people (and the demonization of those who threaten their project) all but eclipses any conceivable strife between the political relationships that persist between 'citizens' and the ethical relationships that might oblige them to 'aliens.'

However, if theology has effectively sacralized the present paradigm, it may yet furnish means for resisting it. Manifest Destiny sacralizes American popular sovereignty (over and against the demand of the other) by asserting

---

oowharrich/. The explicit, racially-coded language that accompanied American appeals to providence are on dramatic display in William H. Wharton's remarks on Texan independence, "The justice and benevolence of God will forbid that the delightful region of Texas should again become a howling wilderness, trod only by savages, or that, it should be permanently benighted by the ignorance and superstition, the anarchy and rapine of Mexican misrule. The Ango-American race is destined to be forever the proprietors of this land of promise and fulfillment. Their laws will govern it. Their learning will enlighten it, their enterprise will improve it." (p. 236)

31   Cuéllar, "Contesting State Violence," 55.
32   "Ethos of the U.S. Customs and Border Protection Agency," in U.S. Customs and Border Protection, *Vision and Strategy 2020: U.S. Customs and Border Protection Strategic Plan*, 2020.

the American people's messianic purpose in history. It legitimizes imperial aspirations by making imperial politics the mechanism of human redemption. But this is not the only way to construe the relation. To the contrary, Spanish-Salvadoran theologian Ignacio Ellacuría proposed that the messianic is not made manifest in the advance of elite power or great moments of historical progress. Instead, it concerns itself with those whose suffering 'progress' necessitates. The Messiah makes his place amidst the people crucified for the sake of the *Pax Romana* or the *Pax Americana*. Amid this 'pueblo crucificado,' the paschal mystery comes to be known as the divine rejection of any claim "that many [must] suffer so a few may enjoy, that many [must] be dispossessed so that a few may possess."[33] Yet, PTD has strewn the valleys of the Sonoran with the dry bones of the suffering and dispossessed. In line with Ellacuría's messianic theology, this book sees in them a crisis of legitimacy for the present political order. They testify that the American project of self-determination has not brought to fruition the messianic mission but instead repeated its crucifixion. Can any resurrection follow in its wake?

4   Between Worlds

If the fantastic effort of politics entails the creation and maintenance of that world in which we long to live, then to stand in the wake of this effort's failure is to stand at the point of transition between worlds. In the borderlands, the notion that we find ourselves between worlds attains a distinctive plausibility. Viewed as solid lines on political maps, borders and states appear as though they are timeless facts not up for negotiation. However, this illusion condenses into thin lines the thick histories of concrete practice by which borders are established and maintained. In the borderlands, this illusion loses its aura of self-evidence. In her landmark study, *Borderlands / La Frontera,* Gloria Anzaldúa conceives the borderlands as a place of transition between worlds. Her point is not simply geographical. "The US–Mexico border," she explains, is "*una herida abierta* [an open wound] where the Third World grates against

---

33   Ignacio Ellacuría, "The Crucified People: An Essay in Historical Soteriology," in *Ignacio Ellacuría: Essays on History, Liberation, and Salvation,* ed. Michael E. Lee (Maryknoll: Orbis Books, 2013). C.f. Kyle B.T. Lambelet, *¡Presente! Nonviolent Politics and the Resurrection of the Dead* (Washington, DC: Georgetown University Press, 2019). Developing a political theology from the School of the America's watch, Lambelet has already made compelling use of Ellacuría's 'pueblo crucificado' in defense of a 'messianic political theology' counterposed to imperialism.

the first and bleeds."[34] Those who inhabit this wounded land, *los atravesados* [the border-crossed ones], intermingle in a 'new mestizo' the 'American' with the 'Mexican,' the European with the indigenous, and the past, shaped by conquests, with the present, wracked with violence. The upshot of this intermingling is a people and place that is neither American nor Mexican, European nor indigenous, past nor present. This intermingling keeps the borderlands in a state of constant transition by keeping the constitutive geographic, subjective, racial, and temporal disjunctions in irresolution.

The securitization of the border aspires to resolve this irresolution by bringing to bear the power of the nation-state. However, the effort to resolve the disjunctions only exacerbates the wound. In the Sonoran Desert, the border and the state are simultaneously at their most and least real. State power is acutely manifest in the law's regulation of bodies and patently incongruous with the site of its exercise. The processes of state-making and nation-building are encountered concretely in border fencing, surveillance towers, highway checkpoints, helicopters, uniformed officers, and predator drones. Yet they are refuted by the expanse of an environment that makes them appear like unnatural obstructions.[35] For those who must endure its searing heat and navigate its maze, the Sonoran Desert is eminently more real than the 'United States' or 'Mexico.' Seeing the borderlands as a place between worlds, as does Anzaldúa, invites ethical, political, and theological reflection not only about *what ought to be* but about *what is* and *what might yet be*.

Shifting theological reflection to the borderlands' vantage empowers possibilities present but not yet fully developed in Christian ethical responses to migration. By no means have Christian ethicists passed over the phenomenon of migration in silence. Nor have they failed to note the difficulty of squaring Christian ideals with the international system of nation-states. Dana Wilbanks early noted national borders' incompatibility with Christianity's universalist commitments.[36] Likewise, Kristin Heyer has suggested that enacting these

---

34 Gloria Anzaldúa, *Borderlands / La Frontera: The New Mestiza* (San Francisco: Aunt Lute Books, 1999), 25.

35 C.f. Jessica Auchter, *The Politics of Haunting and Memory in International Relations* (New York: Routledge, 2017), n.b., 89–126. Auchter observes the performative, memorializing function of border walls. These walls state the state, revealing its contingency. By their activity, they draw the primordial event of the state's foundation into the present, revealing the ongoing character of its creation. Moreover, the exigency of national security which accompanies this work of creation underscores its vulnerability and the possibility that things might be arranged otherwise.

36 Dana Wilbanks, *Re-Creating America: The Ethics of US Immigration & Refugee Policy in a Christian Perspective* (Nashville: Abingdon Press, 1996).

commitments would mean adopting a form of transnational solidarity that is bound to be subversive in nature.[37] Nevertheless, a kind of 'realism' that seeks to adapt Christianity's more radical potentials to the present order has predominated in the present literature. The upshot of this effort is a political theology that, on one hand, defends the legitimacy of the nation-state as a provision of divine sovereignty for subduing violence and disorder in a fallen world, while, on the other, seeking to restrain the state's most excessive efforts with an appeal to the humanity that the outsider and its members share in common. However, since PTD's implementation, immigration policy has proven exceptionally resistant to change, leading some critics to despair of the legislature's ability or willingness to abide by such restraints.[38] Faced with the proposition that theological ethicists are impotent to move the usual centers of political agency, resisting despair requires searching for novel forms of political agency. One means of doing this is to challenge that account of the 'real' that places legislatures at center-stage and to embrace instead the tensive space between worlds and, by extension, the possibilities presented by the activists and advocates at work there.

5   Argument Summary

Throughout this book, I use the term 'political theology' in several senses. Perhaps most fundamentally, I take the term to describe a constellation of symbols, discourses, and practices that, together, constitute and place within a transcendent frame, an account of the broader realities that are the setting for the endeavors of individual actors and the political associations of which they are a part. This setting demarcates the bounds of the possible and the impossible. Further, as it situates human endeavor within transcendence's frame, a political theology supplies the narrative vantage in which the normative significance of human action is to be determined. In this sense, a political theology comprises a world and *Weltanschauung* that incorporates ethics, politics, history, and ontology in a narrative that conceives and acts upon material history under the shadow of the millennium. It is in this sense that Manifest Destiny may be said to be a political theology. Likewise, it is in this sense that PTD could be said to instantiate a political theology. However, as competing

---

37   Kristin Heyer, *Kinship Across Borders: A Christian Ethic of Immigration* (Washington, D.C.: Georgetown University Press, 2012).

38   See, for instance, Miguel De La Torre, *Embracing Hopelessness* (Minneapolis: Fortress Press, 2017).

'political theologies' enter into tension, we may add two further significations to the term. First, 'political theology' may describe an analytic approach that seeks to make explicit the (potentially implicit) constellation of elements that constitute such a *Weltanschauung*. In this sense, the foregoing represents an exercise in political theology. Second, however, as the analytical task turns to normative criticism and proposal, 'political theology' connotes a field of discourse in which theological metaphors provide the language and logic for moral dispute. In both of these senses, this book presents a political theological project.

I divide the argument of this book into three major parts. The first of these sections comprises a pair of essays that serve as preliminaries for the arguments of the subsequent sections. Chapter One seeks to uncover a set of 'realist' presuppositions that provides the political theological backdrop for much of the contemporary Christian ethics of migration. By attending to these presuppositions, I seek to clarify how this political theology informs the discipline's operative conception of political agency and how it has led some scholars to despair at the possibility of morally meaningful political change. Chapter Two serves as a note on method and the connections between political theology, ethics, and aesthetics that emerge in the context of the borderlands. Authors and activists alike, I contend, premise the possibility of political change on the ethically transformative power of remembrance—of encounters with the dead. However, if the work of remembrance is to be effective, it must take care in its aesthetic representations of the dead or risk generating grim spectacles that reproduce and normalize PTD's violation of migrant bodies. In pursuit of sound practice, I turn to the work of a pair of borderlands artists for direction.

Part Two of the book, which comprises the third and fourth chapters, seeks a reckoning with the disappointment wrought by the catastrophic failure of the United States' border enforcement strategy. In these chapters I argue that this failure is not the consequence of PTD's inability substantially to reduce the number of unlawful entries occurring at the border. Rather, the strategy's profound failure is its contempt for our embodiment and its cunning effort to obscure the relationship between migrants and citizens. Chapter Three sets the stage for this argument by refuting the notion that we live in a world of 'neighbors' and 'strangers.' Rather, with an eye to Hannah Arendt's reading of the story of Cain and Abel, which she interprets as a fable about the emergence of the political, I argue that these 'strangers' are better understood as 'estranged siblings.' As Arendt argues, the body politic has its genesis in a rejection of the ethical ties that bind the social body and, by extension, the freedom constitutive of the political is secured in a moment of 'fratricide.' However, whereas Arendt presents the violation of the social body as a 'problem of beginning,' I argue that a complete reading of Genesis' fourth chapter shows it to be a problem that recurs continually in the present, haunting the polity with the good denied and uncovering the contradiction sewn in our humanity.

Chapter Four then seeks to conceive PTD as a form of fratricide that divides bodies politic through the continual and repeated violation of the social body. Further, I argue that PTD's distinctive approach not only violates the social body, but also nihilates the political good it seeks to uphold. By making the natural environment the primary agent of law enforcement, it obscures the boundaries between city and wilderness, law and violence, freedom and necessity. Despite the strategy's best efforts to persuade us that migrant mortalities are either consequences of blind chance or justified interventions to halt the advance of criminal outsiders, the bones in the Sonoran permit neither of these explanations to succeed. Instead, the dead attain a political afterlife as they confront us with the strategy's conceits, intentionality, and contempt for our embodiment. Thus, Part Two of the book offers a provisional answer to the project's orienting question: the bones may indeed live, but it is unclear whether our political project, as presently understood and pursued, can live along with them. If there is to be any redemption, then our political project must be imagined otherwise than it is now.

Part Three of the book, which comprises Chapters Five and Six, represents an effort to sketch a form of normative borderlands politics premised on compassion rather than contempt. To this end, I turn to a text that has enjoyed considerable resonance with ethicists and humanitarians in the borderlands, the parable of the Samaritan (Lk 10:25–37). An inversion of the form of subjectivity that grasps its freedom through fratricide, chapter three develops an account of subjectivity constituted by its approval of a demand that comes to it from without. That is, in the parable of the Samaritan, I find a subject formed not in the nominative but in the accusative; a subject defined not by freedom unalloyed but by a responsibility whose ambit is oriented and delimited by a good incarnate in the life of the other. For this subject, the law becomes the means of articulating this relationship of responsibility. Nevertheless, I contend, this good's embodiment makes it radically particular; thus, rather than sanctifying the positive law by directing it to norms supplied by some higher law, it discloses simultaneously the law's ends and limits, seeding it with eschatological longing.

Lest this vision of subjectivity appear politically inert, I turn in Chapter Six to the case of one self-styled borderland Samaritan and the trial court as a theater for political agency. In the United States v. Scott Warren, I contend, we see a contemporary instance in which the other's ethical demand collides with the law. However, this collision results neither in the law's undoing nor its total reconciliation with the other's demand. Instead, at the point of collision, the language of rights, particularly the citizen's rights of conscience, provides a means for making the demand legible to the polity. Building on the work of scholars who see in the case a precedent for something like a 'right of rescue,' I argue that the case reveals an interstitial space wherein the law's deference to the citizen's right of conscience challenges the state's power to exclude and preserves the possibility of political coalitions whose bounds are not determined by citizenship and alienage. In this interstitial space, we glimpse a politics ordered otherwise than our own, in which the citizen's responsibility to the migrant enacts a different sort of reconciliation with our humanity.

Of course, redemption glimpsed at the limits of the law is not a reassurance of self-determination's compatibility with compassionate responsibility. Ultimately, this argument cannot resolve in some higher unity the contradictions revealed by PTD's failure. Neither our humanity nor that law which would reconcile us to it can be relieved of persistent non-identities. Or rather, *we* cannot relieve these contradictions for ourselves. We may only glimpse their relief. Thus, I conclude this book with a brief reflection on the necessity of hope. "*Mortal*, can these bones live?" The exchange between Ezekiel and the divine sets in stark relief the differing possibilities available to human and divine agency. Thus, the satisfaction of our desire for redemption and our resistance to despair relies on a form of hope dedicated to the possible impossibility that we do not act alone.

PART 1

Realism, Bodies Politic, and Bodies Remembered

∴

CHAPTER 1

Contesting Realism in the Christian Ethics of Migration

On the State of a Conversation

> [*R*]*ealism*, views the world as composed of distinct political com-
> munities. Each one of these communities is independent and sov-
> ereign, and each one pursues its short- and long-term interests in
> the international system[.]
>
> —MARK AMSTUTZ, *Just Immigration*

∴

1 Introduction: Christian Ethics and Political Theology

Few, in good faith, would argue that a Christian ethics of migration (or any
other ethics) should not strive for realism. Migration is not an abstract phenomenon. It takes place in geographic, political, and legal space.[1] Migrants not
only move between points demarcated by latitude and longitude, they cross
over international lines and jurisdictional boundaries. We come to know them
(and they come to know us) in the names they acquire in the crossing. The leg-
ibility yielded by these names—'alien,' 'refugee,' 'illegal,' 'asylum-seeker,'—is
not abstract or indifferent. Instead, it posits legal, social, and political realities
that assert who is to be admitted and who is to be excluded, whom the polity
must shelter and whom it may remove. To fail to account for any of these realities would be to produce an ethics inattentive to the power structures within
which migrants and citizens must live. Such an ethics might yield lofty ideals unsullied by compromises with contingent powers. However, these ideals
would be as vacuous as they would be impracticable.

---

1 On the significance of legal and political contexts for contemporary conceptions of migra-
tion, see Rainer Bauböck, "Mobility and Migration: Physical, Contextual, and Perspectival
Interpretations," in *Contested Concepts in Migration Studies* ed. Ricard Zapata-Barrero, Dirk
Jacobs, & Riva Kastoryano (New York: Routledge Press, 2022): 167–181.

This charge of impracticability is precisely what international relations scholar Mark R Amstutz levels against Christian perspectives on migration. In his 2017 study, *Just Immigration*, Amstutz divides the field of immigration ethics into two broad categories.[2] On one side are the 'realists.' Amstutz judges that these scholars take seriously the rules that the international order posits to govern the game of migration. Further, Amstutz deems that they properly acknowledge collective self-determination's normative legitimacy for justifying these rules. On the other side are the cosmopolitan 'idealists,' who disregard the international system of nation-states and envision a unified world of global citizens. By Amstutz's assessment, the Christian perspective on migration, especially insofar as it is organized by universalizing convictions like the kinship of all human beings, lies in the idealist camp.[3] However, as it slides into this intellectual camp, it loses sight of the political order as we know it. Consequently, Christianity's cosmopolitan tendencies may equip it to offer moral guidance in the private sphere but not political counsel in the public sphere. The problem with the Christian perspective on immigration policy, then, stems from its failure to offer moral provisions informed by and amenable to a realistic assessment of the context in which migration occurs.

While many Christian ethicists have cast doubts on the international order's ability to implement Christian ideals, and although others have expressed concern that their ethics are impracticable, Amstutz's criticisms overlook several critical presuppositions that inform most contemporary Christian Ethics of migration. My aim in this preliminary essay is to uncover these presuppositions. In so doing, I seek to demonstrate their consistency with a form of 'realism' that has long informed Christian ethics. My purpose, however, is not straightforwardly to vindicate Christian ethicists to critics like Amstutz. Instead, I hope to demonstrate that theological reflection not only informs our response to 'the real' but also informs our understanding of 'the real' itself. The 'real world' is not a brute empirical fact, an aggregation of episteme readily legible for neutral acts of description. On the contrary, the 'real world' only emerges as our intuitions of empirical phenomena are conceptualized and organized with the help of concepts, symbols, and metaphors—including *theological* ones. A fact

---

2   Mark R. Amstutz, *Just Immigration: American Policy in Christian Perspective* (Grand Rapids: William B Eerdmans Publishing Company, 2017).

3   N.b., Amstutz, 97–100. Among the theological ethicists that Amstutz cites in support of this claim are Dana Wilbanks and Kristin Heyer, who, in turn, argue for relatively free transnational migration and forms of solidarity that traverse borders. See Dana Wilbanks, *Re-Creating America: The Ethics of US Immigration in a Christian Perspective* (Nashville: Abingdon Press, 1996); & Kristin Heyer, *Kinship Across Borders: A Christian Ethics of Immigration* (Washington, DC: Georgetown University Press, 2012).

is a thing fashioned, and theology plays a role in the fashioning. Addressing the shortcomings of Christian ethics of migration, then, does not require, as Amstutz contends, limiting its jurisdiction to the realm of private counsel. Nor does it require a theological acquiescence to the set of possibilities latent in a so-called 'realist' account of the world. Instead, it requires a critical reconsideration of the political theological commitments that inform such descriptions and lend plausibility to the sense of 'realism' that attends them.

As Robert Heimburger argues in *God and the Illegal Alien*, Christian ethics of migration generally lack an explicit political theology.[4] Heimburger's book seeks to alleviate this problem by articulating one. My contention here is that the political theology that Heimburger articulates makes explicit a set of 'realist' presuppositions that have informed most studies to date. These presuppositions include, first, the tacit acceptance that the international system of nation-states constitutes the primary 'real' to which Christian ethics must accommodate itself. Second, and connected to the first, is the operative assumption that these nation-states are the principal bearers of *effective* agency in the story of migration. Third is the notion that this context determines what is possible and impossible for moral actors. My intention in this essay is not to question the value of realism but rather to scrutinize this set of assumptions, which constitute the world that this theology either actively posits or tacitly accepts. That is, in this preliminary essay, I seek to identify the contours of one political theology better to clarify how the one sketched out in the following chapters furnishes an alternative.

2   Christian Realism

It is unlikely that Amstutz's 'realism' and the 'realist' stance adopted by so many Christian ethicists in contemporary discussions of migration could be shown to be siblings in a common intellectual genealogy that originates with the works of Hans Morgenthau. Nevertheless, this stance does recall several features of the 'Christian Realism' developed by one of Morgenthau's contemporaries: Reinhold Niebuhr.[5] Niebuhr first articulated this theological vision in

---

4 Robert W. Heimburger, *God and the Illegal Alien: United States Immigration Law and a Theology of Politics* (New York: Cambridge University Press, 2018).

5 Regarding the relationship between the form of realism that came to predominate in twentieth-century international relations and that which now informs much Christian ethics, there are striking connections. Reinhold Niebuhr and Hans Morgenthau shared a close friendship. In an exchange of letters, Niebuhr wrote to Morgenthau, "I am forced to ask whether all my insights are borrowed from Hans Morgenthau." To this, Morgenthau responded, "You raise

response to what he judged the excessive optimism of liberal mainline Protestant theology. His Christian Realism marked an effort to provide a theological ethics chastened by a Christian social theory attentive to the realities of the human condition. What Niebuhr believed his liberal counterparts to have missed was the full anthropological and sociological significance of the doctrine of sin.[6] Their social ethics, in turn, offered a set of provisions premised on a faulty description of the actors by whom, and on whose behalf, they would be carried out. In recovering the anthropological and sociological significance of the doctrine of sin, Niebuhr sought to provide a revised ethics and a revised account of the world in which they would be enacted. In effect, this effort produced the outlines of a political theology that accounts for the role of the nation-state, the exigency that justifies its exercises of power, and the connection between material history and eschatology.

For Niebuhr, the human condition is a paradoxical one. We are simultaneously rational beings, capable of self-transcendence and self-determination, and natural creatures, subject to the constraints of finite existence. Niebuhr contends that the intellectual history of human self-understanding reflects an effort to alleviate the vexing problem that this paradox presents.[7] At various turns, we have sought to identify ourselves with one side of the paradox or the other. The classical view of humanity emphasized our rationality—the romantic view our naturality. However, no such simplified view is untroubled by anxiety. Anyone who would define our humanity according to our rationality cannot but be troubled by the capacity for animalistic brutishness to which our war-torn history testifies. Anyone who would reduce our humanity to our mere naturality must reckon with the peculiar phenomenon that a human animal is an animal constantly determined to inscribe some meaning into its existence. Contrary to these reductive errors, Niebuhr found in the

---

the question 'whether all my insights are borrowed from Hans Morgenthau,' I have asked myself the same question with reference to you, and I am sure I have the far better argument." On this intellectual relationship see Daniel Rice, "Reinhold Niebuhr and Hans Morgenthau: A Friendship with Contrasting Shades of Realism," *Journal of American Studies* 42 (2008): 255–291.

6   C.f. Walter Rauschenbusch, *A Theology for the Social Gospel* (Louisville: Westminster John Knox Press, 1945). Like Niebuhr, Rauschenbusch believed his theology to be built on a working partnership with "real social and psychological science." (p. 5). However, Rauschenbusch saw his social gospel as centrally concerned with "the eradication of sin and the fulfillment of the mission of redemption." (p. 31) However, it is precisely human agency's effectiveness for this 'eradication,' and by extension the conditions of redemption, that Niebuhr's Christian social theory calls into question.

7   Reinhold Niebuhr, *The Nature and Destiny of Man: A Christian Interpretation*, Vol I, II vols (London: Nisbet & Co LTD, 1941).

biblical understanding of human beings an effort to preserve the paradox by insisting that human beings are at once made in the 'image of God' but *made* creatures, nevertheless.[8] Thus, human beings possess the defining capacity for self-transcendence and self-determination. However, even as our capacity for self-transcendence gestures toward a source and end of human life that lies somewhere beyond the finite world, it nevertheless fails to grasp or define this source and end, and, thus, in its failure, this very capacity reinscribes our creaturely finitude. Crucially, the possibility of sin arises within this paradoxical condition.

In Niebuhr's interpretation, human sinfulness does not stem from rationality's capitulation to base carnal desires. Biblical literature, after all, insists that the creation is good. Our creatureliness is no less a part of our goodness than the *imago dei*. On the contrary, sin is most essentially a rebellion against our creatureliness—our determination to be God and not God's image. Niebuhr writes:

> Man is an individual, but he is not self-sufficing. The law of his nature is love, a harmonious relation of life to life in obedience to the divine center and source of his life. This law is violated when man seeks to make himself the center and source of his own life. His sin is therefore spiritual and not carnal, though the infection of rebellion spreads from the spirit to the body and disturbs its harmonies also.[9]

Niebuhr does not judge this 'seeking' to be a simple error. Instead, it entails a self-deceiving 'will to power' that stems from and corrupts our capacities for self-transcendence and self-determination. Like other animals, human beings are subject to the contingencies of nature. Unlike other animals, however, humans are distinctly aware of the insecurity this produces and seek, by their power, to alleviate it. This seeking passes into sin as we overreach the limits of our creatureliness and inevitably seek "security at the expense of other life."[10] Niebuhr supposes that this rapacious self-assertion takes many forms. It gives rise to avarice and the extractive abuse of the natural environment for its resources. It shows itself in the desire to dominate others and, by the force of their multitude, safeguard one's life and possessions from external threats. Implicit in both instances is a mendacious conflation of our capacities for self-transcendence and self-determination with our desire to be self-sustaining

---

8   Ibid, n.b. 161–189.
9   Ibid, 17.
10   Ibid, 194.

and self-mastered—our desire to be our own creators and gods. The terrible cost of this deceit is born by those subordinated by this will-to-power and, for them, "the perils of nature [are transformed] into the more grievous perils of human history."[11]

Defined as a 'will to power,' sin not only infects the individual but also rends the whole social fabric. On the one hand, Niebuhr argues that the desire for self-sufficiency gives rise to the structures of domination and organs of power constitutive of modern states. Yet, it also puts competing classes and states at enmity with one another. "The group," Niebuhr writes, "is more arrogant, hypocritical, self-centered, and more ruthless in the pursuit of its ends than the individual."[12] "The egotism of racial national and socio-economic groups," he explains, "is most consistently expressed by the national state, because the state gives the collective impulses of the nation such instruments of power, and presents the imagination of individuals with such obvious symbols of its discrete collective identity, that the national state is most able to make absolute claims for itself, to enforce those claims by power and to give them plausibility and credibility by the majesty and panoply of its apparatus."[13] As the aggregate of individual agents, the social group expresses sin's collective effects, amplifying and exacerbating human insecurity and rapaciousness. Thus, sin's rebellion against the divine replaces the harmonious relation of life to life with a cacophony of warring voices.

Thus, for Niebuhr, the doctrine of sin sets the context for all our political and ethical endeavors. "The society in which each man lives," he writes at the outset of *Moral Man and Immoral Society*, "is at once the basis for, and nemesis of, the fulness of life which each man seeks."[14] It is the basis of genuine fulfillment in that humans were made to live with one another. Yet it becomes the nemesis of this fulfillment as it confuses collective fulfillment with narrow self-sufficiency and provides the setting for conflictual wills and competing powers. Niebuhr does not suppose that sin completely undoes our filial impulses to care for our relations. He even grants that, by dint of our intelligence, we have found ways to extend this impulse beyond their filial ties to include the rights and needs of other people. However, Niebuhr judges it a fact of human history that as human groups grow, our best moral insights become less and less effective in restraining the aggregation of our vices. "For all the centuries of experience,"

---

11   Ibid.

12   Ibid, 221–222.

13   Ibid, 222.

14   Reinhold Niebuhr, *Moral Man and Immoral Society: A Study in Ethics and Politics* (New York: Charles Scribner and Sons, 1936), 1.

he writes, "men have not yet learned how to live together without compounding their vices and covering each other 'with mud and with blood.'"[15]

In the context of the political association, restraining the sinful will to power requires a check more forceful than conscience. Ultimately, Niebuhr reasons that power acknowledges its best ideals only when a superior power threatens its vital interests. Therefore, he concludes, there exist no stable political associations free of coercion—however subtle its exercise may appear:

> Ultimately, unity within an organized social group, or within a federation of such groups is created by the ability of a dominant group to impose its will. Politics will, to the end of history, be an area where conscience and power meet, where the ethical and coercive factors of human life will interpenetrate and work out their tentative and uneasy compromises.[16]

Niebuhr judges this dictum as being no less accurate of democracies than dictatorships. A democratic minority may appear to accept the majority position because they have been persuaded. However, a vote is abided not because it persuades but because it signals the majority's superior social power. Nevertheless, in his appraisal of politics, Niebuhr does not, for this reason, suppose that political power, even coercive power, cannot be judged to be in the service of better or worse ends. Contrary to stringent political realists, Niebuhr rejects the idea that peace is nothing more than a stalemate between inscrutable interests. However, it is a warning meant to chasten our visions of progress by reminding us of the tragic irony that sin sews in every political action.

As long as sin endures, we cannot return to a society governed by nothing more than the law of love. In the interim, justice, not love, must be the polity's orienting good. Given the material and immaterial inequities that are the consequence of human sin, the task of political justice is to achieve a (more) equitable distribution of the physical and cultural goods necessary for human flourishing. If the remediation of sin means resisting domination, then "social conflict which aims at greater equality has a moral justification which must be denied to efforts which aim at the perpetuation of privilege."[17] In so far as an exercise of political power is oriented toward this aim, it posits a countervailing force against sin's destructive inertia. Nevertheless, Niebuhr concedes that whatever political justice we may achieve in this history is always incomplete and impermanent. "The oppressed," as Niebuhr suggests, may "have a higher

---

15   Ibid.
16   Ibid, 4.
17   Ibid, 234.

moral right to challenge their oppressors than these have to maintain their rule by force."[18] Nevertheless, in its coercive conflict with the inertial force of human sin, justice becomes a testament to sin's endurance no less than its remediation. The presence of coercive force is, in itself, at odds with the law of love, which is human beings' proper guiding factor. Even the justified use of force, however subtle its means, cannot help striking a ringing, discordant tone in what is supposed to be the harmonious relation of life to life.

To return to the matter at hand, the preceding remarks on sin and the project of political justice suggest three implications that, in turn, provide the theo-political backdrop for contemporary Christian ethics of migration. The first may be drawn from the doctrine of sin's dialectical counterpart, the doctrine of salvation. If the problem of sin is not limited to the individual but affects the whole of our social life, then the story of redemption is not the mere province of narrow biography but also of social and political history. Second, with our eyes on history's grand stage, our attention lands less on single individuals and more often on the powerful political entities capable of wielding sufficient force to restrain the social aggregates of our worst impulses.[19] Third, if Christian ethicists want their arguments to precipitate substantive change, they must address these arguments to the leaders who have their hands on the levers of power. Nevertheless, this fact limits what they can reasonably hope to achieve. If political justice is always achieved through coercive force, and if coercive force can only achieve stalemates and partial victories, then history cannot achieve complete redemption through progressive advances toward the good. No such straightforward advances are ever truly made. Instead, our history must be judged to take on a tragic character. The ironic nature of political power means that final redemption must be disjoined from human

---

18   Ibid, 234.

19   This point is perhaps best illustrated by Niebuhr's applied ethics, like his comments on the Manchurian controversy in *The Christian Century*. In this series of essays, Niebuhr advocates for American intervention against Imperial Japan's invasion of Manchuria. Consistent with his understanding of political justice, Niebuhr judges that the cause of the oppressed in Manchuria enjoyed a moral priority over Japan's imperial interests. However, when he imagines intervention on China's behalf, he does not have in mind a collective action of private Christian citizens. Rather, he advocates action by the United States itself. That is, for Niebuhr, this crisis of justice is not a story about disaggregated individuals, but rather about China, Japan, and the United States. It is a story about nation-states. See Reinhold Niebuhr, "Must We Do Nothing," in *The Christian Century: Representative Articles, Editorials, and Poems Selected from More than Fifty Years of the Christian Century*, ed. Harold E. Fey & Margaret Frakes (New York: Association Press, 1962), 222–227.

endeavor and deferred to the eschaton.[20] To borrow a turn of phrase from another political theologian, Christian Realism envisions the eschaton not as the *telos* of our historical striving but as its limit.[21] Nevertheless, if Christian ethics is to attain any measure of realism, its proponents have no choice but to articulate their visions within the constraints of this tragic history. Perhaps they may reasonably hope that their arguments would persuade leaders to bring to bear the force necessary to restrain injustice. However, if they are to avoid the pain of contradiction, they cannot equate the imposition of restraint with the progressive unfolding of the reign of God.

3   Realism and the Christian Ethics of Migration

If not explicitly stated, this (or a structurally homologous) theo-political back-drop makes itself known in much of the contemporary Christian ethics of migration. By and large, these projects approach the issue of migration from the vantage of the international system of nation-states.[22] To date, six monographs on the Christian Ethics of migration have come to publication. The earliest of these books, published in 1996, just after the current legislative framework for immigration enforcement was passed, is Dana Wilbanks' *Re-Creating America*. Almost two decades later, three more books were published: Kristin Heyer's *Kinship Across Borders* and Susanna Snyder's *Asylum-Seeking, Migration, and Church* in 2012, and Ilsup Ahn's *Religious Ethics and Migration* in 2014. Not long after that, concurrent with Amstutz's chastisements in *Just Immigration*, Tisha M. Rajendra published her 2017 study titled *Migrants and Citizens*. The most recent of these books, published in 2018, is Robert W. Heimburger's *God and the Illegal Alien*. Contrary to Amstutz's criticisms and consistent with real-ist attention to the historical role of the nation-state, these studies treat the international system of nation-states as the basic real within which migration occurs and to which ethics must be addressed. Although they may acknowl-edge a possible aversion in Christianity to political institutions like borders, as does Wilbanks, they often present their arguments as interventions in a tragic

---

20   For a concise articulation of Niebuhr's eschatology, see Reinhold Niebuhr, *Faith and History: A Comparison of Christian and Modern Views of History* (New York: Charles Scribner and Sons, 1949), n.b., 120–138.

21   C.f. Walter Benjamin, *Reflections: Essays, Aphorisms, and Autobiographical Writings*, ed. Peter Demetz (New York: Schocken, 1986), 312.

22   Of the book-length studies published on the Christian Ethics of Migration, Heyer's *Kinship Across Borders* constitutes a notable exception to this pattern.

history—not as visions of a progressively emerging eschatological world without borders.

Consistent with realist assumptions about power and agency, they tend to address their arguments primarily to the legislators positioned at the national center.[23] Of all these scholars, Ahn is the most explicit about this intended audience. In the opening pages of *Religious Ethics and Migration*, he writes, "Although this book may be categorized and cataloged as a monograph in religious ethics ... I imagine that my readers would be those who work in the areas of civil and public services as well as those who participate in enacting and implementing public policies."[24] "They," he continues, "are the ones who can *actually* impact the lives of many undocumented migrants through their positional powers."[25] This little adverb conveys much. What Ahn makes explicit is the view that 'actual' political agency depends on positional power. More precisely, it depends on a positional power that is to be found among the legislature. Operating at a distance from such positions, private Christian citizens or non-governmental organizations, however well-intended they may be, cannot expect their actions to bring about real, lasting change. They do not have the agency to do so.

Even where scholars have not made this point as explicitly as Ahn, their arguments suggest a similar accounting of political agency. Wilbanks' social ethics furnish a set of principles designed to inform a more just US immigration and refugee policy. Such reforms must inevitably fall to the legislature (or else to executive action) to complete. Likewise, Rajendra's theory of justice is meant to convict the United States of its distinctive responsibility for upholding the rights of Central and South American migrants. Given the federal government's plenary power in matters of exclusion, removal, and admission, it is difficult to imagine what it would mean to see this responsibility fulfilled without congressional action that creates novel policy.[26] However, by making policy reform the central means of alleviating the immigration crisis, Rajendra

---

23   Or, as is the case in Snyder's work, the religious communities positioned to change the minds of their constituents.

24   Ilsup Ahn, *Religious Ethics and Migration: Doing Justice to Undocumented Workers* (New York: Routledge University Press, 2014), 3.

25   Ibid. [emphasis mine]

26   In a 2021 interview with Brite Divinity School's Borderlands Institute, Rajendra made several such proposals including withdrawing from the use of for-profit immigration detention centers, reforming and rethinking the mission of the US Customs and Border Patrol, and treating asylum as a right rather than treating asylum-seekers as criminals. See Tisha Rajendra, "Justice as Responsibility: Migration, History, and Ethics," Film, December 2, 2021, https://youtu.be/hY-ud1ZXxrI?feature=shared.

and Wilbanks implicitly reproduce the same realist assumptions that Ahn explicitly states.[27] Political agency is a positionally dependent phenomenon that lies with the legislature.

Heimburger's book, however, offers the most developed political theology for its ethics and, consequently, the best opportunity to elaborate the realist presuppositions at work in the present conversation. Contrary to the most unalloyed forms of Realpolitik, Heimburger rejects the notion that we live in "a world without universal right, where governments fend off threatening foreigners to preserve their own sphere of justice."[28] Instead, like Niebuhr, Heimburger situates his account of politics in the larger dynamic of sin and salvation playing out on the historical stage. In Heimburger's telling, this history stretches from the Garden of Eden to the gates of the New Jerusalem. Moreover, these biblical images are paradigmatic for his account of the state and the extent of its legitimacy. The Garden of Eden prefigures the idea of a 'kept place,' but one whose keeping, before the entry of sin, depends in no way on coercive force. The garden is given to the first humans to steward, and they accomplish this task with the power of their word alone. In this respect, the Garden of Eden does not yet resemble the walled states we know today. However, it does secure the legitimacy of some form of 'keeping' against the criticism that all forms of political division and rule are consequences of the fall. What the fall precipitates, instead, is the association of rule with force. This association is prefigured by the Angels, who must keep the garden's boundary with a flaming sword. The coincidence of rule and force finds full expression as the humans living in the world beyond the garden must find weapons of their own. "No longer do human beings guard just by fending off animals," Heimburger notes, "they have to fend off fellow human beings who are 'thieves and murderers.'"[29]

It is precisely this dynamic that informs the biblical image of Enoch, the first city. Cain establishes Enoch as a city of refuge—after murdering his brother Abel. For the crime of fratricide, God had condemned Cain to wander in the lands of Nod. However, certain that anyone he might meet would know his

---

27 Strikingly, since publishing *Religious Ethics & Migration*, Ilsup Ahn has made direct appeal to a revised form of Christian Realism in arguments regarding Christians' responsibility for and social engagement with Honduran migrants. In making his case, Ahn points to Rajendra's arguments in *Migrants and Citizens* as exemplary of the tack that such an approach would take. See Ilsup Ahn, "Christian Realism, Human Vulnerability, and the US Immigration Crisis," *CrossCurrents* 71 (2021): 115–136.
28 Heimburger, *God and the Illegal Alien*, 95.
29 Ibid, 97. Here, Heimburger is glossing Martin Luther's account of the fall of humankind. C.f. Martin Luther, *Luther's Works*, vol. 1 (St Louis: Concordia Publishing House, 1958).

crime and kill him, Cain judged this itinerancy a death sentence. Enoch's walls
were to be a shelter from the cycles of vengeful bloodletting triggered by the
fratricide. Enoch, then, emerges in response to the problem of sin. Ironically,
however, it replaces the divine mark of protection that God places on Cain
with a peace premised on the threat of overwhelming reprisal. Cain's descen-
dant, Lamech, declares, "If Cain is avenged sevenfold, truly Lamech seventy-sevenfold." (Gen. 4.24) As for Niebuhr, the use of coercive force typical of
the political is at once a restraint against sin and a mark of its historical effects.
If the kept garden images a city without sin, Cain's walled refuge is a sign of the
cities to come. "The guarding of cities," Heimburger concludes, "is a divine provision to protect human life."[30] Yet, it is a provision whose legitimacy is born
out of dire necessity.

However, in Heimburger's interpretation, the first city does not establish in
the beginning what must be so in the end. In the image of the New Jerusalem, Revelation depicts a city that is haunted neither by Cain's crime nor by
Lamech's threat. Here is a city that is walled yet open. Whereas Enoch's walls
are a bulwark against violence and a monument to human sinfulness, the New
Jerusalem's walls are a sign of harmony and order. With sin redeemed and
the threat of violence dissipated, its gates are thrown wide. Christian legislators, Heimburger suggests, may act in anticipation of this vision in one way
or another. They might conceive of their borders as sites of encounter rather
than boundaries against invading aliens. Nevertheless, the total embrace of
this ideal is neither possible nor morally commendable before the eschaton.
As long as sin endures, states must guard their borders. If Heimburger does not
go as far as Luther, who encouraged contemporary leaders to act as if God did
not exist, he nevertheless clings to the Niebuhrian conviction that they must
act with the awareness that sin does.[31]

Like Niebuhr, Heimburger suggests that political justice does not consist of
the elimination of coercive force but in its alignment to justified ends. In the
context of border policing, states have a right and obligation to act as 'humble guards' over their territories and their inhabitants. The divine provision
of state sovereignty, in this view, derives from the state's duty to secure the
common good. As such, people arriving at a state's borders may indeed be
required to seek its permission before entering. Moreover, the state's obligation
to restrain violence may sometimes permit the state to deny such requests.
However, Heimburger rejects the notion that states should enjoy such absolute
sovereignty as would render their decisions in these matters uncontestable. To

30   Heimburger, *God and the Illegal Alien,* 104.
31   Ibid, 105ff.

the contrary, Heimburger sets hard limits on the grounds to which a state may appeal in legitimizing acts of exclusion. The need to restrain violence may permit exclusions in the interest of public safety. A state—or, more importantly, its people—have a legitimate interest in the exclusion of violent criminals, invading militants, or persons engaged in the trafficking of narcotics. However, if the political community is not the summum bonum, then it cannot so easily justify exclusions to protect jobs, hoard wealth, or preserve culture.[32] In these instances, the divine preference for the orphan, the widow, and the sojourner must predominate. Hence, the state has a limited role in protecting its territory. Still, it must not be so arrogant as to equate narrow visions of economic or cultural self-preservation with the divine work of redemption.

The result of Heimburger's effort is a political theology remarkably similar to Niebuhr's. Our history is a story of tragedy. We have passed from the garden to Enoch and from Enoch to nation-states bristling with arms. The flaming sword, wielded by the angels, pales in comparison to the host of artillery, drones, jets, tanks, and other armaments that fortify our territories today. Contemporary nation-states stand well prepared to deliver on Lamech's promise of seventy-sevenfold violence. Within this story of tragedy, nation-states discover their role in constraining the cycles of violence introduced by humanity's fall into sin. Yet, like the flaming sword outside Eden, the very means by which they restrain violence are a sign of the fall with which they contend. Consequently, nation-states enjoy a measure of sovereignty. However, as we await the coming of the New Jerusalem, this political sovereignty cannot claim any form of ultimacy. Our present politics stand under the judgment of God, who is ever drawing nearer. As such, whatever sovereignty the state may claim is yet subject to divine justice—a justice paradigmatically expressed in care for the widow, the orphan, and the sojourner. Thus, for Heimburger, the state occupies its place in salvation history insofar as it acts as a 'humble guard' against the violence at its gates.

In *God and the Illegal Alien*, Heimburger has made a novel contribution to the Christian Ethics of Migration.[33] His theology of politics not only responds

---

32   Ibid, 146.

33   Among the book's triumph's is the legal history it provides for the category of the 'alien.' Heimburger traces this term's emergence from its early appearances in Common Law through its various treatments in US Law. Although this topic does not immediately occupy us here, Heimburger's care with the legal materials reveals this category's historical contingency and the shifting places it has occupied in US Law. The upshot of this effort is an argument for dispensing with the term that draws at once theological and legal justifications. For further remarks on this aspect of Heimburger's book, see my review of *God and the Illegal Alien* in the *Journal of Law and Religion* 35 (2020): 341–344.

to critics like Amstutz, who accuse scholars of overlooking the legitimacy of the international system of states, but it also brings to the surface the set of theological reasons built into our account of the 'real.' No more for Heimburger than for Niebuhr is theology an exclusively ideal discourse incapable of rendering descriptions of the world in which we live. On the contrary, theology contributes to our understanding of the real, framing our conceptions not only of *what ought to be* but *what is*. Moreover, for Heimburger, just as for Niebuhr, an apt understanding of ourselves, our political associations, and the trajectory of our histories depends on an adequate accounting of the doctrine of sin.

Yet, Heimburger grants 'walled states' their role in salvation history only as he sets aside more radical strains in Christian theological imaginaries. Heimburger, that is, conducts his theological exegesis of Genesis and Revelation in conversation with four 'trusted interpreters': Martin Luther, Jean Calvin, Jacques Ellul, and Oliver O'Donovan. These figures, especially Luther and Calvin, are doubtless standard bearers in the Protestant tradition. However, in prioritizing these voices, Heimburger leaves aside those that might press us to see, in the biblical text, the possibility of a world ordered otherwise than our own.[34] Consequently, even as it uncovers the intersections of theological ideals and material reals, Heimburger's political theology drives a wedge between history and eschatology that effectively insulates the present order from the Reign of God to come.[35] In doing this, Heimburger does not depart the intellectual company of fellow Christian ethicists but instead helps to explain the dawning sense of hopelessness that is coming to characterize the Christian ethics of migration.

4   Hopelessness in the Borderlands

Where theology is walled off from reconfiguring our accounts of the 'real,' it also appears to be ineffective in moving the consciences within it. United

---

34   One might reasonably wonder, for instance, how Heimburger's theology of politics would change were it to draw on more radical reformers, like Luther's opponent Thomas Müntzer. C.f. Thomas Müntzer, *Sermon to the Princes* (New York: Verso, 2010).

35   Beyond theological discontents such as this one, there are discontents that communitarian political philosophers might reasonably bring to Heimburger's argument. First among these might well be the idea that a state cannot exclude an outsider on the grounds of cultural self-preservation. As Michael Walzer explains (and as we shall take up in considerable detail in subsequent chapters), self-determination entails not only freedom in *what* a state will do with its power, but in *whom* a state will determine itself to be. Thus, to prohibit exclusions on the grounds of cultural preservation seems not to be a qualification of a state's capacity for self-determination, but rather its total abrogation.

States immigration policy has undergone little substantive change in the last thirty years—likewise, the humanitarian crisis in the southwestern border-lands. Under successive presidential administrations, the doctrine of pre-vention through deterrence has continued to justify the securitization of the US–Mexico line. Undoubtedly, President Donald Trump revived the border's significance as a site of political theater. Still, construction of his long-prom-ised wall neither began nor ended with his first tenure in the Oval Office.[36] In October of 2023, it was reported that construction was ongoing.[37] All the while, migrant mortalities have continued with little sign of abating. Among Christian ethicists, years without meaningful policy change have led some to despair about the possibility of justice—especially among those who live in or spend considerable time in the borderlands.

In a 2021 interview at Brite Divinity School in Fort Worth, Texas, Rajendra remarked that in the years since publishing Migrants and Citizens, she had come increasingly to embrace a 'Niebuhrian' insight earlier articulated by Karen Lebacqz.[38] Namely, all our discussions of justice begin in an unjust world, where injustice poses an ever-present danger, and the fight against injus-tice is relentless. "In this vale of tears," Rajendra remarks, "we do have fleeting moments of justice ... and we should rightfully look for them as something to be celebrated and affirmed."[39] However, she continues, we must also concede that any such victory will be partial and temporary. Doubting the likelihood of federal reforms that would bring about lasting change, she proposes that we must discover our ethical task in works of love that render more humane a world borne down by pervasive systemic injustice that will not go away.[40] For Rajendra, however, love does not excel justice. Instead, the work of love is an effort to cope with justice's impossibility.

To illustrate this point, she recounts the story of an immigrant couple that was preparing to cross the US border. As they made their preparations, the couple planned to get married. This bond would lend them some form of legal claim to one another in the event of their interdiction. What these migrants were owed was the right to seek asylum safely. However, in their desert crossing,

---

36   Nor were President Trump's calls for border fencing novel. Much of the fencing erected by the Trump administration was merely a replacement for old fencing the construction of which traced at least as far back as the Secure Fence Act of 2006.

37   Eileen Sullivan and Colbi Edmonds, "Biden, the Border, and Why a New Wall Is Going Up," *The New York Times*, October 6, 2023, sec. U.S., https://www.nytimes.com/2023/10/06/us/border-wall-biden.html.

38   Rajendra, "Justice as Responsibility." C.f. Karen Lebacqz, *Justice in an Unjust World* (Min-neapolis: Fortress Press, 1987)

39   Rajendra, "Justice as Responsibility."

40   Ibid.

this right would fall into doubt. Federal authorities would likely meet them as criminals rather than asylum-seekers. Moreover, this right was something other than what their attorney or their community could give them. So, their community gave them a wedding instead. The ceremony was complete with a cake and a band. This sort of action, Rajendra goes on, is what she has in mind when she speaks of 'solidarity' as 'political love.' A wedding certificate would have sufficed their legal objectives. Hosting a complete wedding and reception was unnecessary. However, it was a testament to their union's status as a domain of human practice that involves more than the official relationship that the law names. Solidarity, that is, is the declaration of migrants' humanity in the face of a border regime under which they are routinely dehumanized.

Nevertheless, for Rajendra, such shows of solidarity are declarations not only of migrant humanity but of intractable injustice. They are love's expression in a history that, as Niebuhr suggests, is fundamentally tragic. "We love knowing that justice is not possible," Rajendra explains, "knowing that we cannot, at this time and in this place, meet our responsibilities to these migrants."[41] It is not as though Rajendra considers these shows of solidarity morally insignificant. Nevertheless, these declarations of humanity occur under the failure to provide migrants with the safety that is their just desert. Love is the expression of a responsibility foreclosed. Works of love, that is, may attain an ethical significance, but this significance stands in stark relief to the genuine political efficacy upon which justice relies.

Miguel De La Torre puts the issue more forcefully in his monograph, *Embracing Hopelessness*.[42] Theologians who hope to persuade leaders in the national legislature face the impossible task of convincing the United States to abandon the very policies that have made it rich. The criminalization of migration, De La Torre argues, is part of a larger neo-colonial strategy that seeks to extract wealth and resources from Latin American nations while stopping their citizens from following these goods north.[43] Migrant mortalities in the Sonoran and the host of maladies faced by migrants across the US interior, then, are not bugs in an otherwise well-intended system. They are the features. The US, in De La Torre's final judgment, is an empire, and it is one that Christian ethicists cannot reasonably hope to persuade. Whatever justifications they may provide

---

41   Ibid.
42   Miguel A. De La Torre, *Embracing Hopelessness* (Minneapolis: Fortress Press, 2017).
43   This same dynamic is reflected in De La Torre's more narrative work *The US Immigration Crisis: Towards an Ethics of Place* (Eugene: Cascade Books, 2016). Here, De La Torre narrates the stories of migrants who have been carried (often surreptitiously) across the United States in their effort to eke out a meager living.

for pursuing one course of action or another, they cannot overcome the motivational force conveyed by national self-interest. Instead of hoping for reform, De La Torre concludes that Christian ethicists must embrace hopelessness. If, indeed, the international system of states provides the fundamental reality to which Christian ethicists must respond, then in De La Torre's view, true justice is decidedly out of the question. Where Rajendra counsels acts of love that assert migrants' humanity, De La Torre commends an ethics *para joder*, that is, interventions that cannot precipitate lasting change but nevertheless gum up the works of an insidious imperial machinery. If the machine cannot be stopped, it can at least be slowed down.

"The *joderon*," the practitioner of De La Torre's ethics, "is one who becomes a royal pain in the ass, purposely causes trouble, constantly disrupts the established norm, shouts from the mountaintop what is supposed to be kept silent, and audaciously refuses to stay in his or her assigned place."[44] "To *joder*," De La Torre continues, "is to create instability, upsetting the prevailing panopticon social order designed to maintain the law and order of the privileged."[45] Defined in these terms, this ethics is negative in its function. It opposes the unjust system that refuses to be reformed and declares its inhumanity but does not posit a new order. Where Rajendra sees at least fleeting victories that are to be commended and celebrated, De La Torre sees none. History has taught us that victory is not possible. It has taught us not of God's presence but of God's absence. "We strive forward," De La Torre concludes, "not because we hope to succeed (because we won't) or because we cling to a biblical belief that a promise was offered; we move toward justice because we have no other choice if we wish to define ourselves as human."[46] With the hope of success precluded, this self-definition and ethical action, in general, can be known only in acts of negation. To practice an ethics *para joder*, then, is the task of the Christian ethicist and of the humanitarian in the borderlands. To aspire to do more would be to lose touch with reality.[47]

---

44   De La Torre, *Embracing Hopelessness*, 150.
45   Ibid.
46   Ibid, 152.
47   It should be noted that De La Torre insists that an ethics *para joder* is not only an ethics that "f*cks with the prevailing power structures," it is also "an effective response to the consequences of Eurocentric globalization, the oppressive normativity of social structures, and the pain of the domestication of communities of color." (p. 150) Nevertheless, De La Torre's argumentation leaves us to question in what this *effectiveness* consists and upon what it is conditioned. If De La Torre's ethics, after all, permits something else than an unmitigated embrace of hopelessness, then it presses us to question anew the grounds

Must Christian ethicists embrace hopelessness? Are we capable of nothing more than loving (or, perhaps, spiteful) yet futile revolts against some indefatigable and malicious force that cannot be overcome? The despair that has come to infect the Christian ethics of migration is not superficial. De La Torre and Rajendra are no strangers to the borderlands. De La Torre, as he notes in his book, has taken part in direct actions with humanitarian organizations in Arizona, including No More Deaths. His work carries considerable credibility among their members.[48] The common presupposition underlying both of their positions, however, is that political agency lies elsewhere than with these borderlands actors. That is, both in *Migrants and Citizens* and in *Embracing Hopelessness*, the achievement of justice is handed over to actors at the national center. It is Congress that must reform the border patrol and change immigration policy—and it is Congress that refuses to move. However, realism's despair may be avoided if realism's presuppositions regarding the locus of agency can be revised. The effort to empower such a revision, in turn, lies close to the heart of the present analysis and its political theological project.

5   An Eschatological Imperative

Doubtless, as De La Torre and Rajendra suggest, there is real cause for frustration and, perhaps, even hopelessness in the US–Mexico borderlands. Nevertheless, the borderlands also present us with a distinct epistemological context for construing our political reality and the possibilities and limits present therein. This setting at once confirms and refutes the reality of the international line, confronting us with its contingency. Here, we meet neither the border nor the system of states that it implies as brute facts. Instead, we discover them as claims that must be asserted. Border enforcement is not the enforcement of a natural boundary that preexists policing activity but rather a work of statecraft

---

of our political agency and how they may become available to actors in the borderlands. Indeed, this book is an effort to pursue just this line of inquiry.

48   In a conversation I shared with Rev. John Fife, former pastor of Tucson's historic Southside Presbyterian Church, one of the pillars of the 1980s Tucson Sanctuary Movement, and an organizer for Humane Borders and No Más Muertes, De La Torre's was the only name that was mentioned. Recounting an effort to intervene against Operation Streamline, Fife recounted a story of several church members lashing themselves to a bus that was meant to deliver a group of migrants back to Mexico. These were *joderones*, actively disrupting an inhumane system. In Fife's estimation, De La Torre's ethics had accurately captured the feeling in the borderlands.

that must constantly construct and reconstruct that edifice, which is the bulwark between nations and polities. This construction is sometimes literal, as with the erection of concrete and steel fencing. At other times, it is more figurative, as is the case when migrants are captured in high-tech surveillance systems or interdicted by border patrol officers. "On the border," as Jessica Auchter eloquently puts it, "the state states itself."[49] However, this statement is not final. If it were, continued policing would be unnecessary. Instead, against the state's self-assertion, migrant crossings and the work of transborder organizations posit the possibility of another politics, one defined by crossing rather than dwelling.

To critics like Amstutz, who might doubt theology's ability to achieve a realistic description of migration's context, the borderlands bear witness to the fact that the international system of collectively self-determining nation-states is shot through with as much unreality as reality. It is by no means obvious that those whom Amstutz labels 'realists' have a monopoly on 'realism.' As political philosopher Wendy Brown suggests in *Walled States, Waning Sovereignty*, we may now find ourselves in a distinctly 'post-Westphalian' reality.[50] Brown's contention is not that nation-states have ceased to exist but that they are passing away. With the prefix 'post,' then, she seeks to describe a present that is conditioned, on the one hand, on a reality that is increasingly slipping into the past, and, on the other, another that is only now beginning to break across history's horizon. That is, the securitization of national borders suggests that we find ourselves in a moment of historical transition wherein the contours of the real are the subject of active contest. At this point of transition, the dispute between so-called 'realists' and 'cosmopolitans' is not a fight between the real and the ideal. Instead, it is a dispute over the nature of the real itself.

Participants in this dispute, Christian ethicists need not adopt a realist political theology that commits itself to the international system of nation-states. Neither ought one suppose that making the borderlands the epistemic context for the work of theological reflection should require departing from the biblical literature. The Hebrew Bible and the Christian Scriptures speak not only about walled cities but also about sojourners and the roads on which

---

49   Jessica Auchter, *The Politics of Haunting and Memory in International Relations* (New York: Routledge, 2014), 91.

50   Wendy Brown, *Walled States, Waning Sovereignty* (New York: Zone Books, 2010), 22ff. Brown writes, "in a post-Westphalian order, sovereign nation-states no longer exclusively define the field of global political relations or monopolize many of the powers organizing that field, yet states remain significant actors in the field, as well as symbols of national identification." (p. 24)

they spend their lives. Abram and Sarai, Moses and the Hebrews, the exilic diaspora, Jesus' disciples, the apostle Paul, and Christ himself are depicted primarily in crossing rather than dwelling. It is no accident that the sojourner is included as a character of particular concern in the Levitical Holiness codes. In the outsider, a theo-political community of sojourners encounters not an alien but one of their own. In the Pauline Epistles, moreover, the very problem of eschatology is a problem addressed to a people who find themselves within the present order but not of it. Eschatological reflection begins in the space between worlds and the time between the times. In the borderlands, Christian theology finds a setting that offers a material reminder of its origins and radical political potentials.

Furthermore, if, as the Niebuhrian tradition suggests, 'realism' requires accounting for the doctrine of sin's full anthropological and socio-political significance, the borderlands underscore and enrich our sense of this doctrine. Indeed, in security regimes like PTD, we can witness the contempt for contingency that Niebuhr associates most essentially with sin. Our creatureliness includes our existence as embodied animals and, therefore, our existence as animals vulnerable to thirst, hunger, exposure, and one another. PTD weaponizes this embodiment. It sews enmity between migrants and their bodies, making our creatureliness an object of contempt. However, as a law enforcement regime rather than a bare aggregate of individual actions, PTD also offers a chilling confirmation of sin's ability to infect our social structures. As Kristin Heyer rightly identifies, the United States immigration and enforcement apparatus itself comprises a structure that alienates and dehumanizes migrants, subverting their dignity.[51] PTD, we might say, is not merely the consequence of sinful volitions but expresses sin in its very structure. Thus, shifting the locus of our reflections away from the national center and toward the borderlands allows us to render sin's full significance concretely.

In the subsequent chapters, I seek to sketch a political theology capable of navigating the Scylla and Charybdis of hopelessness and deluded optimism. To avoid the latter problem, I aim to accommodate Christian Realism's sober appraisal of the human condition and its implications for the limits of our ethical projects. In this respect, I strive for 'realism.' Nevertheless, better to resist the temptation to despair, I will reject the three 'realist' presuppositions described in the preceding pages. That is, I will not begin from a vantage that centers on the international system of states, nor will I insist that meaningful

---

51   Heyer, *Kinship Across Borders*, n.b., 14–17.

political agency is the exclusive province of those who occupy positions of legislative power. I do this not to preserve the moral purity of an impracticable idealism. Instead, I pursue this project because the 'realism' these presuppositions constitute stands out of joint with the reality of the borderlands. However counterintuitive, I will contend that by turning our eyes to this dynamic place between worlds, we will be better positioned to identify conditions for political agency that have been largely overlooked and glimpse the possibility of a world ordered otherwise than our own.

CHAPTER 2

The Remembrance of Dismembered Bodies

A Remark on Method

> Five men stumbled out of the mountain pass so sunstruck they
> didn't know their own names, couldn't remember where they'd
> come from, had forgotten how long they'd been lost ...
>
> —LUIS ALBERTO URREA, *The Devil's Highway*

∴

1 Mortalities on the Margins and the Danger of Spectacle

Since its publication in 2004, Luis Alberto Urrea's book, *The Devil's Highway*, has become a touchstone for literature about migration in the southwestern borderlands. It recounts the true story of five migrants who were intercepted by an agent of the Border Patrol near its Welton Station on May 24, 2001.[1] They were surviving members of a group of twenty-six men and boys who, five days earlier, had crossed from Mexico into the United States. By the end of the fifth day, only twelve remained among the living. The Sonoran claimed fourteen as its share. At the time, the story of the 'Wellton Twenty-Six' caught national attention. Appearing in the *New York Times* and *Washington Post*, it shed light on a gruesome reality of which many Americans living in the interior were unaware. Blending the talents of the journalist, the poet, and the novelist, Urrea's book reproduces in graphic detail the journey's effect on migrants' bodies. With these troubling images, Urrea sought to ensure that the light national media had cast on the Wellton Twenty-Six (and the crisis of which their story was a part) would not be fleeting.

While the fate that befell the Wellton Twenty-Six is frighteningly common, it is quite uncommon that it is made the center of media attention. From time

---

1 Luis Alberto Urrea, *The Devil's Highway: A True Story* (New York: Little, Brown, and Company, 2004).

to time, a story breaks into the news cycle.[2] However, the sporadic coverage of such stories leaves the impression that such occurrences are exceptional. Despite this impression, these stories are only the visible flashpoints in a long-standing humanitarian crisis that takes place just beyond the view of the public eye. Those like Urrea, who would draw attention to the crisis of migrant mortalities, face the challenge of bringing visibility to deaths that occur on the geographic and political margins.

However, the same harsh landscape that resists migrants' advance also resists those who would document and memorialize the lives it claims. As migrant traffic shifts into remote wilderness corridors, migrant mortalities are pressed further from view. Thus, the real human cost of securing the US–Mexico line—the cost paid in migrants' bodies—is largely invisible. Organizations committed to tracking migrant deaths, however, have done important work in recording this cost. Still, even as they reveal the crisis' scale, staggering reports of thousands of dead test our capacities for comprehension and compassion. These numbers are impersonal, without narrative. By retelling individual stories, works like Urrea's endeavor to humanize the crisis and to render in concrete detail realities that might otherwise feel distant or abstract. However, they are resisted in their efforts not only by the landscape itself but by a law enforcement regime that is designed to disappear migrants in the desert's expanse.

PTD is an aesthetic project designed to cope with a political imperative of its own. Abandoned to the wilderness, the ever-growing ledger of the dead counts the human cost of maintaining the present political order. This cost cannot be dismissed as a matter of political indifference. As Erika Doss suggests, the bodies of the deceased, unburied and ungrieved, present the polity with a life frighteningly 'out of order.'[3] Migrant remains, abandoned in the desert, provide a gruesome reminder of the violations that mark the thresholds of the

---

2   Perhaps the most recent example came in June of 2022, when over 50 deceased migrants were discovered in the back of a box truck in San Antonio Texas. This story found its way onto the pages not only of local papers, but national outlets including CNN, the Washington Post, and the New York Times. See James Dobbins, Miriam Jordan, and J. David Goodman, "Texas Migrant Deaths: 51 Migrants Dead After Overheated Truck Is Abandoned in Texas," *The New York Times*, June 28, 2022, sec. U.S., https://www.nytimes.com/live/2022/06/28/us/texas-migrants-dead; Arelis R. Hernández, Nick Miroff, and Maria Sacchetti, "46 Migrants Found Dead in Texas inside Sweltering Tractor-Trailer," *Washington Post*, June 28, 2022, https://www.washingtonpost.com/nation/2022/06/27/migrants-dead-texas/; & Ray Sanchez, Nicole Chavez, & Priscilla Alvarez, "On a Texas Road Called 'the Mouth of the Wolf,' a Semitruck Packed with Migrants Was Abandoned in the Sweltering Heat," CNN, June 29, 2022, https://www.cnn.com/2022/06/29/us/san-antonio-migrant-truck-deaths/index.html.

3   C.f. Erika Doss, *Memorial Mania: Public Feeling in America* (Chicago: University of Chicago press, 2010)

body politic. They attest that the bounds of American territory and identity are not produced and maintained without severing some part of the social body and creating an obscene remainder of nonmembers. This remainder points to the contingency not only of the bodies of the disowned but of the body politic itself, positing the possibility that life could—and perhaps should— be ordered otherwise. If the polity is to maintain the present order, the dead must be pressed to the margins of visibility. The obscene remainder must be disappeared.

Situating political theological reflection in the borderlands bears great promise. However, realizing this promise means joining figures like Urrea not only in ethical and political protest but also in aesthetic projects designed to rupture the regimes of visibility and invisibility that PTD enforces. The bodies in the wilderness must be recovered and brought to light. Implicit in the remembrance of these dis-membered bodies is the possibility of an encounter that would precipitate a form of politically transformative ethical experience. As Alexandra Délano Alonso and Benjamin Nienass propose, practices of public mourning can serve to conjure the ghosts that haunt the borderlands.[4] By calling the dead from the wilderness and into the streets of the polity, the work of mourning draws the violation into view and allows the dead to demand a reckoning from the living. This remembrance, this reckoning between the polity's members and the disavowed, bears within it the possibility of a re-membering of the body politic; a renegotiation of the bounds of membership that traverses the international line and the boundary between the living and the dead. The question that borderlands activists, authors, scholars, and journalists face is *how* to go about this work.

The range of methods so far employed stretches from the figurative to the concrete. Barbara Sostaita has demonstrated how the seemingly innocuous act of planting crosses at the sites where migrants have died can provide an occasion for ethically and politically transformative encounters with the dead. Her 2016 essay, 'Making crosses, crossing borders,' offers a careful analysis of the aesthetic interventions being made by Arizona artist Alvaro Enciso.[5]

---

4   Alexandra Délano Alonso and Benjamin Nienass, "Deaths, Visibility, and Responsibility: The Politics of Mourning at the US–Mexico Border," *Social Research* 83 (2016): 421–451. See also Ulrich Schmiedel, "Mourning the Un-Mournable? Political Theology Between Refugees and Religion," *Political Theology* 18 (2017): 612–27. Writing in the European context, Schmiedel's work suggests that public burial rituals for deceased migrants declare the grievability and the dignity of otherwise 'ungrievable' lives; lives that many European governments are happy to let slip unnoticed beneath the waves of the Mediterranean.
5   Barbara Sostaita, "Making Crosses, Crossing Borders: The Performance of Mourning, the Power of Ghosts, and the Politics of Countermemory in the U.S.-Mexico Borderlands," August 18,

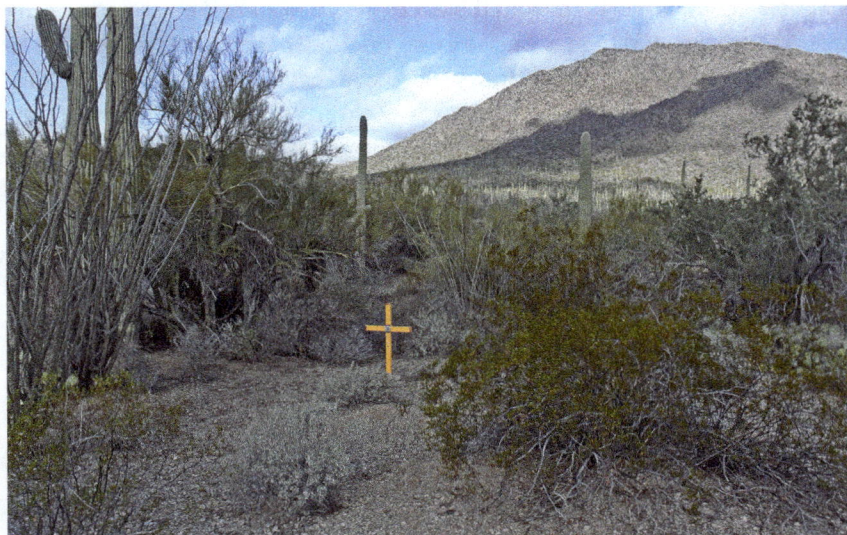

FIGURE 5   Alvaro Enciso, *Cross for an Unidentified Male Migrant*
SOURCE: ALVARO ENCISO, *CROSS FOR AN UNIDENTIFIED MALE MIGRANT*, 2022,
SCULPTURE, DONDE MUEREN LOS SUEÑOS, DIGITAL MULTIMEDIA PROJECT

Working in tandem with the Samaritans, a network of borderland humanitarians, Enciso designs, creates, and plants crosses in places where migrants
have died. These crosses provide a material interruption in the landscape that
grants visibility to the lives that the polity attempts to disappear. Moreover,
as symbols of state-sanctioned violence, these crosses also evoke the largely
invisible enforcement regimes that have brought about these disappearances.[6]

Crosses like Enciso's can be found in demonstrations across the borderlands. They appear not only in the desert but also in city squares. In Tucson, for
instance, on El Día de Muertos, the Coalición de Derechos Humanos organizes
an eight-mile processional through the city's south side.[7] Participants carry
crosses, one for each migrant who has died in the desert during the year. Some
bear names and many others have the label *desconocido/a*. At the procession's
end, the crosses are joined with those from previous years, producing a collection that numbers in the thousands. Just as Enciso's crosses aim to facilitate an

---

2016, https://mavcor.yale.edu/conversations/mediations/making-crosses-crossing-borders-
performance-mourning-power-ghosts-and.

6   Sostaita takes care to remind her readers that before it was transformed into a symbol of
    Christian faith, the Cross was a method for capital punishment under the Roman Imperium.

7   See Alonso & Nienass, "Deaths, Visibility, and Responsibility," 433–437.

encounter between the living and the deceased, the Coalición's crosses signify the dead's presence. Whereas Enciso's artwork draws the viewer's attention to the wilderness, the Coalición's draws those who have been left in the wilderness back into the city's streets. Their overwhelming number depicts with clarity the staggering scale of the crisis—or so the demonstrators hope.

However, fearing that the subtlety of such messages might be lost on most viewers, other activists have opted for more direct forms of representation. Both in the borderlands and at protests in the national center, some activists have traded crosses for placards emblazoned with images of decaying migrant bodies. In Texas, for instance, members of the Border Network for Human Rights affixed images of migrant remains to sections of border fencing along Interstate 10. Set in opposition to the spectacles of criminality that serve to legitimize border security efforts, Alonso and Nienass suggest that these graphic images constitute "counter spectacles" that demand redress.[8] On the one hand, these images display in grisly detail the violence that PTD perpetrates against migrants' bodies. They bring the work of mourning to highly populated areas and hold before the public eye the inhumanity of the present border enforcement regime. On the other hand, these direct methods of representation also bring to our attention the distinctive dangers that accompany this sort of aesthetic intervention.

However well intended, the effort photographically to disinter the dead risks reproducing the same racialized violence that it protests. Most of these images depict black and brown bodies. Yet they are arrayed before what is often a primarily white gaze. Saidiya Hartman, in her 1997 study, *Scenes of Subjection*, warns that gruesome spectacles such as these can inure just as easily as inspire indignation at the body's violation.[9] Hartman opens her book with a series of reflections on a scene frequently cited and reproduced in accounts of antebellum and reconstruction era America: the savage beating of Frederick Douglass' Aunt Hester. It was this 'terrible spectacle' that introduced Douglass to the horrors of slavery, and Hartman concedes that it is one of the "most well-known scenes in the literature of slavery."[10] However, she refuses to quote it at any length herself. To do so, she warns, would risk plunging the spectacle into a repetition that would not only desensitize us to its effects but normalize the brutalization of black and brown bodies. Like the 'terrible spectacle' that

---

8   Ibid, 437–439. C.f. Nicholas De Genova, "Spectacles of Migrant 'Illegality': The Scene of Exclusion, the Obscene of Inclusion," *Ethnic and Racial Studies* 36 (2013): 1180–1198.

9   Sadiya Hartman, *Scenes of Subjection: Terror, Slavery, and Self-Making in Nineteenth Century America* (New York: Oxford University Press, 1997).

10   Ibid, 4.

Douglass describes, the placards in the borderlands are held up in the hope that they will awaken the polity to PTD's inhumanity. However, at a border that is considerably more open to those who are not marked as racialized others, this hope cannot be divorced from the anxiety that the image might acclimatize the viewer to violence rather than compel them to stop it.

This problem is central to the purposes of this book. It raises a methodological issue that must be addressed. Indeed, I hope this book will do more than offer a description of PTD. I hope it will permit, however indirectly, an encounter with the lives it takes and, in doing so, provide a prelude to responsible action. In one form or another, then, this project, too, must find a way to bring the dead present without succumbing to a macabre fascination with gory spectacles that fix the eye on ravaged bodies. Thus, the present analysis finds itself at the juncture not only between ethics and political theology, but also between ethics and aesthetics. In this chapter, I aim first to introduce the theory of ethical subjectivity that will inform much of the subsequent argumentation. Second, I seek to elaborate on how this account of ethical subjectivity makes aesthetics a matter of first concern. Third, I appeal to the work of borderland artist and writer Valerie Lee James.[11] In her work, I identify an aesthetic strategy that confronts us with the dead's ethical demands without making their bodies the objects of a disinterested or prurient gaze.

2   The Ethical Demand

This book affixes its argument to the conviction that our ethical subjectivity is constituted and oriented in an experience of demand.[12] To borrow Søren Kierkegaard's formulation, the ethical subject is not an 'I' that announces itself in the nominative, but a 'You' constituted in the accusative.[13] That is, I set out

---

11   Although I focus here on James' sculpture, she is also widely published, having contributed to the *Yale ISM Review*, *America Magazine*, *Open Democracy*, the *Global Sisters Report*, the *Society of Southwestern Authors Storyteller Magazine*, *She Magazine*, and *The Hummingbird Review*. Several of James' written works, including pieces on the 'Art of Asylum' and 'Spiritual Activism on the Border,' can be found on her website https://artandfaithinthedesert.com.

12   In subsequent chapters, I will seek to elaborate in more concrete terms how this demand is conveyed to us, the good that it reveals, and the extent to which law can render this good legible to the polity. In this essay, I will settle for sketching out Critchley's relatively formal account of ethical subjectivity's structure, a structure that cannot be clarified without his tandem concept of ethical experience.

13   See Søren Kierkegaard, *Works of Love,* trans. Howard Hong and Edna Hong (Princeton: Princeton University Press, 1998).

from the conviction that ethical subjectivity does not consist in the lonely identification and ordering of goods but rather in negotiating our relationship with a good under whose address we are always already found. Moreover, this address does not come to us in abstraction but approaches us concretely in the person of the other. In her, we are confronted with our mutual interdependence. We are confronted with our ability either to take part in the preservation of this life or else, whether actively or passively, to participate in its destruction. Whatever freedom we possess cannot be defined apart from the choice to accept our mutual interdependence as a good for which we are responsible or to protest it as a contemptible encumbrance. This account of ethical subjectivity, as a dialectical relationship founded in an experience of approval and demand, builds on a confluence of ethical traditions that find compelling expression in Simon Critchley's concise study, *Infinitely Demanding*.[14]

Critchley articulates his account of ethical experience in response to a problem of moral motivation that he diagnoses at the core of ethical systems built on principles of autonomy.[15] This problem emerges in the effort to differentiate what Immanuel Kant calls 'hypothetical imperatives' from what he terms 'categorical imperatives.' Kant calls 'hypothetical' any imperative or rule an actor adopts merely because she desires some associated end and has chosen to act on that desire.[16] Imperatives so formed are insufficient for a robust ethics, Kant judges, because they are purely subjective. Before a rule can bind our wills, it must attain a measure of objectivity distinct from the ends produced by transient desires. So, if they are to constrain our worst impulses, this is precisely what ethical rules must do. That is, ethical rules must be 'categorical,' binding on human actors under their status as rational agents. Before any moral proposition can attain motivational force, it must attain a *facticity* distinct from the agent's subjective, transient desires.

For his part, Kant attempts to solve this problem by appealing to what he calls 'the fact of reason,' our experience of reason's claim as something other to us. However, the problem with this solution for many post-Kantians is that by introducing this dimension of 'otherness' into moral reasoning, Kant appears to introduce a contradictory moment of heteronomy into an ethics

---

14   See Simon Critchley, *Infinitely Demanding: Ethics of Commitment, Politics of Responsibility* (New York: Verso, 2012). Critchley's book, for its part, draws heavily on the works of Knud Ejler Løgstrup, Emmanuel Levinas, and Alain Badiou.

15   Critchley, *Inifinitely Demanding*, 26–37. To demonstrate the pervasiveness of this problem, Critchley points to the challenge of accounting for the 'fact of reason' in Kant's philosophy and subsequent interpretations of his work.

16   Immanuel Kant, *Critique of Practical Wisdom*, trans. Mary Gregor (New York: Cambridge University Press, 2015), 18.

committed to autonomy. At this point of contradiction, many post-Kantians see a breakdown in the system. Critchley, however, sees in this contradiction a vital insight. 'Ethical experience,' Critchley insists, is precisely an experience of 'hetero-affectivity,' in which we feel ourselves moved not by a good we appoint for ourselves but by one that approaches us from without. Contrary to those who would hold to an orthodox understanding of autonomy, Critchley's theory prizes precisely that 'ethical experience' which suspends rather than confirms the sovereignty of the 'I.' This suspension is the beginning of our ethical subjectivity, not its undoing.

Critchley does not seek to explain precisely of what the subject's good does or must consist. Instead, satisfied to generate a formal account of ethical subjectivity, he leaves the matter open. We might think, Critchley explains, of 'the good' in any number of ways: the Mosaic Law in the Bible, the good beyond being in Plato, the resurrected Christ in Paul and Augustine, the moral law in Kant, *et cetera*.[17] However we conceive the good, what Critchley finds crucial is that we appreciate that we do not, in fact, produce our moral identities in isolation through Archimedean acts of self-legislation. Rather, we come to understand ourselves as moral actors as we find ourselves under the address of another and meet her demand with approval. As Critchley puts it, "an *ethical subject* can be defined as a self relating itself approvingly, bindingly, to the demand of its good" and "this demand of the good *founds* the self ... is the fundamental principle of the subject's articulation."[18] Attempting to account for the problem of moral motivation, then, leads Critchley to an account of ethical subjectivity in which the moral actor is defined from the outset by its relation to some other.

We may turn to the marital relationship as an illustration of this point. In the marital relationship, individuals become a distinctive kind of subject only as the ambit of their responsibility comes to be defined by the fact of their relationship to some specific other. To take on the name 'husband,' 'wife,' or 'partner' is to declare one's binding approval of the claim made upon them by some other 'husband,' 'wife,' or 'partner.' Consequently, whatever it means to be a 'good' partner or a 'bad' partner is unintelligible apart from one's fidelity or infidelity to the relationship that this approval confirms. Tellingly, the pain accompanying a marital transgression is not the consequence of one's betrayal of some abstract code of marital duties. It is instead the acute pain of breaking faith with one's partner—the pain that accompanies a betrayal of this particular good—and, by extension, the pain of standing at enmity with the identity

17   Critchley, *Infinitely Demanding*, 16.
18   Ibid, 20.

that one's relationship to this good bestows. Likewise, for the ethical subject. If we articulate our moral self-understanding in light of that which we approve as our good, then our moral self-understanding comes to be bound up with the pleasure or pain that accompanies our fidelity or infidelity to this fact. Moral propositions, by extension, attain their motivational force from the relation of fidelity or infidelity that their adoption would produce within our subjectivity. With this in mind, we may define ethical subjectivity in more complete detail as a form of relationship that begins in an experience of active receptivity to the demand of some good, in light of which we understand ourselves as moral actors and with which we may either stand in good faith or bad faith.[19]

However, even as Critchley's theory of ethical subjectivity provides us with a structure for understanding moral motivation, it also reveals a point of moral vulnerability where ethics and aesthetics converge. Experiences of hetero-affectivity are conditioned on our ability actually to encounter some other. If my wife is to be that good that orients my responsibilities as a husband, then it is critical that I actually meet her. To stipulate such a point in the context of a (potential) romantic relationship is so obvious as to verge on the comical. However, if ethical subjectivity depends on encounters, then we must acknowledge the contingency and chance that permeate the very possibility of our self-understandings as moral agents. Furthermore, we must take seriously how these contingencies can be manipulated and exacerbated by political regimes designed to control the movements of bodies.[20] Such a regime enforces itself on the borderlands. This regime is the very reason that artists like Enciso and activists like the members of the Coalición and Border Network must find ways to bring the dead present—to lend visibility to an 'invisible crisis.' They must

---

19   However, if ethical subjectivity is defined in relation to a good, it is worth specifying that this relation may be one of approval or of rejection. If the marital relationship provides a useful illustration for conceiving a subjectivity formed by approval, we might also consider divorce as an illustration for a relationship formed by rejection. A name like 'ex-husband' does not erase the good of the former partner. It only negates this good's ability to make a continuing claim on our sense of responsibility. This point is of particular importance in the context of migration, since the bounds of the body politic are defined no less by its relation to those whom it excludes than those it admits.

20   Theodor Adorno's criticisms of Søren Kierkegaard's doctrine of love target precisely the naïve assumption that we will encounter and see our neighbor as a matter of course. The occurrence of such encounters Kierkegaard entrusted to the hand of divine 'governance.' The problem, as Adorno rightly observed, is that between the ethical subject and the hand of the divine often intervenes the hand of state governance. Writing amid the Nazis' rise to power, Adorno was keenly aware that state governance could not be trusted with this task. See Theodor W. Adorno, "On Kierkegaard's Doctrine of Love," *Studies in Philosophy and Social Science* 8 (1939): 413–29.

stage their aesthetic interventions because, in the Sonoran Desert, PTD threatens to determine the shape of our ethical subjectivity by enforcing a distinctive 'distribution of the sensible' that precludes encounters between citizens and migrants.

3   The Distribution of the Sensible

The political philosopher Jacques Rancière describes the 'distribution of the sensible' in his 2010 study *Dissensus* as "the *nemeïn* upon which the *nomoi* of the community are founded."[21] Here, he defines it as a set of partitions that divide the world and its people into visible and invisible, audible and inaudible, such that sensory experience appears to disclose a shared commons, comprising exclusive parts and corresponding forms of partaking.[22] Before any other form of political distribution can occur, Rancière believes this prior distribution of aesthetic parts and positions must establish the basic sense of empirical reality in which all subsequent distributions will take place. Borderlands scholars have adapted this concept to explain the often-theatrical nature of border enforcement.[23] The function of this theater, they contend, is to frame some lives as criminal, that is, as rightful objects of the laws' power to exclude and separate while encouraging us to see others as subjects rightfully deserving the laws' protections. Better appreciating what may be problematic about such framing requires an appreciation of the more fundamental issue Rancière believes the distribution of the sensible is meant to cover up.

By Rancière's definition, politics does not consist first in the exercise and struggle to possess power, but rather in "a mode of action put into practice by a specific kind of subject and deriving from a particular form of reason."[24] More precisely, what defines the political subject is its partaking in "the fact of ruling and of being ruled."[25] This activity of partaking, however, suggests a paradoxical form of action in which the political subject is both the agent and object of its activity.[26] This reflexive relationship, Rancière explains, signals a rupture in our conventional logics of rule, which suppose a more linear,

---

21   Jacques Rancière, *Dissensus* (New York: Continuum, 2010), 44. The "ten theses" that make up the book's first chapter had previously been published as a standalone article in *Theory & Event*. See Jacques Rancière, "Ten Theses on Politics," *Theory & Event* 5 (2001).

22   Rancière, *Dissensus*, 44.

23   See De Genova, "Spectacles of Migrant 'Illegality.'"

24   Rancière, *Dissensus*, 27.

25   Ibid, 29.

26   Ibid.

hierarchical model, a model in which a subject with a determinate superiority, a ruler, acts upon a subject with an equally determinate inferiority, the one ruled. Even as it stands at odds with the partaking that defines its subject, this logic of *archē* now dominates contemporary politics. Ironically, pursuing political stability has led many political orders to attempt to cover up that political subject, which would rupture and destabilize their organizing logics. In this context, the 'distribution of the sensible' is vital to our political life. It attempts to repair its ruptures by creating and maintaining a world of sense wherein some appear to possess such a determinate superiority and others the corresponding inferiority.

However, it bears stating that this role also makes the 'distribution of the sensible' a field of contest over the bounds of the visible and the audible. Before the ones that the distribution excludes may fight for rights, they must first fight to be seen and heard. Thus, the prospect of political change depends on their ability to interpose themselves into the distribution.[27] This struggle, Rancière contends, finds paradigmatic expression in the tension between the demonstrator and the police.[28] The demonstrator, in Rancière's view, is tasked not only with asserting her rights but rather creating a disruption in the logic of *archē* and declaring herself as a political subject in the first place. It is no mere coincidence, Rancière argues, that Aristotle saw the capacity for speech as one of the defining characteristics of the *zōon politikon*. By asserting their place in the public square, the disenfranchised and dispossessed assert themselves as subjects with the talent to speak and the capacity to partake in ruling. Determined to make visible what is not supposed to be seen, they produce a rupture in the distribution of the sensible and, amid the accepted consensus about what is and can be, produce tremors of 'dissensus.' Against such demonstrators, the police's first task is not to arrest each demonstrator but to break up the crowd. Her remark is not the accusative "you there." Instead, it is the dismissive, "Move along, there is nothing to see here." From the conflict between the demonstrator and the police officer, we learn that it is not the enforcement of some specific law that provides the most fundamental motivation for police action. Instead, it is the preservation of the possibility of law itself, and this exigency underscores the contingency of that aesthetic order, which is the foundation of the legal order. It underscores that police action must constantly struggle to preserve that *nemeïn*, which is the foundation of all *nomoi*.

Border policing, too, Nicholas De Genova has argued, serves the creation and maintenance of a distinct aesthetic world. "Material practices of immigration

---

27   Ibid, 36.
28   Ibid, 37ff.

and border policing," De Genova writes, "are enmeshed in a dense weave of discourse and representation and generate a constant redundancy of still more of these languages and images."[29] Law, on the one hand, provides the discursive terms and conditions for identifying things like borders, surreptitious entries, and illegal aliens. However, law alone is insufficient to bring these entities into empirical reality. Instead, the accumulation of border fencing, surveillance towers, law enforcement personnel, and other assets, all serve to produce a scene where the agents of the legal order are increasingly visible and the 'illicit' or 'illegal aliens' who would challenge this order, are increasingly invisible—except in spectacular moments of high-speed chases and interdictions. PTD's aesthetic success is to dominate the terms on which people living in the borderlands see migrants and to predispose them to meet these migrants as criminals worthy of suspicion and repulsion.

Under PTD's distribution of the sensible, legal constructs like citizens, the borders that bound their territory, and the illegal aliens that transgress these bounds, are made to appear as objects of sense experience no less a part of the natural world than saguaros, acacias, jaguars, or scorpions. This is not to say that actual migrants do not make their way to populated areas without being caught. Rather, it suggests that the spectacles' effect reinforces the likelihood that on the occasions that migrants are encountered, they are not perceived as possible political subjects. Approaching from the desert, it is almost as though they are creatures of the wilderness. They are agents of the anarchy, violence, and disorder that rule there. For an actor so framed, even to be seen is not yet to be seen as human. To be apprehended in this way is to be apprehended as no less 'alien' to political society than a scorpion or a jaguar. It is to fail to be seen by the polity and thus to have one's life removed to a place of exception. In this place of exception, one may be subjected to the law's rule without any claim to be subject over it.

To return to the issue of ethical subjectivity, then, if our encounters with one another are subject to such pernicious aesthetic mediation, we cannot take for granted the possibility of the sorts of ethical experiences that Critchley makes essential. PTD works to occlude such experiences in myriad ways. First, if recognizing the migrant as a subject of moral concern depends upon our ability to encounter them in physical space, then by diverting migrant traffic into wilderness corridors, PTD would effectively preempt any such encounters. Second, as prevailing discourses frame these lives as disanalogous to our own, even when an encounter occurs, they change the conditions of the encounter

---

29   Nicolas De Genova, "Spectacles of Migrant 'Illegality,'" 1181.

to negate the form of ethical experience that would challenge this framing. Third, in the instance that the migrant is only encountered after her death, then even if the second problem can be overcome, it is compounded by the issue of discerning what it would mean to become an ethical subject constituted in the face of a good that has already been lost. What might fidelity look like in this context? By what practices would it be enacted?

The aesthetic interventions described above attempt to grapple with this constellation of problems in different ways. However, each one also relies, in its own way, upon the eloquence of bodies to resist the aesthetic frames posited in PTD's distribution of the sensible. This strategy is likely most evident in interventions that utilize images of migrant remains. The remains depicted in these images are emphatically *not* political subjects. They represent the reduction of human life to biological material that, if not for the photographer, would be allowed to disappear into the desert landscape unwitnessed and ungrieved. If the remains depicted in the photographs are to be recognized as subjects of *moral* concern, however, then it will be because the viewer brings something to the image that allows her to see precisely that which is not depicted: the fullness of the migrant's humanity and its connection to their own. Indeed, for some viewers, seeing these images might also bring to light the awareness that their bodies, too, could be abandoned to such a fate. The image might spark an awareness that its subject and its viewer, by virtue of their embodiment, participate in a common humanity to which the Sonoran environment is indifferent. Thus, it would resist the dehumanization that PTD works on migrant bodies and provide the conditions for ethical experience.

However, even if it is granted that the fact of human embodiment provides a necessary condition for our perception of another as a potential subject of moral concern, it is not obvious that it provides, on its own, the sufficient condition for eliciting our approval. 'Criminals' and 'enemy combatants,' no less than 'immigrants' or 'asylum-seekers,' are fellow embodied creatures. However, how we understand our responsibility to an 'enemy combatant' or an 'asylum-seeker' differs considerably based on the narrative frames contextualizing our encounter. Insofar as prevailing political discourses provide viewers with such narrative contexts, there is no reason that the direct representation of migrant remains, on its own, should be more effective than more abstract approaches. On the contrary, a viewer who sees the border as the frontline in a war of civilizations or the hedge between the political world of law and order and the anarchic violence of the natural world may interpret these images as artifacts of justice served. The direct approach may bring about an encounter. Still, it cannot, on its own, account for the distance interposed between the migrant's life and the member's, the distance between encounter and ethical experience.[30]

Enciso's aesthetic strategy differs in that it relies less on the bodies of the migrants and more on the members' bodies. That is, as Sostaita observes, Enciso does not place most of the crosses on his own. Many are carried into the desert and planted at their appointed sites by Anglo-American volunteers. Whereas the viewer of an image may apprehend its object relatively passively, these volunteers must take on a more active relationship with the artworks they carry. In adopting this role, the volunteers experience first-hand the desert's heat, its rugged terrain, and its effects on the human body—on *their* bodies. Moreover, by stepping away from their daily lives and taking the time to sojourn into the desert, the volunteers suspend the standard patterns of movement and routine that order their days. Thus, Sostaita argues, they are beckoned to join the fallen migrants in an intimate experience of life lived out of order:

> Not only are migrants 'betwixt and between' their home and receiving countries and life and death, [Enciso] and his team are also liminal entities in the sense that they engage in a "state or process which is betwixt-and-between the normal, day-to-day cultural and social states and processes of getting and spending, preserving law and order, and registering structural status."[31]

Critchley contends that ethical experience is an experience of hetero-affectivity, of being affected by another. Sostaita notes that those who bear the crosses into these liminal spaces are often moved to tears, to prayer, and to reflections on their own suffering. Together, these responses establish commonalities between the volunteers' lives and those lost. This shared experience, then, presses volunteers into a social space no longer defined by the labels that

---

30   C.f. also Judith Butler, *Frames of War: When Is Life Grievable?* (New York: Verso Press, 2009); & Susan Sontag, *Regarding the Pain of Others* (New York: Farrar, Straus, and Giroux, 2003). Judith Butler and Susan Sontag have each written persuasively about the problem of positionality in the interpretation of violent images. Neither our humanity nor the horror of the violence that besets it is a self-evident phenomenon. As Sontag writes, "To an Israeli Jew, a photograph of a child torn apart in the attack on the Sbarro pizzeria in downtown Jerusalem is first of all a photograph of a Jewish child killed by a Palestinian suicide-bomber. To a Palestinian, a photograph of a child torn apart by a tank round in Gaza is first of all a photograph of a Palestinian child killed by Israeli ordnance."

31   Sostaita, "Making Crosses, Crossing Borders." Here, in this passage, Sostaita adopts the language of Victor Turner. See Victor Turner, "Frame, Flow, and Reflection: Ritual and Drama as Public Liminality," *Japanese Journal of Religious Studies* 6 (1979): 465–499.

the majority society imposes. In this undefined space, the volunteer's body becomes a clearing in which an ethical experience can occur between the mourner and the one mourned. Although I do not expect my work here to achieve the same visceral effect that Enciso's has for his volunteers, I intend, albeit in writing, to stage a similar kind of intervention.

4   "Las Madres/No Mas Lágrimas:" a Metonymic Encounter with the Dead

The aesthetic struggle Enciso and fellow artist activists undertake represents an effort to achieve ethically transformative 'dissensus' amid PTD's distribution of the sensible. Like Rancière's demonstrators, their interventions insist on making visible—even articulate—that which is not meant to be seen. Enciso's artwork endeavors to do this by appealing to the eloquence of bodies but without arraying the remains of abused bodies before our eyes. However, if

FIGURE 6   Valerie Lee James, *Las Madres/No Mas Lágrimas*.
SOURCE: LEAD ARTIST VALERIE LEE JAMES WITH ARTIST-COLLABORATORS: ANTONIA GALLEGOS, CESAR LOPEZ, AND DEBORAH MCCULLOUGH, LAS MADRES / NO MAS LÁGRIMAS, 2006, SCULPTURE, PIMA COMMUNITY COLLEGE, TUCSON

THE REMEMBRANCE OF DISMEMBERED BODIES

Enciso's work generates much of its affective power from literally drawing volunteers into places that are 'betwixt and between the normal,' can one working in the written medium do the same? In this section, I want to highlight the work of one more borderland artist, Valerie Lee James, who models a form of metonymic representation open not only to her artistic medium of sculpture but also to prose.

Las Madres/No Mas Lágrimas was installed on Pima Community College's east campus in 2005. The piece engages a haunting play of presence and absence, and it is in this play that its power to affect dissensus lies. The life-sized statues portray three mothers standing at the desert's edge. Their eyes are closed in sorrow, and their hands crossed over aching hearts. Each one serves as a memorial for more than one thousand migrants who have lost their lives in the corridors that pass through the Sonoran. As a mother implies a child, the figures invoke these sojourners' presence through visual metonymy. However, their connection to these migrants runs deeper. It is not only that the mothers' presence implies the absent children. The statues are composed of found materials, scraps of pants, shirts, and backpacks that have been discarded on the migrant trails. Consequently, as Jessica Auchter notes, "the bodies of the mothers are literally constituted by the attributes of the children."[32]

As James explained in an interview with *Tucson Weekly*, her home in Amado, Arizona, sits near a heavily trafficked migrant trail, and each day, she and her dogs walk the nearby arroyos.[33] On these walks, she finds the supplies for her artwork. Many of James' installations keep these found objects intact, carefully arranging them into makeshift memorials. However, to create *Las Madres/No Mas Lágrimas*, James adopted a different approach. After collecting the abandoned possessions, she combined them with desert plant material to form a malleable pulp. She then backed this material with plaster and rebar to give the mothers their form. When each statue was completed, she coated each layer of cloth pulp with natural tree resin that, for a time, would protect the material from the desert heat. The result is a trio of organic statues that now stand exposed and vulnerable to the natural environment. Since the sculptures' installation, the environment has taken its toll, causing the resin to rise, melt, and drip down the mothers' faces. As the resin deteriorates, it allows the

---

32   Jessica Auchter, *The Politics of Haunting and Memory in International Relations* (New York: Routledge, 2014), 108.

33   For a brief spotlight on James' life and art, see Margaret Regan, "Tales From the Outskirts: Amado," Tucson Weekly, accessed October 24, 2023, https://www.tucsonweekly.com/tucson/washed-into-the-land/Content?oid=2096094.

FIGURE 7   Detail of Valerie Lee James, *Las Madres/No Mas Lágrimas*
SOURCE: LEAD ARTIST VALERIE LEE JAMES WITH ARTIST-COLLABORATORS:
ANTONIA GALLEGOS, CESAR LOPEZ, AND DEBORAH MCCULLOUGH, *LAS
MADRES / NO MAS LÁGRIMAS*, 2006, SCULPTURE, PIMA COUNTY COMMUNITY
COLLEGE, TUCSON

artifacts it once protected to return to the desert and gives the impression that the statues are crying for the children who have slipped from their reach.

Although James' sculpture may lack the same references to state-sponsored violence that Sostaita observes in Enciso's work, it retains its commitment to somatic experience. Auchter notes that this piece achieves its political effect by situating resistance in the mothers' bodies.[34] The statues' distressed surfaces depict in real time the Sonoran environment's impact on the people who attempt to cross it. Slowly succumbing to the sun and the wind, the statues illuminate "both the body's biological struggle for life in the harsh desert conditions, and the body's biopolitical struggle for qualified life in a zone of indistinction where certain bodies matter and others fade into the desert."[35] Thus, James dramatizes PTD's cunning effect for the viewer.

Nevertheless, the bodies conspicuously absent from this deeply visceral encounter are the migrants' own. *Las Madres/No Mas Lágrimas* is saturated with absence. The three mothers' eyes are closed as if to underscore that the thousands of migrants for whom they stand have long ago passed from view. James does not attempt to depict them. Instead, she challenges her viewers, standing face to face with the mothers they leave behind, to reckon with that absence. Composed of found materials, the mothers are the traces of traces. Scraps of clothing and artifacts from the migrant trail do not make their former owners physically present. They tell us exceedingly little about them. We may know that someone has passed this way. However, we do not know who that person was. We do not know why they undertook the journey. We do not know whether they reached their destination or fell short somewhere in the landscape beyond. They are so close that we might touch the hem of their garment, but not close enough to capture within our gaze.

And yet, those whom spectacle renders unapproachable through direct depiction, *Las Madres/No Mas Lágrimas* brings intimately close by indirect depiction. The piece's effect on its viewers is to populate their imagination with the ones the statue declines to portray. Moreover, James' decision to sculpt *mothers* interrupts any swift identification of the dead as 'criminals,' 'combatants,' or some other suspect class. Instead, this particular metonym invites us to think of the dead first as *children*. Thus, against the frames supplied by prevailing political discourse, James asserts one of her own. Though these women do not move, through them, their children are allowed to make the approach

---

34   Auchter, *The Politics of Haunting and Memory in International Relations*, 108ff.
35   Ibid, 107.

that PTD denied. The memorialized dead haunt the viewer's subjectivity and, in so doing, they confront the viewer with a choice. We may resist the dead's advance and seek to exorcise the ghosts. We may return these children to the same oblivion that PTD has cast them. Or, if this temptation can be resisted, we may bear the dead along with us. We may choose the haunting and make the dead our responsibility. To choose the haunting is to blur the lines between inside and outside, self and other, life and death. Thus, it is to become the transformed, ethical subjects, laid open to otherness, that Critchley sees as the catalyst for radical political change.

5   Metonymy in the Scriptural Imaginary

Although it refuses the direct representation of their bodies, James' use of metonymy in representing the dead is not an instance of evasion. Instead, it carefully addresses the complex of relationships between an image, its frame, and its meaning. What an image means depends on the antecedent narratives that frame it. James chooses the mother for her metonym. In so doing, she challenges us to think of migrants as children rather than invaders or criminals. This metonymic framing device carries moral implications with it. Combatants are to be repelled. Criminals are to be separated from the community. Children are to be nurtured and cared for. In this book, I will undertake a similar aesthetic strategy, appealing to three scriptural narratives to reframe theologically the relationship between the ethical and the political, members and non-members, the living and the dead. I will draw on Ezekiel's vision of the valley of dry bones, the story of Cain and Abel, and Luke's parable of the Samaritan. Each of these passages supplies a narrative imaginary, a set of metonyms, by which to recast the meaning of what is occurring in the US–Mexico borderlands.

    In appealing to these passages, I am informed by two hermeneutical commitments. First, I read these texts not only as reflections on transcendence but also on history. In line with interpreters like Jacob Taubes, I seek in these texts the political potentials brought along in theological metaphors.[36] In Ezekiel's

---

36   C.f. Jacob Taubes, *The Political Theology of Paul* trans. Dana Hollander (Stanford: Stanford University Press, 2004). For additional examples of such an approach, see Alain Badiou, *Saint Paul: The Foundation of Universalism* trans. Ray Brassier (Stanford: Stanford University Press, 2003); Giorgio Agamben, *The Time that Remains: A Commentary on the Letter to the Romans,* trans. Patricia Daley (Stanford: Stanford University Press, 2005); Giorgio Agamben, *Pilate & Jesus,* trans. Adam Kotsko (Stanford: Stanford University Press, 2015). Authors like Taubes, Badiou, and Agamben are, by no means, the first to identify biblical scriptures' interests in this-worldly political arrangements. This

vision, I am taken with the this-worldly connection between collective human endeavor and the discernment of our humanity. In Genesis, the relationship between the political and the social body. In Luke, the relationship between law and compassion. In none of these texts do I mean to excise the political kernel from the theological chaff. To the contrary, I seek a theological vantage of the political that situates the polity, its possibilities, limits, and ends within a broader eschatological story of human beings, their kinship with one another, and their relation to the divine.

Second, I am committed in my reading of these texts to accentuate that which is 'other' and 'strange.' As Gregory Cuéllar has argued, the borderlands have come to be known and controlled under a language and practice of enforcement that dehumanizes the 'other'—more precisely, the non-white 'other.'[37] We might wish to insist that these 'others' are not so unlike us. That is, we might wish to insist that their dehumanization is only justified by providing some false difference that renders their moral status subordinate to the members'. However, this strategy is accompanied by risk. By insisting on that which is familiar, those advocating for outsiders risk rendering difference and particularity morally insignificant. By negating these characteristics in favor of some abstract or disembodied commonality, they risk advancing a hegemonic notion of the human in their very effort to dispute it. Rather than resisting dehumanization by beginning with what is shared between the insider and the outsider, the member and the non-member, Cuéllar advises another strategy, 're-sacralizing the other,' reading her experience against the grain of dominant

---

list leaves aside, for instance, the growing body of Post-Colonial and Decolonial biblical scholars who read the New Testament material as colonized literature responding to the distinctive political situation created by Judea's subordination to the Roman Empire. What I find distinctively intriguing about these (primarily philosophical) interpreters of the biblical texts is their decidedly normative projects. In their exegetical treatments of the New Testament Literature, Taubes, Badiou, and Agamben have sought to interpose the scriptural political imaginary into our own and, in the remembrance of this imaginary, to identify its revolutionary potentials for the present moment. While some bible scholars have met their work with suspicion C.f. *Paul in the Grip of the Philosophers: The Apostle and Contemporary Continental Philosophy* ed. Peter Frick (Minneapolis: Fortress Press, 2013), I align with others, like Alain Gignac, who have found in these readings an opportunity to re-examine the scriptures' theological claims from novel vantages that do not share the same hermeneutical commitments and assumptions that predominate in much biblical scholarship. See Alain Gignac, "Taubes, Badiou, Agamben: Contemporary Receptions of Paul by Non-Christian Philosophers," in *Reading Romans with Contemporary Philosophers and Theologians*, ed. David Odell-Scott (New York: T&T Clark, 2007), 155–211.

37 Gregory Cuéllar, *Resacralizing the Other at the US–Mexico Border* (New York: Routledge, 2020)

discourse and elite power. From this hermeneutical perspective, Cuéllar invites us to consider that which the polity and its laws attempt, yet fail, to name. Moreover, by identifying the sacred with the 'other'—with the 'strange'—this vantage drives a wedge between that which the polity dignifies and that which possesses sanctity, bringing about a form of dissensus and opening up a tensive space for the renegotiation of identities and responsibilities. This appeal to the 'strange' and the 'unnamed' does not necessitate abandoning the notion that we participate in some common human condition then. However, it does suggest that whatever commonality at which we may arrive must lie on the other side of our reckoning with alterity. By re-sacralizing the other, we come to see the sacred in that which is other—both in the outsider and in ourselves. Thus, we encounter theological claims' radical power for reconfiguring the political and our relationship with it.

Thus, I seek in biblical imagery metonyms for rethinking our contemporary situation. Moreover, just as James' depiction of mothers allows the dead to make their approach while challenging the frames under which we might be accustomed to receiving them, I seek in these biblical images means of rethinking the relationship between the political and the ethical, the familiar and the strange, the citizen and the alien, and the living and the dead. In conjunction with Ezekiel's Valley of Dry Bones, the remembrance of the dead is connected with the problem of political redemption. However, whereas one vision of American progress necessitates the outsider's figurative and literal death, Ezekiel proposes that the polity's redemption is inseparable from their reconciliation with the lives denied. Likewise, Abel's ghost becomes a metonym for these very same lives, refuting the notion that the political can be separated from the social without producing a lingering, disquieting moral remainder. Finally, the figures of the Samaritan and the sojourner provide images of what such a reconciliation might look like and upon what grounds it would be premised.

Just as the works of borderlands artists like James and Enciso leverage the power of their artistic mediums to foster transformative ethical experiences, I rely on the power of theological metaphor. As a writer, I am reticent either to claim the sculptor's talent to cultivate transformative imagery or the poetic excellence of someone like Urrea. Instead, I rely on the power of theological metaphor. Rather than seeing these metaphors as mere illustrations that render more accessible otherwise challenging concepts, I assume, alongside great theological writers like Kierkegaard, that metaphors orient rather than illustrate. Scripture doesn't merely tell us something. It provides powerful heuristics for organizing our experiences of ourselves, others, the political, and the divine. In the introduction of this book, I argued that, as the political theology of Manifest Destiny deploys them, theological metaphors function in this way, albeit sometimes to pernicious effect. In the following pages, I seek to uncover their redemptive qualities as they empower us to remember the dead and open the way to a remembrance of the social and political bodies.

PART 2

Cain and Abel

∴

Now Abel was a keeper of sheep, and Cain a tiller of the ground. In the course of time Cain brought to the Lord an offering of the fruit of the ground, and Abel for his part brought of the firstlings of his flock, their fat portions. And the Lord had regard for Abel and his offering, but for Cain and his offering he had no regard. So Cain was very angry, and his countenance fell. The Lord said to Cain, "Why are you angry, and why has your countenance fallen? If you do well, will you not be accepted? And if you do not do well, sin is lurking at the door; its desire is for you, but you must master it."

Cain said to his brother Abel, "Let us go out to the field." And when they were in the field, Cain rose up against his brother Abel and killed him. Then the Lord said to Cain, "Where is your brother Abel?" He said, "I do not know; am I my brother's keeper?" And the Lord said, "What have you done? Listen, your brother's blood is crying out to me from the ground! And now you are cursed from the ground, which has opened its mouth to receive your brother's blood from your hand. When you till the ground, it will no longer yield to you its strength; you will be a fugitive and a wanderer on the earth."

—GENESIS 4.2b-12

CHAPTER 3

Politics Haunted

> Whatever brotherhood human beings are capable of has grown out of fratricide, whatever political organization men may have achieved has its origins in crime.
>
> —HANNAH ARENDT, *On Revolution*

•••

> Listen! Your brother's blood is crying out to me from the ground!
>
> —GENESIS 4.10

∴

1   Strangers or Estranged Siblings?

Borders are places of beginnings and endings. As lines in political space, they mark where one territory begins and another ends. As lines in juridical space, they demarcate the limits and reaches of jurisdictions. Here, one power meets with another and goes no further. As lines in social space, they parse the world into a constellation of places that are not merely the provinces of political and juridical powers but also the dwellings of peoples and nations. In this respect, borders are also places for the beginning and ending of relationships. At these lines, peoples meet with one another in trade, partnership, cultural exchange, military conflict, and the provision of aid. Viewed as bright lines on political maps, they tempt us to think of the international system of sovereign nation-states as timeless, seamlessly fitted to and coeval with the communities and continents upon which they are super-imposed. Depicting a world where dwelling is the norm and not crossing, they also tempt us to think of the outsider as a 'stranger,' one 'alien-born,' as if from another world.

Yet, borders are places of beginnings and endings not only in the words' spatial senses but also in their temporal senses. They are evocative of the oldest of political institutions. As is widely noted by political philosophers, the Greek word *polis* appears to have derived its name from the ring wall that divided the public square from the *agora* and the *oikos*. The etymological link is suggestive.

© BRYAN M. ELLROD, 2025 | DOI:10.1163/9789004721524_005

The emergence of the body politic, it seems, is possible only after the assertion of that boundary, which distinguishes it from the larger social body. This
notion has gained increasing plausibility with the proliferation of border fortifications that has occurred in recent decades. As Jessica Auchter puts it, constructing border walls recalls "the originary moment of the state."[1] To recall
this 'originary moment' is to conjure the very beginning of a people's shared
history. However, it is also to envision what lies before and, perhaps, what may
come after. At the borderline, the state emphatically asserts its empirical reality in concrete and steel. However, as the construction of new walls late in the
country's history reminds us, this statement is made in *medias res*. A border
may be a beginning, but the international system of states is not timeless, and
the state's statement is no instance of *creatio ex nihilo*.

Thus, a border is a tacit acknowledgment of the prior history from which
our own has emerged. It is an implicit acknowledgment that there was a time
when the body politic was not, and, by extension, that there may yet come a
time when the body politic is no longer. This acknowledgment does not come
without anxiety. Increasingly, in the United States, the southwestern border
has become a place where the nation (or rather certain understandings of
'America') believe they are glimpsing their end. "We, as a country, either have
borders or we don't," wrote then-candidate Donald Trump in typically blunt
terms, "if we don't have borders, we don't have a country."[2] Citizens are encouraged to believe that what is at stake in acts of border enforcement is more
than the fate of this or that migrant, but the very form of life to which they are
accustomed. Thus, this border anxiety freights the encounters between citizens and migrants with such weight that it is as if the fate of our polities—and
the future of the world as we know it—would be decided by the terms of their
meeting and parting. In the face of this exigency, the state must persistently
state itself, again and again, in opposition to the forces of historical entropy.

In the southwestern borderlands, these statements have been received
as wounds. The US–Mexico line, writes Gloria Anzaldúa, is *"una herida abierta* where the Third World grates against the first and bleeds."[3] Viewed from
the historical long view, this wound is still fresh. The present location of the
US–Mexico line was only fixed after 1848, when the Treaty of Guadalupe

---

1   Jessica Auchter, *The Politics of Haunting and Memory in International Relations* (New York:
    Routledge, 2017), 92.
2   Trump, Donald. X Post. November 12, 2015, 7:50 AM (https://twitter.com/realDonaldTrump/
    status/664787273184108545)
3   Gloria Anzaldúa, *Borderlands / La Frontera: The New Mestiza* (San Francisco: Aunt Lute
    Books, 1999), 25.

Hidalgo brought an end to the United States' rapacious invasion and conquest of Mexican territory.[4] With the treaty, The Republic of Mexico ceded more than half of its territory to the United States.[5] Many people who inhabited this territory were expelled or allowed to leave with their possessions. However, more than one hundred thousand Chicanx people who occupied the territory were made citizens by conquest.[6] Anzaldúa refers to these people as *los atravesados,* 'the border-crossed ones.'[7] Forcibly grafted into the United States' newly expanded body politic, *los atravesados* testified in blood and bone to the complex of histories through which the new border was asserted. The blood of these new Americans intermingled the 20,000-year-old Indigenous heritage of the Cochise civilizations with the European heritage of the Spanish settlers that had invaded in the sixteenth century AD. They were to be inscribed into a citizenry that would redefine their social status vis-à-vis the Anglo-American settlers making their way west. They would become strangers on their own land. Transported, with the stroke of a pen, from Mexican to United States territory, they testified that a border is stated, enforced, and preserved against

---

4   It is not entirely clear which country fired the first shots in this conflict. After The Republic of Mexico declined the United States' offer to purchase a majority of its northern territory, the United States moved a military force into contested territory between the Rio Nueces and the Rio Grande. Whether this force or the Mexican force with which it met began the fight, the US made the skirmish a pretense to begin a military march that would carry its soldiers to the gates of Mexico City. With the Treaty of Guadalupe Hidalgo, the United States would ultimately pay just $15 million to take the 525,000 square miles that Mexico had, prior to the conflict, refused to sell.

5   Even after 1848, the international line would continue to be adjusted and renegotiated. With the Gadsden Purchase in 1854, the United States would acquire an additional 30,000 square miles in what is now Arizona and New Mexico. By this time, all that marked the location of the international line was a series of 53 boundary markers. Some consisted of little more than piled stones and, with time, both sides made reports of the markers being moved or destroyed. It would take until 1892 for the International Boundary Commission, led by Colonel J.W. Barlow of the United States and Jacobo Blanco of Mexico, to settle the matter.

6   Under the terms of the Treaty, those that did not accept citizenship were expelled.

7   Anzaldúa, *Borderlands / La Frontera,* 25ff. Channeling the epithets of Anglo-American citizens, Anzaldúa describes *los atravesados* as "the squint-eyed, the perverse, the queer, the troublesome, the mongrel, the mulato, the half-breed, the half-dead; in short, those who cross over, pass over, or go through the confines of the normal." Though they were (and still are) considered 'transgressors' and 'aliens' by many of the Anglo-American citizens that came to settle the southwestern borderlands, Anzaldúa is quick to correct that these people did not migrate *to* the United States. They did not cross over the border from the 'strange' into the normal. Their ancestors had been in the land since at least 1000 BC (the first humans had arrived in the land in 35000 BC). They had only been made 'strange' as the border crossed over them and rendered them 'aliens' in their own homes.

the memory of what came before and the uneasy apprehension of what might come next. They testified to the problem of beginning.

In Western political philosophy, the story of Cain and Abel has served as an allegory for the problem of beginning. Interpreted as a prelude to Cain's establishment of the first human city, Enoch, the fratricide appears to prefigure that violence, which inevitably marks the threshold between the political present and the pre-political past. Likewise, as Cain is taken to provide the prototype for a political subject defined by self-determining freedom, the fratricidal act represents freedom's bloody liberation from the bonds of natural and moral necessity. Indeed, the fratricide represents a troubling crime that lingers at the threshold of our historical memory. However, as the story effectively removes this violation to some primordial beginning, it facilitates a measure of closure, insulating the polity from its corruption and freedom from responsibility. Insofar as this allegory is allowed to frame our thinking about our history, it allows us to concede that the alienation of *los atravesados* is indeed regrettable. However, we may add, it was a necessary moment in history's progression to the state of the world as we know it today. And, after all, that event is in the past. It is no more a part of our twenty-first-century life than the crimes committed by the first-born children of Adam and Eve.

Of course, as Anzaldúa points out, *los atravesados* are not gone. They continue to inhabit the borderlands. Moreover, the Treaty of Guadalupe Hidalgo did not really achieve closure, and the borderlands continue to be a place in a state of constant transition. The region has come to be a setting for large-scale migrations. The descendants of those who were expelled at the end of the war have begun their return, making their way north to their ancestral homelands. As this return brings them back to the US–Mexico line, they cause to recur the very same alienations that created *los atravesados*. They carry into the present what was supposed to be past. In so doing, they give the lie to the reading of Genesis 4 just described. My contention in this chapter is that even if the story of Cain and Abel can be read as a story about the emergence of the body politic and its defining form of subjectivity, it may not be read as a story about closure. Instead, a more complete reading of Genesis 4 reveals a tale about haunting and fratricide's inability to liberate freedom from its responsibility for the good of the life denied.

2   Fratricide: a Problem of Beginning

In the story of Cain and Abel, Hannah Arendt believed that Western thought had crystallized a chilling truth about the origins of our political associations:

Cain slew Abel, and Romulus slew Remus; violence was the beginning and, by the same token, no beginning could be made without
using violence, without violating ... The tale spoke clearly: whatever
brotherhood human beings are capable of has grown out of fratricide, whatever political organization men may have achieved has its
origins in crime.[8]

For Arendt, the primordial fratricide illustrated that part and parcel to the primordial constitution of the body politic was a disavowal of responsibility; a
disavowal that had to be judged a violation. For Arendt, then, Genesis 4 signals
a fundamental tension between the freedom paradigmatic of political life and
the responsibilities enjoined upon us by the other's ethical demand. Coming
to terms with Arendt's understanding of this violation (and its apparent inevitability) permits a clearer understanding of the tensions between the relationships constitutive of our ethical and political subjectivities.

For Arendt, fratricide's most profound meaning and inevitability derive
from the polity's struggle to wrest its distinctive form of life from the bonds of
necessity. Political life, she contends, is fundamentally a life of collaborative,
free 'action' between human beings. Distinct from the activities of 'labor' and
'work,' which ultimately function to sustain the biological processes of human
bodies, Arendt uses the term 'action' to denote the human capacity to make a
beginning of something new—an *archē*—worthy of historical remembrance.[9]
While Arendt does not suppose labor and work are worthless, their direction to
the tireless maintenance of physical life subjects them to the rule of necessity.
Political action, on the other hand, affords humanity a bid at immortality in
defiance of this rule. From this perspective, the value of labor and work derives
from their role in supporting the conditions for politics' *vita activa*. Individuals,
of course, will eventually pass away, and the toil by which they lived will be forgotten. However, the polity they constitute by virtue of their action promises
to long outlive them.

Therefore, preserving the *vita activa*'s integrity requires separating it from
the life of labor and work. "Of all the activities necessary and present in human
communities," Arendt explains in an approving citation of Aristotle, "only two
[are] deemed to be political, ... namely action (*praxis*) and speech (*lexis*), out
of which rises the realm of human affairs [and] from which everything merely

---

8   Hannah Arendt, *On Revolution* (New York: Penguin Books, 1990), 20.
9   Hannah Arendt, *The Human Condition* (Chicago: The University of Chicago Press, 1998), 7ff.

necessary or useful is strictly excluded."[10] The merely 'necessary' and 'useful,' Arendt judges, are the province of individual households and their aggregate, the social. These domains of human activity rightly occupy themselves with the routines necessary for meeting our biological needs of shelter and suste- nance. However, such activities are cyclical by nature. Those who are hungry or thirsty may be sated but inevitably will become hungry and thirsty again. The routines constitutive of the social are trapped in an eternal return of the same, prohibited from making a beginning of anything new. Hence, as Arendt explains in *The Human Condition*, their exclusion necessitates the passage from the household to the public square.[11]

This passage, however, is not easily achieved, in thought or in practice. Pointing to the tendency in Western political philosophies to equate the *zōon politikon* with the *animal socialis*, Arendt identifies a problematic inclination to reduce the political to the social, the public forum to the bare aggregate of households.[12] This intellectual conflation, however, is to the detriment of actual political institutions. Recalling the follies of the French Revolution, Arendt warns against the dangers of occupying politics with problems proper to the social. She argues that Maximilien Robespierre's shortcoming was that he was "haunted and driven" by the "passion of compassion."[13] Thus, he doomed the French Revolution by his desire not only to throw off the bonds of the old monarchy but to remedy the widespread poverty that had left so many of the French people to live in squalor.

"The magic of compassion," Arendt writes, "was that it opened the heart of the sufferer to the sufferings of others, whereby it established and confirmed the 'natural' bond between men [*sic*]."[14] On Arendt's understanding, compas- sion's distinguishing qualities are immediacy and particularity. It speaks to the heart, and its message is decisively concerned with the suffering of *this* or *that* person. In attempting to generalize the experience of compassion, the revolutionaries added to the ideals of *liberté, egalité,* and *fraternité* an unshak- able concern for the pitiful mass of *les misérables.* But compassion's was a dark magic and by closing the distance between subjects, compassion also elim- inated that space which is the place of politics. At best, Arendt concludes,

---

10   Ibid, 25. C.f. Aristotle, *Politics,* III. Here, Aristotle elaborates his suspicions regarding the compatibility of the life of the citizen and the life of the laborer, concluding that the pol- ity relies for its possibility on a laboring class that, nevertheless, must be excluded from its citizenry.
11   Arendt, *The Human Condition,* 28–37.
12   Ibid, 23.
13   Arendt, *On Revolution,* 71.
14   Ibid, 81.

compassion's particularity provides insufficient basis for establishing lasting political institutions. At worse, as was the case under Robespierre's Committee on Public Safety, its immediacy chafes against the long, drawn-out processes of law and politics and opts for "swift and direct action ... with the means of violence."[15] By attempting to legislate compassion, the fledgling French republic destroyed both law and compassion and collapsed into the anarchic and anomic reign of terror. However, if violence is not to be the polity's end, then it must be its beginning.

In this context, Arendt offers her gloss of Genesis 4, identifying Abel's murder as a necessary condition for founding the first city, Enoch. On the surface, Cain's murder of Abel reproduces the literal bloodletting involved in revolutionary struggle. However, the distinctive crime of fratricide signifies something more fundamental than the simple act of killing. It takes place within the household, severing the bonds constitutive of the social. By killing his brother, the founder of the first city extricates himself from that domain of life whose distinguishing concern is the care of human wants and needs.[16] Treated within this setting, the act of fratricide inflicts its wound not only on the victim's body but also on the social body. It represents the subject's refusal of the necessity that rules the household and her disavowal of responsibility for those routines which would lash her to the interminable cycles of biological life. The killing of Abel, that is, represents the threshold between freedom and the rule of necessity. It is the bloody initiation of the *vita activa*.

To be clear, the fratricide itself is not the *archē* worthy of historical remembrance. It endures in memory as tragedy, not as achievement. Contrary to the deliberative speech that animates political action through persuasion, violence achieves its objectives with mute coercion. Insofar as the political order prizes deliberative speech over coercive force, it cannot legitimize the fratricide. Consequently, it must be judged a crime no more welcome in the polity than in the household. Nevertheless, to condemn the act is not to deny its necessity. By putting to death the cyclical toil required for the maintenance of biological life, this crime furnishes a liberating moment of *an-archē* that ruptures the rule of necessity and opens a clearing in which the political may emerge. Hence, Arendt concludes, whatever political organization human beings may have achieved, must have its origins in crime. Violence is the beginning and the threshold into the political has seldom (if ever) been crossed without it.[17]

---

15   Ibid, 87.
16   Arendt, *The Human Condition*, 30.
17   Between *The Human Condition* and *On Revolution*, we are presented with two accounts of the boundary between the household and the political. In *The Human Condition*,

Arendt's concept of fratricide and its relation to the political illuminates why the ethical relationship, as I have construed it in this study, is not so easily reproduced in the political. If the ethical relation is defined by its approval of a demand communicated by an embodied other, then it binds our ethical subjectivity to a good whose affirmation does not permit indifference to biological life.[18] The life of ethics, in this respect, does not resemble the *vita activa* but rather a life of compassionate labor. If allowed to spill into politics, the ethical relation threatens to deteriorate the boundary between the social body and the body politic, the *vita activa,* and the life of labor. To be haunted by compassion, as was Robespierre, is to be moved by the good of precisely those lives the political cannot accommodate without descending into interminable violence. Compassion may indeed be a virtue, but it is a virtue that brings upon us our end. Fratricide may indeed be a crime, but it is a crime that makes a new beginning possible. The possibility of politics is secured by that original violation that refuses the good to which compassion cleaves. Furthermore, the longevity of its institutions requires that we exorcise the ghosts. Therefore, the political must be defended from that ethical relationship that would bring these ghosts present. In Chapter Five, I will refute the assertion that compassion must inevitably descend into anomie. For now, I am determined to show that the problem of fratricide cannot be relegated to the past. If only for the self-determining political subject, the ethical demand recurs constantly in the present and, with

---

Arendt describes law (*nomos*) as that which maintains the boundary between them. In *On Revolution,* violence effects the boundary. The coincidence of law and violence was an issue of considerable interest to one of Arendt's philosophical contemporaries, Walter Benjamin. In his landmark essay, "Critique of Violence," Benjamin observed violence's fundamental role both for enforcing legal regimes and for establishing them, speaking of 'law-preserving' and 'law-creating violence.' For Benjamin, these historical realities were a cry for redemption—a cry for a kind of 'divine violence' that would revoke the legitimacy asserted in the violence of the law. See Walter Benjamin, *Toward the Critique of Violence* (Stanford: Stanford University Press, 2021).

18   In this specification of the ethical relation, I render it more narrowly than does Simon Critchley. For Critchley, we might articulate our ethical subjectivity in relation to a range of (potentially disembodied) goods: "mosaic law in the Bible, the Good beyond being in Plato,... the Good as the goal of desire for Aquinas, the practical ideal of generosity for Descartes,... the greatest happiness for the greatest number for Bentham and Mill, the moral law in Kant [&c]." (See Simon, Critchley, *Infinitely Demanding* [New York: Verso Press, 2007], 16ff) Thus, in my account of the ethical relation, I draw nearer to one of Critchley's theological inspirations, Knud Ejler Løgstrup, who develops his theory of the ethical demand through a phenomenological approach that turns on a concern for human vulnerability and interdependence. (See Knud Ejler Løgstrup, *The Ethical Demand* [Notre Dame: University of Notre Dame Press, 1997], 8–28) However, I will seek to justify this narrower rendering over the course of the following chapters.

it, the crime of fratricide.[19] The notion of such a recurrence finds theological warrant when Arendt's reading of Genesis 4 is amended to include not only Cain's agency but that of the divine—and that of the dead.

3   Abel's Ghost: a Theological Case for Haunting

In Arendt's view, the story of Cain and Abel is essentially the same as that of Romulus and Remus. They are differentiated only by the languages of their transmission. Arendt underscores this implicit equation by her willingness, in shorthand, to refer to them as a single 'tale' that speaks clearly a singular moral. Furthermore, with this equation, Arendt establishes a causal relationship between fratricide and the emergence of the political. Likewise, as causes precede effects, she creates a temporality that seems to imply that fratricide is a problem of 'beginnings' and not an enduring problem for the political present. However, this equation depends on an exegetical conceit that leaps over the time between the fratricide and the foundational act. As Ted A Smith has pointed out, the time that Arendt omits is the time in which God acts.[20] Consequently, the story's theological elements and their bearing on the political are effectively written out. However, when this conceit is dispelled, the theological may be reintroduced, and Arendt's reading may be complicated by the ghostly endurance God secures for Abel.

At least as Dionysius of Halicarnassus conveys the story in his *Roman Antiquities*, Arendt's interpretation of Remus' murder appears sound.[21] The murder

---

19   Whether or not Hannah Arendt was herself an advocate of politics of self-determination I don't mean to settle here. The concept does not figure particularly prominently in *The Human Condition* or *On Revolution*. Further, some commentators have even premised Arendt's appeal on her severance of the concept of self-determination from that of freedom. See Joan Cocks, "On Commonality, Nationalism, and Violence: Hannah Arendt, Rosa Luxembug, and Frantz Fanon," *Women in German Yearbook* 12 (1996): 39–51. Nevertheless, I find the tension between freedom and responsibility illumined in Arendt's account of fratricide a useful tool for understanding the troubled relationship between ethics and politics premised on self-determination. What Arendt helps us to appreciate in the tension between the sovereignty of nation-states and the ethical demands of outsiders is a tension between two fundamentally different forms of subjectivity: one ordered by freedom from necessity and the other founded by the other's demand.

20   Smith examined the theological and political consequences of this conceit as they bear on the concept of sovereignty in Ted A Smith, "The Mark of Cain: Sovereign Negation and the Politics of God" *Modern Theology* 36 (2020): 56–73.

21   I rely in this chapter on the version of the story relayed in Dionysus of Halicarnassus' Roman Antiquities. See Dionysius of Halicarnassus, *Antiquities of Rome*, trans. Earnest Cary, vol. 1, 7 vols. (Cambridge: Harvard University Press, 1937) However, his is not the only

is the direct consequence of an intractable feud regarding which hill should provide the site for the brothers' new colony. This fratricide is the consequence of an expressly political dispute. Romulus wishes to build the colony on the Palatine Hill, and Remus wants to build it at Remoria. They go to the gods searching for a sign that would resolve the dispute, but the signs they receive are ambiguous and do little to settle the matter. Conflict comes to a head, and the rival brothers' parties attack each other. Remus is killed in the fighting, and violence secures the resolution the gods do not provide. Consequently, the act presents itself as the direct solution to the problem frustrating the polity's emergence. With Remus out of the picture, Romulus can build the colony where he pleases. Dionysius does not propose, however, that the strife's political exigency allows Romulus to kill his brother in cold blood. On the contrary, Romulus grieves his fallen brother and buries him at Remoria.[22] Notably, however, the manner of Romulus' mourning supports a sense of closure. The spatial distance between Remoria and the Palatine Hill mirrors a temporal distance between the fratricide, consigned to the pre-political past, and the political foundation it facilitates. Remus' ghost may have haunted the countryside, but not the streets of Rome.

The fourth chapter of Genesis, however, withholds any such separation, along with whatever sense of closure this separation would afford. Like Romulus, Cain kills his younger sibling. However, whereas the dispute between Romulus and Remus is expressly political, the one between Cain and Abel is not obviously so. Genesis 4 vv. 1–7 explain that the tension arises in a ritual setting, as each brother brings an offering to God. Cain, a tiller of the ground, brings a share of its fruits. Abel, a keeper of sheep, brings the best portions of the firstlings of his flock. But God does not hold each brother's oblation in equal esteem. Cain's enmity toward Abel stems from the favor that God shows his younger sibling. This favor might evince a disruption of the normal state of affairs within the household. The subversion of the primogeniture's rights is a motif that recurs in the Pentateuch. Nevertheless, Cain's status as the eventual founder of the first city nowhere comes directly into question. Consequently, it is difficult to suppose that Abel's murder stands in any direct causal relationship with the founding of Enoch. The pericope fails to provide an obvious

---

account of the fratricide. Ovid and Livy too provide variations on the story. See Ovid, *Fasti*, trans. James George Frazer (New York: G.P. Putnam's Sons, 1931); & Titus Livius, *History of Rome*, vol. 1, 14 vols., Livy in Fourteen Volumes (Cambridge: Harvard University Press, 1976).

22   Ovid also suggests that Romulus regrets his brother's death, unsuccessfully "smother[ing] his rising tears" and lovingly granting his brother funeral honors. See Ovid, *Fasti*, Book IV, 'April 21: The Parilia.'

analogy with the story of Romulus and Remus. Yet, even if one permits the analogy, a more critical distinction remains to be made.

Unlike Romulus, Cain does not bury or mourn his brother. Determined to be rid of him, Cain leaves Abel's bloodied body in the field. Death, however, does not silence Abel, and his blood cries out from the ground. This cry reaches the ears of God, prompting a divine intervention far more decisive than the ambiguous oracles presented in the story of Romulus and Remus. God confronts Cain on Abel's behalf: 'Listen!' This is the command that meets Cain. Even as Cain refuses to be his brother's keeper, the divine sovereign amplifies Abel's cries.[23] Cain is charged to keep them forever ringing in his ears. "And now," God declares to Cain, "you are cursed from the ground, which has opened its mouth to receive your brother's blood from your hand." (Gen. 4.10) This declaration ruptures Cain's identity. The one for whom the ground was once a co-conspirator now finds in it an adversary.

Instead of hiding the crime, the soil spits it back at him. "When you till the ground, it will no longer yield to you its strength," God continues, "you will be a fugitive and a wanderer on the earth." (Gen. 4.12) With this sentence, God negates the fratricide's power to emancipate the living brother from fraternal obligations. It reinforces the bond, albeit in the form of a haunting. The charge to remembrance and subsequent curse give Abel an afterlife that Remus never receives. Cain slays Abel. Nevertheless, it is the one who dwells and not the one who wanders who is left behind in the field. This reversal alienates Cain from his former identity, thrusting him towards his brother's. By assuming Abel's itinerancy, whatever his protest, Cain becomes his brother's keeper. Or perhaps Abel keeps him. Although he would go on to establish Enoch, the city would be a haunted place. Cain would forever be a wanderer—his identity would always be riven by his little brother's call.

With Arendt, we might suppose that Cain, like Romulus, seeks freedom from responsibility for his brother. The text bears out this much (whether or not the text makes this freedom paradigmatic of the *eu zen* of politics). In both

---

23   C.f. Smith, "The Mark of Cain." In his own treatment, Smith casts the text slightly differently. On Smith's reading, God's sovereignty is most powerfully illustrated in the mark that God places upon Cain. This mark, a warning of retribution for anyone who would harm Cain, evinces a form of negative sovereignty that revokes the fratricide's ability to define subsequent history. Smith's contribution should not be understated. His account of negative sovereignty permits a fundamental rethinking of the relationship between ethical goods and political institutions. My intention is to amend appreciatively rather than to reject. Whereas Smith emphasizes the negative, I seek to reintroduce a measure of positivity—even if the good posited can never fully be reintegrated into a political relationship premised on collective self-determination.

cases, the life of the other presents itself as a potential encumbrance—perhaps even an encumbrance that would stifle the political community's emergence. The act of fratricide negates this encumbrance. The upshot of this negation, presumably, should be freedom. However, if Genesis 4 presents a distinctive theological insight regarding our politics, it is this: whereas Romulus' mourning facilitates a closure that establishes a threshold between past and present, responsibility and freedom, the divine imperative to listen ensures that, for Cain, the past spills continually into the present. The curse that makes Cain a wanderer reveals that fratricide does not release freedom from responsibility, the political from the ethical. Instead, it allows the good of the life denied to endure as a kind of dialectical excess, and this excess defines freedom's ambit. A political theology informed by Genesis 4 must confront the political with this good's haunting endurance in the present. In so doing, it should stir up longing for a reconciliation that a political life premised on self-determining freedom alone cannot provide. It should incline us to listen to the disruptive, ethical demands crying out to us from the ground.

4   Troubled Closure: Haunting and the Politics of Self-Determination

In *Spheres of Justice*, Michael Walzer provides a sense of how this haunting is expressed in contemporary political philosophies organized around the ideal of collective self-determination. As historian Jörg Fisch observes, over the last century, the ideal of collective self-determination has come to enjoy near unanimous approbation, now standing as a peremptory norm of international law.[24] It describes at once a normative framework in which to evaluate just political action and the process of identification by which the political subject discloses

---

24   On the ideal's history, see Jörg Fisch, *The Right of Self-Determination of Peoples: The Domestication of an Illusion* (New York: Cambridge University Press, 2015); Eric D Weitz, "Self-Determination: How a German Enlightenment Idea Became the Slogan of National Liberation and a Human Right," *American Historical Review* 120 (April 2015): 462–496; & Brad Simpson, "Self-Determination and Decolonization," *The Oxford Handbook of the Ends of Empire,* ed. Martin Thomas & Andrew S. Thompson (New York: Oxford University Press, 2018), 417–430. Whereas Fisch and Weitz center their attention on self-determination's development in European thought, Simpson emphasizes the global south's role in contributing to the concept's meaning. Against scholars who claim that anti-colonial and decolonial movements merely adopted the language of self-determination as a rhetoric for legitimizing their aims, Simpson explains that these movements played a considerable role in shaping the term's meaning.

its shape. Nevertheless, despite the ideal's ubiquity in contemporary political discourse, few political philosophers have offered so clear and compelling an account of this structure and process as has Walzer in *Spheres of Justice*. Moreover, few others are so helpful in resisting the feeling of false triumphalism to which the ideal's preeminence might incline us.

One possible rival to Walzer is John Rawls. However, I leave his work aside in this chapter because Rawls' theory of justice presupposes a closed society whose members "enter only by birth and exit only by death."[25] Consequently, Rawls does not deal with the phenomenon of migration at any considerable length. He comes closest in *The Law of Peoples*. However, here, he argues that migration is merely a consequence of failed states. If the international community were constituted entirely of liberal and decent societies, he argues, the phenomenon of migration would disappear altogether.[26] Rawls' response to the question of migration, then, is the mere restatement of his general political philosophy. This philosophy is set not in our history but in the history of some 'realistic utopia.' On the other hand, Walzer's methodological commitment to analyzing nations as historically enduring communities of shared values produces considerably more careful thought about the interconnections between migration and self-determination. Walzer allows us to see that collective self-determination is impossible apart from a dialectical process of identification and alienation that works through acts of admission and exclusion. Moreover, he allows us to see how the ethical demand makes its presence felt in this dialectic's moments of troubled closure, where a non-identity erupts between what he refers to as 'political justice' and 'moral necessity.'

For Walzer, the ideal's normative structure sets out from the conviction that all human beings are 'culture-producing creatures' that "create and inhabit worlds of shared meaning."[27] To be subject to a power that strips us of this

---

25   John Rawls, *Political Liberalism* (New York: Columbia University Press, 1996), XLIII.

26   John Rawls, *The Law of Peoples* (Cambridge: Harvard University Press, 1997); c.f. Karoline Reinhardt, "No Migration in a Realistic Utopia? Rawls' The Law of Peoples and the Topic of Migration" (49th Societas Ethicas, August 23–26, 2012, Lucian Blaga University, Sibiu, Romania).

27   Michael Walzer, *Spheres of Justice: A Defense of Pluralism and Equality* (New York: Basic Books, 1983), 3. Walzer's language should be read as an emphatic assertion of the equality of all peoples and the universality of human dignity. To speak of humans as 'culture producing creatures' is to evoke and overturn invidious theories like the Nazi account of race, which divided humanity into racial groups defined either as 'founders of culture,' 'bearers of culture,' or 'destroyers of culture.' See Adolf Hitler, *Mein Kampf* trans. Ralph Manheim (Boston: Mariner Books, 1999), 290.

capacity is to be dehumanized. Therefore, political justice requires that the organs of state power would be responsible to this creativity:

> [The] principle of political justice is this: that the processes of self-deter-mination through which a democratic state shapes its internal life must be open, and equally open, to all those men and women who live within its territory, work in the local economy, and are subject to local law.[28]

Where this principle is applied, collective self-determination becomes an extension of individual self-determination, and nations become "communi-ties of character, historically stable, ongoing associations of men and women with some special commitment to one another and some special sense of their common life."[29] Political governance, in turn, becomes the mechanism of these communities' self-realization on the historical stage. If, for Arendt, the political is defined according to the *vita activa* of deliberation and creation, for Walzer, this creativity is always concerned with producing and preserving moral worlds that are at once the *vita activa*'s object and context. Thus, we call a given society 'just' when "its substantive life is lived ... in a way faithful to the shared understandings of its members."[30]

However, this account of collective self-determination's normative struc-ture makes the question of membership an issue of paramount importance. "What we do with membership structures all other distributive choices," Walzer explains, "it determines with whom we make choices, from whom we require obedience and collect taxes, and to whom we allocate goods and ser-vices."[31] "Admissions and exclusions," in a word, "suggest the deepest mean-ing of self-determination ... without them, there could not be communities of character."[32] The distribution of membership establishes the very bounds of that political subject that acts in the world. Nevertheless, Walzer does not imagine or appeal to any primordial distribution of membership. Instead, his philosophy begins *in medias res*, depicting collective self-determination as a process that takes place in the present through ongoing decisions of admission and exclusion. Consistent with his principle of political justice, Walzer argues that it is up to a society's present members to determine whom to admit and on what grounds:

---

28   Walzer, *Spheres of Justice*, 60.
29   Ibid, 62.
30   Ibid, 313.
31   Ibid, 31.
32   Ibid, 62.

We who are already members do the choosing, in accordance with our own understanding of what membership means in our community and what sort of community we want to have. Membership as a social good is constituted by our understandings; its value is fixed by our conversation; and then we are in charge (who else could be?) of its distribution.[33]

Admissions, then, occur based on a resemblance. Membership may be extended because the members and the non-member share a meaningful measure of political, religious, cultural, linguistic, national, or even ethnic affinity.[34] Concerning those who do not bear any such resemblance, self-determining political associations enjoy a 'right of closure.' To deny them this right would mean stripping them of their ability to make exclusions. Forced to admit anyone that appeared in their territory, the bounds of their identity would cease to reflect their defining traditions and nihilate the notion of self-determination itself. The political subject would be crushed under the tyranny of the other.

Nevertheless, Walzer does not believe the right of closure to be absolute. Beyond the particular commitments that define relationships within the political community, Walzer acknowledges a measure of responsibility that persists between human persons as such. Although he does not attempt to provide a philosophical basis for these responsibilities, he considers our 'sense' that the stranger might be entitled to our hospitality, assistance, and goodwill as one of our history's hard-earned insights.[35] It implies that the polity's encounter with the outsider cannot be treated as a matter of moral indifference. Beyond (or perhaps more correctly, before) the political relationship, there is an ethical relationship that demands from us a reckoning. Thus, the right of closure comes to be qualified by what Walzer refers to as the 'principle of mutual aid.'

In encounters between strangers, Walzer suggests that this principle obliges us to provide positive assistance, including the provision of refuge, if and only if the following two conditions are met: First, it must be the case that one of the parties desperately needs aid, and second, the risks and costs of extending

---

33   Ibid, 32.
34   Ibid, 46–47. Walzer expresses unease at this final possibility in his treatment of the 'White Australia' policy. His repudiation of this policy, however, does not yield a categorical repudiation of ethno-nationalism, only its validity for territories already occupied by an ethnically diverse population. This limited rebuke should not be read as Walzer's toleration for ethno-nationalism, only a limitation of his historical, comparative method.
35   Ibid, 32–33. Walzer distinguishes his own position from John Rawl's, who attempts to ground our responsibility to the stranger on a kind of Kantian categorical imperative. Walzer, for his part, is satisfied to accept the slow emerging historical distinction between strangers and enemies.

it must be judged tolerably low for the other party.[36] Whereas the first condition expresses our responsibility to address the vulnerability of fellow persons, the second condition attempts to temper this responsibility so that it does not overwhelm communal independence. Walzer explains:

> Groups of people ought to help necessitous strangers whom they somehow discover in the midst of their path. But the limit on risks and costs in these cases is sharply drawn. I need not take the injured stranger into my home, except briefly, and I certainly need not care for him or even associate with him for the rest of my life. My life cannot be shaped and determined by such chance encounters.[37]

This final sentence is telling. The fundamental risk implicit in extending aid is that helping the necessitous other would fundamentally change our identity. Walzer's treatment of the relationship between members and non-members transposes the tensions that Arendt locates in the polity's internal relationships to its external boundaries. Compassion might become the death of freedom, and our autonomy might succumb to that 'tyranny of the good' from which Arendt believed politics needed to be liberated. Consequently, the urgency of the other's need furnishes a necessary but insufficient condition for extending hospitality. The polity must also judge the cost of extending the aid to be tolerable.

Strikingly, however, Walzer does not suggest that fidelity to the principle's second condition releases us from our ethical responsibility to the other. On the contrary, he argues that hospitality to necessitous others is often "morally necessary," even as "the right to restrain the flow remains a feature of communal self-determination."[38] The principle of mutual aid does not justify the self-determining community vis-à-vis the stranger. It only signals the tension between the ethical relationship on one side and the political relationship on the other. The ethical relationship may indeed expose us to an experience of heteronomy, but this experience cannot be squared with a political relationship that abides by a more autonomous structure. Committed to his theory of political justice, Walzer concludes that "the principle of mutual aid can only modify and not transform admissions policies rooted in a particular community's understanding of itself."[39] The precise meaning of this conclusion is

---

36   Ibid, 33.
37   Ibid.
38   Ibid, 51.
39   Ibid.

difficult to discern, but it feeds the anxiety that the decision to exclude might amount to a form of fratricide. The defense of communal independence necessitates the transgression of an incarnate good that the polity can neither accommodate nor deny.

For Walzer as for Arendt, fratricide marks the boundaries of the body politic. It is the moment of negation following the dialectical collision of freedom and necessity. It locates the political subject's emergence at the point of divergence between political justice and the necessitous other's demand. Moreover, for Walzer and Arendt, there are instances in which this release must be judged a violation. Where Walzer and Arendt differ is in the temporality they assign to the crime. For Arendt, who fixes her attention on 'the problem of beginning,' it marks a point of transition between a pre-political past and a present wherein the *vita activa* of politics has been made possible. For Walzer, on the other hand, this dialectical process cannot be consigned to the past and takes place in present decisions of admission and exclusion. Each encounter with an outsider poses anew the possibility that the embodied good they bear along would make its claim on the polity's distinctive self-understanding. With each exclusion, the polity refuses responsibility for this good. In many instances, this refusal may prove to be benign. But every asylum-seeker and weary migrant cannot be accommodated purely by virtue of their need. Therefore, as Walzer is keenly aware, 'political justice' and 'moral necessity' will not always coincide. In the moments that their non-identity is revealed, the good of the life denied lingers in excess of the dialectic—haunting the polity.

What does acknowledging this transgression mean for our understanding of the process of self-determination? First it shifts the so-called stranger's place in self-determination's dialectic. If the process of identification moves through decisions of admission and exclusion, and if the other's approach prompts these decisions, then the other is not simply an 'outsider' or 'stranger' to the process. Instead, she provides the process of self-determination with one of its necessary conditions. To refer to the other as a 'stranger' or to suggest that, by chance, she is serendipitously discovered along the polity's path understates this dialectical intimacy. Strangers are not somehow discovered. Rather, they are *created* by the decisions of exclusion that confirm their estrangement from the political body and the political body from the social body.[40] Self-determination is not a clean process. It produces a remainder. Second, this remainder lingers, threatening to destabilize the self-determining political

---

40   If the language of 'discovery' must be retained, then, at the very least, it must be conceded that the polity discovers not only the stranger in the midst of its path, but itself in the midst of its encounter with the other.

subject. As Walzer helps us appreciate, to exclude the other is not actually to deny the good of her life. Nor even is it to cancel our responsibility for her. Instead, it is to make the good into a kind of dialectical excess. This excess, incarnate in bodies disavowed at the boundaries of the political, testifies to the contingency of our bodies politic. If the claim this good makes upon us is permitted to linger, then we permit it to reveal the contingency of the polity's identity. We allow it to insist that the polity's identity could and perhaps should have been formed otherwise.

5   A Riven Condition

In the preceding, I have sought to illustrate that ethical subjectivity and political subjectivity describe distinct forms of self-understanding differentiated by how a self (or collective self) comes into a relationship with its good. By extension, I have proposed that ethical and political subjectivity may be distinguished according to their axiological structures. Whereas ethical subjectivity is articulated in a moment of heteronomy, political subjectivity abides by a structure far more reminiscent of autonomy. That is, just as the autonomous individual constitutes herself according to the maxims she derives through practical reason, the self-determining society's internal life is shaped according to the values that its members hold in common. These values are not imposed from without but emerge from the members' creative activity. The self-determining political subject, therefore, finds its orienting good in the freedom to create, unconstrained by unwelcomed encroachments. The ethical subject, on the other hand, prizes responsibility over unalloyed freedom. She articulates her self-understanding in response to an ethical demand that comes from without, de-centers her autonomy, and exposes her to a good embodied in the life of the other.

Despite these distinct axiological structures, the dialectics of freedom and responsibility developed in the preceding discussions of fratricide suggest that these two forms of subjectivity nevertheless represent differing outcomes of the same dialectic. Whether it belongs to a society's origins or occurs in the present, the apparent necessity of fratricide indicates that the political subject, no less than the ethical subject, is constituted in an encounter with the other. For the self-determining society, the other's exclusion determines the bounds of the community's identity. Nevertheless, where this exclusion sets self-determination at odds with moral necessity, it reveals our subjectivities' instabilities. Moreover, the ongoing nature of this dialectical process puts them at perpetual risk of collapsing into one another. A society may seek to dispel fratricide's criminality by narrowing the boundaries of ethical responsibility so that they do not extend beyond the members of the political association (or those with whom they share cultural affinities). When this occurs, the ethical relationship is eclipsed by the political relationship. However, the political association may also allow freedom to succumb to the demand of the other. In responding to her demand, we risk discovering that encountering the other would mean experiencing the alterity in our own identities—and allowing it to redefine our self-understanding. Thus, our political subjectivity would be destabilized and reformulated by what Simon Critchley calls ethical experience's 'anarchic meta-politics.' Yet, as this reformulation is infused with the heteronomy of the ethical demand, it threatens to undo the very possibility of self-determination.

What the preceding argumentation should help us to appreciate, however, is that the human condition is one riven by contradiction. It is not that the *animal socialis* becomes the *zōon politikon* in a moment of dialectical progression. We are at once the *animal socialis*, ruled by necessity from without, and the *zōon politikon*, governed by freedom from within. This duality reveals itself in the tension between our ethical and political subjectivity. We might be tempted to suppose that to realize its redemptive potential, the law must resolve this contradiction. However, it may also need to find a way to resist the demand for identity and to leave the contradiction unresolved. Turning in the next chapter to the case of Prevention Through Deterrence, I will argue that in the instances that the law seeks to overcome the contradiction by canceling one of its terms, the result is not reconciliation but alienation. In the Sonoran Desert, the consequent alienation is lethal not only for the excluded other but also for the polity.

For now, I will restate the point that has been my principal preoccupation throughout this chapter: exclusions are never complete. They always produce a remainder. Even as the law's system of nomination attempts to insulate the polity from this remainder, its triumphs are only partial victories. No one is just a 'citizen' or an 'alien.'[41] These names do not exhaust the fullness of our humanity.

---

41   C.f. Seyla Benhabib, *Another Cosmopolitanism* (New York: Oxford University Press, 2006). As Seyla Benhabib persuasively notes in *Another Cosmopolitanism,* peoples have a 'dual identity' as "an *ethnos*, as a community of shared fate, memories, and moral sympathies, on the one hand, and as a *demos*, as a democratically enfranchised totality of all citizens, who may or may not belong to the same ethnos, on the other." (pp. 67ff) Both Rawlsian liberalism and Walzerian communitarianism slide into error in the instances that this dual identity is collapsed. In Part Three of this book, I will return to this complexity, particularly as it is revealed by the movements of compassion. The case that I make for the compassionate interpretation of law, in turn, might be read as a form of what Benhabib calls 'democratic iteration' and 'jurisgenetic process.'

Where they inevitably come up short, the commonalities of vulnerable, interdependent creatures make themselves known. These commonalities are closer to us than our language and put to us an ethical demand from which we can never entirely escape. Anzaldúa describes the emergence of *los atravesados* through a process of alienation. However, what is revealed in our encounter with the other is that alienation is not exclusively the experience of the presumed outsider. In alienating the other, we, too, alienate ourselves. We are, all of us, in a sense, border crossed. Even if we displace the suffering that this condition produces disproportionately onto those we name 'alien,' the truth remains.

It is a truth from which we cannot hide. Only in our encounters with our estranged siblings do we become known to ourselves as ethical and political subjects. But ours is a riven condition, marked by enduring non-identities. We, like Cain, may meet this non-identity with enmity and see our interdependence as contemptuous encumbrance rather than common trust. We may refuse to become our brothers' keepers. Yet, like Cain, we may find that, whatever effort we may make to be rid of them, these estranged siblings will keep us. Their ghosts may haunt us. Haunting, however, is a difficult fate to accept. I now turn to the Sonoran Desert and the fratricides that occur in the dust of its valleys. I now turn to PTD's disastrous attempt to exorcise the ghosts.

CHAPTER 4

Exorcising the Ghosts

The people must fight for the law as for the city wall.
    —HERACLITUS, Fragment 44

∙∙∙

And when they were in the field, Cain rose up against his brother
Abel and killed him.
    —GENESIS 4.8

∙∙
∙

1   Prevention through Deterrence as Practical Solution

At the United States-Mexico line, where two bodies politic divide, the boundaries of American territory and identity are maintained through the disavowal
and violation of migrant bodies. Although we are given to think of the world as
an international system of nation-states parsed up according to the process of
collective self-determination, this process does not achieve an even division.
It produces a remainder. This remainder demonstrates self-determination's
dialectical entanglement with the demand of the excluded other, revealing a
non-identity between political subjectivity and ethical subjectivity and giving
rise to the anxiety that the former could and, perhaps, should be constituted
otherwise than it is. In the borderlands, we are reminded that this remainder
is no abstract sum. It is incarnate in the persons undertaking perilous journeys
on dangerous ground. Many do not survive the undertaking, and their remains
challenge our national self-understanding. Though we might be inclined to
think of migrant mortalities as the consequence of ill fortune or foolish gambles, these deaths are better understood as fratricides. In this chapter, I aim
to lay out the anatomy of this fratricide as it plays out in the southwestern
borderlands.

What neither Arendt nor Walzer resolves theoretically, Prevention Through
Deterrence (PTD) determines to settle in practice. First, in the law and then
in the landscape, migrants are stripped of their ability to make any kind of

demand on the polity. Their alienage under the law denies them any scheme of rights that would safeguard them against the federal government's plenary power in matters of exclusion and removal. PTD radicalizes this denial, instrumentalizing the Sonoran Desert and enacting the plenary power doctrine through enforcement actions that identify sovereignty with the power to make live and let die.[1] Like Cain, who called his brother into the field to hide his crime, PTD tempts migrants ever deeper into the desert's vast expanse, consigning them to an anonymous demise. However, just as the ground betrayed Cain, the Sonoran betrays the law enforcement agencies that entrust it with their work. As its rugged landscape is deputized into the work of law enforcement, the law inherits the antinomian violence of nature. Consequently, that political institution, meant to act as a wall between the polity and the wilderness, obscures the distinction instead. In the last, bones discovered in the valleys of the Sonoran raise the unsettling possibility that the law, which was to reconcile us with our humanity, reveals instead our inhumanity. Thus, PTD's success becomes its downfall. Blood cries out from the ground. Like Cain, we are marked for our act. We are haunted by the bodies we seek to disavow, and we cannot exorcise the ghosts.

Therefore, in this chapter, I seek to make three points. The first and second regard PTD directly. First, this border enforcement strategy's decades-long failure does not lie in its inability to prevent illicit entries effectively. Rather, the failure stems from the strategy's contempt for human embodiment. Second, this failure is fatal not only for the migrants it victimizes but for our concepts of law and self-determination as well. The same strategy that destroys migrant bodies also mortifies the organizing ideals of the body politic. Thus, even if one embraced the strategy's contempt for migrants' lives, this contempt would still be a sign that a great effort is failing. Third, and more implicitly, I seek to make a more general point about the law. Against those who would insulate the law from questions of ethics, I propose that a law enforcement regime that makes itself a bulwark against ethical demands is, ultimately, unviable and self-defeating. With this point, I pivot to Part Three of this book, where I will attempt to reconfigure the relationship between the ethical demand, the law, and political right.

---

1 On the identification of sovereignty and the power to make live and let die, c.f. Achille Mbembe, *Necropolitics,* trans. Libby Meintjes (Durham: Duke University Press, 2019).

2 The Making of the 'Alien'

Fratricide begins in the law. At the international line, the encounter between ethical subjects is reframed as an encounter between 'citizens' and 'aliens.' With these names, a crucial distinction is introduced. US law did not coin the term 'alien.' Instead, it is a term inherited from the English Common Law. In his landmark *Commentaries on the Laws of England,* William Blackstone defined the 'alien,' in contradistinction to the 'natural-born subject,' as one born outside of the *ligament* or 'liegence' that binds a subject and the monarch who has dominion over their land.[2] Blackstone conceives of liegence as a natural relationship between a Sovereign and their subject. For the liege-lord, this relationship is expressed in the provision of protection that begins at the subject's birth and does not end until their death. For the liege-subject, it consists in the irrevocable debt of gratitude and loyalty that the sovereign's protection inspires. Thus, liegence does not consist of express oaths but an intrinsic, interminable natural relationship owed from every subject to their sovereign lord.[3] It persists before and after any other oath or declaration of fealty. Consequently, Blackstone supposed that "an Englishman who removes to France or to China, owes the same liegence to the King of England there as at home, and twenty years hence as well as now."[4] Crucially, by defining the relationship in this way, Blackstone interposes between the 'alien' and the 'natural-born subject' a natural and inassimilable difference. To the political community, the alien born comes as if from another world and, whatever they may profess in word or deed, remains forever tied to that world. As such, the figure of the alien, from its inception, is conceived as a figure of divided loyalties and, by extension, of natural suspicion—even enmity.

As Robert Heimburger shows in *God and the Illegal Alien*, this legal concept's place in the history of United States law reflects an effort to grapple with its meaning following its removal from its original conceptual soil.[5] Introduced into a legal system that replaces the natural liege relationship between subject and sovereign with the elective relationship of allegiance between citizens, the

---

2 C.f. William Blackstone, *Commentaries on the Laws of England in Four Books*, Book I, Chapter X (1753).

3 Blackstone does concede that a person who moves to a foreign land may practice a form of 'local liegence.' However, he explains, this relationship is only temporary and begins and ends with their presence in the dominion of the foreign-lord. Moreover, at no point during their sojourn is their liegence to their natural-born sovereign suspended or abridged.

4 Ibid.

5 Robert Heimburger, *God and the Illegal Alien: United States Immgiration Law and a Theology of Politics* (New York: Cambridge University Press, 2018).

alien was removed from the context that provided its initial intelligibility. Consequently, the term's meaning has been gradually refashioned across a legal history that spans the eighteenth, nineteenth, and twentieth centuries.[6] It has taken on various meanings at various turns in this history. In the context of eighteenth and early nineteenth-century naturalization laws, 'aliens' initially appeared to be the stuff of which 'citizens' were to be made. This sense enjoyed justifiable plausibility for a young nation populated mainly by a people with relatively recent immigration heritage. Nevertheless, this conception of the alien was never completely divested of its darker undertones. By the late nineteenth century, as nativist concerns turned Anglo-Americans against migrant laborers considered to be racial others, the aura of suspicion that accompanied the figure of the alien returned to the fore. With this turn, the alien was recast as a figure of enmity whose exclusion was a matter of existential importance to the survival of the political community.

Justice Stephen Field's 1889 ruling on the infamous Chinese Exclusion Case, Chae Chan Ping v. United States, crystalizes this shift.[7] Through a series of agreements culminating in the Burlingame-Seward Treaty of 1868, the United States eased immigration restrictions between the United States and China. At the time of the treaty's ratification, the United States hoped the agreement would be a boon to American trade interests. Though these agreements did not promise to naturalize Chinese nationals in the United States, they intended to afford them protections and access to work, residence, and schooling. However, as the Chinese presence in the United States grew, public opinion about the treaty soured, particularly in California. As Fields writes in the court's majority opinion:

> [The Chinese] remained strangers in the land, residing apart by themselves, and adhering to the customs and usages of their own country. It seemed impossible for them to assimilate with our people or to make any change in their habits or modes of living. As they grew in number each year the people of the coast saw, or believed they saw, in the facility of immigration, and in the crowded millions of China ... great danger that at no distant day that portion of our country would be overrun by them unless prompt action was taken to restrict immigration.[8]

---

6   A a full recounting of this history would far outstrip the scope of the present analysis. For a more complete retelling, see ibid, n.b., 25–44.
7   The Chinese Exclusion Case, Chae Chan Ping v. United States, 130 US 581.
8   Ibid, 595.

Responding to California's perceived plight, the US Congress passed a series of laws from 1882 to 1888 designed to restrict admissions of Chinese laborers. At issue in Chae Chan Ping v. United States was whether the 1888 Scott Act had unlawfully abrogated the terms of the Burlingame-Seward Treaty by valorizing the exclusions of migrants who, under the terms of the treaty, were permitted entry into the United States. In a unanimous decision, the court judged that territorial jurisdiction and the power to exclude aliens were incidents of national Sovereignty. Therefore, the federal government's power in matters of exclusion could not be a matter of controversy or subject to judicial intervention.

Further, the language of Field's decision explicitly grounds that power in the State's right and obligation to repel foreign aggression. "To preserve its independence and give security against foreign aggression and encroachment," Field writes, "is the highest duty of every nation, and to attain these ends, nearly all other considerations are to be subordinated."[9] In the court's eyes, the people of California and the federal legislature held the credible belief that they were facing an 'oriental invasion' that posed an existential threat to their culture. Field argued that all invaders do not arrive armed and uniformed. Some arrive in plain clothes and equipped with little more than the tools of their craft.

> If, therefore, the government of the United States, through its legislative department, considers foreigners of a different race in this country, who will not assimilate with us, to be dangerous to its peace and security, their exclusion is not to be stayed because at the time there are no actual hostilities with the nation of which the foreigners are subject.[10]

Though innocuous in its time, the language of racial difference should be striking to modern readers. What defined these Chinese laborers as potential aggressors were not acts of hostility. It was their race which supposedly rendered them incapable of assimilation into the body politic. This factor alone was sufficient to confirm the threat they posed to the country and reinscribed the notion that the alien was a figure of natural suspicion.[11] By inscribing the

---

9   Ibid, 606.
10   Ibid.
11   C.f. Carl Schmitt, *The Concept of the Political* (Chicago: University of Chicago Press, 2007). Justice Field's line of reasoning, which ties enmity to alterity, makes the citizen-alien distinction an early and disturbing American parallel for Carl Schmitt's later distinction between the 'friend' and the 'enemy.' The enemy, Schmitt writes, is one who is "in a specially intense way, existentially something different and *alien*, so that in the extreme case conflicts with him are possible." (p. 27)

alien in a legal fiction about invasion and defense, Field's opinion reinforced the alien's alterity to the members of the body politic and, as a consequence, her hostility toward them.[12] Moreover, by replacing the difference of liegence with the difference of race, Field's opinion recasts the hostility that supposedly persists between sovereigns with a hostility presumed to exist between races.

With this judgment, the alien was also marked as a legal subject emphatically differentiated from the citizen by her unmitigated vulnerability to the federal government's sovereign power.[13] More than a century later, the alien's exceptional legal status continues to be demonstrated in the procedures that facilitate exclusions and removals in the Sonoran. Here, many migrants are removed from United States territory under a protocol known as 'expedited removal.' This protocol empowers border enforcement officials who have interdicted migrants within 100 miles of the border to remove them from US territory without affording them a hearing in the immigration courts.[14] Ostensibly adopted to reduce strain on the court system, this procedure indicates the enduring force of the federal government's presumptive imperative to deal with migrants expeditiously and the denials of dignity that facilitate its fulfillment.

---

12 On Chae Chan Ping v. United States' enduring significance in contemporary law, see Matthew J. Lindsey, "Immigration as Invasion: Sovereignty, Security, and the Origins of the Federal Immigration Power," *Immigration and Nationality Review* 31 (2010): 591–648; Matthew J. Lindsey, "The Perpetual 'Invasion': Past as Prologue in Constitutional Immigration Law," *Roger Williams University Law Review* 23 (2018): 369–392; Taylor Saito, "The Enduring Effect of the Chinese Exclusion Cases: The 'Plenary Power' Justification for Ongoing Human Rights Abuses," *Asian Law Journal* 10 (2003): 13–36; & Lauri Kai, "Embracing the Chinese Exclusion Case: An International Law Approach to Racial Exclusions," *William & Mary Law Review* 59 (2018): 2617–2662.

13 As Linda Bosniak observes, our contemporary concept of the 'citizen' is not entirely uniform in its denotation. It seems to connote four distinct, if interconnected entitlements: an entitlement to participate in governance, to protection from state power, to membership status, and to a feeling of identity with one's political association. Unlike the citizen, however, the alien bears no legal entitlement to membership status, whether in feeling or in fact. She also lacks the citizen's legal entitlement to protection from state power and her right to participate in the state's governance. On the various traditions and senses combined in our contemporary concept of citizenship and alienage, see Linda Bosniak, *The Citizen and the Alien: Dilemmas of Contemporary Membership* (Princeton: Princeton University Press, 2006).

14 The statutory basis for expedited removal comes from 8 USC 1225 and applies to aliens who arrive at or between ports of entry and are judged by an officer of the border patrol to lack a credible fear of persecution that would otherwise form the basis for a defensive asylum claim.

3   Legal Rights and the Dignification of Demands

Many ethicists are inclined to speak of human dignity as an inherent quality of human personhood. According to this view, to be human is *eo ipso* to possess dignity. To possess dignity, in turn, is to possess a moral status that entitles one to a scheme of rights and protections. Thus, PTD (and other border enforcement regimes) are often criticized for violating *human* rights. However, as Timothy P. Jackson has compellingly argued, the term *dignitas* initially indicated a recognition of status conferred upon persons by their societies.[15] In this sense, dignity denotes a standing that must be earned, or, at least, granted, and one that, presumably, can be lost, revoked, or denied in the first place.

Consequently, Jackson contends that ethicists should differentiate between 'dignity,' which denotes a moral status premised on recognition, and 'sanctity,' which denotes human life's intrinsic and interminable goodness. By introducing this distinction, Jackson presents the possibility that inherent sanctity does not necessitate recognized dignity. Moreover, he warns, in societies that prize dignity-rights over sanctity, sanctity may be transgressed with (legal) impunity where dignity is absent. The history of United States immigration law bears this possibility out. The possession of rights does not depend on one's possession of dignity. Instead, one is dignified, before the law, only as she is conferred that basic scheme of rights that renders her not only an object of but subject over law's power.[16] Yet, for the alien, who is reduced to a mere object of law, the possession of sanctity does little to arrest the advance of government power. Put another way, the goodness of human life, conveyed in the ethical demand, must become legible to the state to make itself felt. It must be dignified. The fratricide perpetrated by the law is not a transgression of dignity but a refusal to dignify.

Joel Feinberg's demand theory helps us to clarify this point. For Feinberg, an individual's possession of a right indicates her capacity to articulate a demand to the state in the language of law. "To have a right," as Joel Feinberg puts it, "is to have a claim against someone whose recognition as valid is grounded in some set of governing rules[.]"[17] According to Feinberg's demand theory, our

---

15   According, at least, to the liberal tradition stemming from Kant, human dignity is connected with human rationality. It is our nature as rational beings that grounds our moral status and, by extension, our social and political status. See Timothy P. Jackson, *Political Agape: Christian Love and Liberal Democracy*, Emory University Studies in Law and Religion (Grand Rapids, Michigan: William B. Eerdmans Publishing Company, 2015).

16   Joel Feinberg, "The Nature and Value of Rights," *The Journal of Value Inquiry* 4 (1970): 245–257.

17   Ibid, 257.

concept of a 'right' contains several interconnected ideas. First, it implies a subject who is the bearer of the right. Second, it implies some claim that establishes a norm for action. Third, it implies an object on whom the claim confers an obligation. For instance, we can see each of these three elements in the context of a contract. The parties to the contract are each the subjects and objects of rights, obliged to specific actions. If I sign a contract to purchase a car, the other party is obliged to deliver the vehicle, and I am required to tender payment. If either of us fails to discharge our side of the contract, we are guilty of transgressing the norm that the other's claim imposes upon us. Consequently, the wronged party would be entitled to seek a remedy for the breach. Pursuing a remedy reveals a fourth component integral to the concept of a right: the claim's validity is grounded in some set of governing rules that transcend it. That is, the object of a right is obliged not only to the subject who makes the claim but also to the more extensive system of rules that conditions its recognition as valid. Hence, when one party to a contract breaches the agreement, the law intervenes on behalf of the other. Fifth, and finally, to be one on whose behalf the law may be invoked is to be dignified by the law. To possess a right, in short, is to bear dignity. To be without rights is to be without dignity.[18]

Understanding a right as an entitlement to protection from state power requires only that we think of the relationship between subject, object, and claim in the context of a social contract rather than a transactional one. On the one hand, by entering into the social contract, we agree to temper or curtail some of our liberties in obedience to laws directed toward the commonweal. In response, the state agrees to provide for security, stability, and the provision of the public good. However, we enter this agreement with the expectation that the body politic will provide not only for security and stability, not merely the enjoyment of superficial comforts, but for the protection of essential liberties. These liberties make a normative claim on the operations of power that order the common life. Thus, the law may afford certain police powers to the state to restrain anti-social and self-destructive behaviors and, in this way, function as a sword that strikes out against those who would threaten the public good. Nevertheless, the law also becomes a shield for the contractors by delimiting the police powers' reach. Where the state overreaches these bounds, the individual members may call on the law to intercede. In so doing, they reassert their dignity before the state's power, interrupting and redirecting the operations of sovereign power by the force of their demand. In this way, the assertion of a right, including and, perhaps especially, in the context of legal

---

18   Ibid.

conflict, declares that the citizen is not merely an object of rule but a subject that participates in the rule determinative of the common life—that she is one who demands and one whose demand carries weight.

A right, then, is a demand made legible in the language of law. Nevertheless, we do well to mark a critical distinction between 'legal rights' and 'ethical demands.' This distinction is apparent in the way that each attains its motivational force. As Simon Critchley conceives it, and as I shall argue in the next chapter, the experience of the ethical demand is an experience of 'hetero-affectivity.' It is an experience wherein the object of the demand is moved affectively by the subject that lodges it such that she desires identity with it. Thus, the pain that attends the transgression of an ethical demand is the pain of breaking faith with that good to which one wills to cleave. Concerning legal right, however, the subject's claim attains its motivational force in connection to some third party—the institution of law. Therefore, the pain attendant to the transgression of a legal right is not the pain of broken faith but rather the penalty or restraint imposed with the law's intercession on the subject's behalf. The ethical subject, then, experiences its good as though it were inherent in the one that embodies it. In the ethical demand, we experience what Jackson calls 'sanctity.' The legal subject, however, is respected on the grounds of her dignity, and this dignity is a status conferred upon her by the law. At stake in one's legal subjectivity, then, is her ability to make her status as a subject of moral concern legible to the state. However, since our legal subjectivity is given from without, it is a point of extreme vulnerability. In systems that attend only to dignity and not to sanctity, those who do not bear legal rights are exposed to distinct danger.

I have already suggested that the alien has emerged as a figure that, at least concerning the federal government's plenary power to exclude and remove, is deprived of any scheme of rights that would dignify her demand. The figure of the asylum-seeker presents a plausible refutation of this claim. Asylum-seekers are aliens. However, they are not immigrants. Instead, they are individuals fleeing persecution, or the credible threat thereof, in their home countries. In the instance that this persecution is the consequence of some immutable quality—race, religion, nationality, membership in a particular social group, or political opinion—the asylum-seeker may request refuge from the United States, regardless of whether they have entered the United States lawfully or not.[19] That is, migrants may assert asylum claims 'affirmatively' by presenting themselves to immigration authorities or 'defensively' after being placed into

---

19   See 8 USC § 1158

removal proceedings.[20] These defensive claims signal an interruption in the operations of sovereign power by which the state's borders are secured and, therefore, appear to function something like a right. The alien that comes to be seen as an asylum-seeker, that is, appears to register a demand that suspends the federal government's plenary power in matters of exclusion and removal. She *seems* to bear a right, irrespective of citizenship status, that dignifies her before the law. However, the various means by which this apparent right is defeated make the asylum-seeker a figure that confirms rather than refutes the precarity that alienage produces. In the borderlands, one must look no further than protocols like expedited removal.

By permitting enforcement officials to remove migrants from US territory without a hearing in an immigration court, expedited removal significantly curtails migrants' abilities to lodge asylum claims. To be granted asylum, migrants must complete a 'credible fear interview' with a representative of the immigration court system. However, to make their case persuasively, migrants must tell a story that satisfies specific statutory requirements. Not only must their stories be factually consistent, they must demonstrate that the migrant is a member of a class protected under the provisions of the law. Further, they must strike the right tone. Throughout the process, the asylum-seeker bears the burden of proving that they should be admitted. The state is not obliged to show that the migrant should be excluded. Consequently, officials conducting credible fear interviews enjoy considerable latitude for disqualifying claims.

> [A] trier of fact may base a credibility determination on the demeanor, candor, or responsiveness of the applicant or witness, the inherent plausibility of the applicant's or witness' written and oral statements ... the internal consistency between the applicant's or witness' written and oral statements with other evidence of record ... and any inaccuracies or falsehoods in such statements, *without regard to whether an inconsistency, inaccuracy, or falsehood goes to the heart of the applicant's claim,* or any other relevant factor.[21]

---

20   The ability to register defensive claims, however, is subject to state control. This point has been demonstrated most recently by the Biden administration's decision to limit the defensive asylum claims available to migrants who have crossed over the southwestern border unlawfully. See The White House, "FACT SHEET: President Biden Announces New Actions to Secure the Border," The White House, June 4, 2024, https://www.whitehouse.gov/briefing-room/statements-releases/2024/06/04/fact-sheet-president-biden-announces-new-actions-to-secure-the-border/.
21   8 USC 1158(b)(1)(B)(iii) [emphasis added]

If a migrant is to succeed under these conditions, they must not only tell a perfectly consistent story with the proper demeanor, but they must also have some measure of knowledge of United States asylum law. However, to expect this of a migrant deprived of legal counsel borders on the absurd.[22] The absence of legal representation afforded to migrants processed through expedited removal hearings, therefore, appears to undermine the law's best moral insights while exacerbating its shortcomings. The policy's stated purpose is to relieve strain on the immigration courts by diminishing the incidence of frivolous asylum claims. However, it also has the effect of circumscribing an alien's ability to make her demand heard.

Thus, in 2020, in the case of Department of Homeland Security v. Thuraissigiam, one migrant's attorneys challenged the legitimacy of expedited removal on the grounds that it violated migrants' rights to due process of law.[23] Vijayakumar Thuraissigiam was a national of Sri Lanka interdicted just 25 yards from the US–Mexico line after entering US territory unlawfully. In a credible fear interview with the intercepting officer, Thuraissigiam expressed a fear of persecution on the grounds of his Tamil ethnicity. The officer did not deem his claim credible and placed him in expedited removal proceedings. This move was subsequently supported by the officer's supervisor and, later, by an immigration judge, before being overturned by the Ninth Circuit Court of Appeals on the grounds that the statutory basis for expedited removal violates the due process clause of the Fourteenth Amendment. This clause stipulates that no state "shall ... deprive any person of life, liberty, or property, without due process of law."[24] The success of Thuraissigiam's defense would turn on an appeal to the constitution that asserted migrants' possession of some scheme of procedural entitlements that includes the right to have their case heard before a judge. Further, the defense asserts that the state must see this entitlement fulfilled and, critically, that expedited removal protocols fail to satisfy this obligation. Thuraissigiam's gambit, in a word, was to seek a constitutional intervention and, in so doing, to demand to be dignified.

However, when Thuraissigiam's case reached the United States Supreme Court, this gambit failed. In a 7–2 decision, the justices ruled that expedited removal did not violate due process. The majority opinion, authored by Justice Samuel Alito, reiterates that "an alien seeking initial admission to the United States requests a privilege and has no constitutional rights regarding his

---

22   This is to say nothing of the problems posed by potential language barriers if the migrant and interdicting officer do not speak the same language.

23   Department of Homeland Security et al v. Thuraissigiam, 591 US_(2020)

24   US Const. amend. xiv, § 2

application, for the power to admit or exclude aliens is a sovereign prerogative."
As such, a credible fear interview conducted by an authorized official constitutes a response to this privilege that is satisfactory for the due process of law.
"An alien," interdicted after crossing the border unlawfully, Alito concludes, "has
only those rights regarding admission that Congress has provided by statute."[25]
However, there is no right to asylum. Though asylum law may afford migrants
a measure of agency, whether the asylum-seeker is admitted or not ultimately
depends on the sovereign's decision as to whether it wishes to dignify her
demand.

This point was reiterated even more recently when, in June of 2024, the
Biden Administration issued an executive order stating that it would place limits on defensive asylum claims from migrants who had crossed the southern
border unlawfully.[26] The limitation imposed by the executive order does not
refer to the merits of any hypothetical claims in question. Instead, it harkens
back to the state's need to be able to restrain the movement of migrants into
its territory, premising the suspension of defensive claims on nothing other
than "high levels of encounters" that exceed the immigration court's ability
to "deliver timely consequences."[27] The asylum-seeker's case is interesting
because it regards a figure that seems to represent a plausible exception to the
plenary power doctrine and one premised on a right that is the legal transcrip-
tion of an expressly ethical demand. To use Walzer's diction, in the figure of
the asylum-seeker, the state's right of closure meets with the duties enjoined
upon it by the principle of mutual aid. Nevertheless, despite the codification
of asylum procedures established by the 1980 Refugee Act, time and again, the
United States refrains from recognizing any legally stated or conferred right to
asylum. In her dissenting opinion to DHS v. Thuraissigiam, Justice Sotomayor
argued that the refusal to acknowledge any such right empowered arbitrary
decision-making in matters of asylum.[28] A similar arbitrariness appears to be
on display in the 2024 executive order.

Once designating the stuff of which citizens were made, a point of contact
between the law and its outside, the name 'alien' now establishes a bulwark
between migrants and the laws' protections. Subject to exception, migrants
occupy a position distinctly exposed to the federal government's power to separate and exclude. Stripped of meaningful rights, it is as if they could make

---

25   Department of Homeland Security et al v. Thuraissigiam.
26   The White House, "FACT SHEET: President Biden Announces New Actions to Secure the
      Border."
27   Ibid.
28   Department of Homeland Security et al v. Thuraissigiam.

no ethical demands upon the polity. They remain, as it were, subjects before
a sovereign. Moreover, they enjoy no dignity before the sovereign, and without dignity, no provision is made to protect the sanctity of their lives. Having
become legible to the polity as 'aliens,' therefore, migrants are already victims
of a kind of political fratricide. Whatever good they embody is the province of
that social body from which the political association labors to extricate itself.

4   Disappeared in the Landscape

PTD completes the fratricide, reifying in the landscape the alienation begun
in the law and disclaiming responsibility for the sanctity of those lives that
the law does not dignify. Whereas alienage renders the outsider's demand
legally illegible through the denial of rights, PTD renders it invisible and inaudible by forcing migrant traffic into remote wilderness corridors beyond the
vision of the public eye. Migrants crossing the US–Mexico line did not always
travel through such remote passages. Before the strategy's implementation,
so-called 'twin cities,' which span both sides of the international line, were
the most common sites of unlawful entries. Most notable among these cities
were places like San Diego-Tijuana, El Paso-Ciudad Juárez, and Nogales. These
urban settings offered easy access to buses, trains, and other transportation
inland while presenting relatively little risk of detection or arrest. Even where
security measures existed, they were comparatively ill-equipped to regulate
migrant traffic effectively. San Diego saw the emergence of a tactic that came,
unfortunately, to be termed the 'banzai run.' The tactic would begin with large
groups of migrants gathering on the Mexican side of the boundary. Knowing
that security checkpoints were insufficiently staffed to catch the whole group,
they would rush them *en masse*. Participants (rightly) wagered that some of
them would be stopped. However, thanks to their overwhelming numbers,
many would be able to slip through.[29] Elsewhere, the crossings were far less
dramatic. In El Paso, migrants could wade across shallow sections of the Rio
Grande, conduct their business, and return home in the same manner. The
perceived vulnerability of these 'twin cities' made their fortification a priority for the Border Patrol's senior leadership. Therefore, PTD's strategy was to

---

29   See Joseph Nevins, *Operation Gatekeeper and Beyond: The War on "Illegals" and the Remak-
      ing of the US–Mexico Boundary* (New York: Routledge, 2002), 155ff.

cut off these traditional points of entry and force "illegal traffic ... over more hostile terrain, less suited for crossing and more suited for enforcement."[30]

For three decades now, the border patrol has accomplished this objective with the aggressive accumulation of enforcement assets in urban areas along the borderline. Since the implementation of PTD, the Border Patrol's budget has swelled from four hundred million dollars in 1994 to nearly $4.9 billion in 2021.[31] This growth in spending has facilitated a dramatic increase in Border Patrol staffing nationwide. In 1994, the Border Patrol employed just over four thousand people. By 2020, the number saw a five-fold increase.[32] The vast majority of these agents have been assigned to enforcement sectors along the southwest border. Between fiscal years 1994 and 2020, the number of agents in the region rose from a meager 3,747 to 16,878.[33] Today, United States Customs and Border Protection is the largest federal law enforcement agency. However, funding increases have also supported efforts to adapt technologies initially designed for use on overseas battlefields to the Border Patrol's domestic needs. These technologies include not only assault weapons, jeeps, and all-terrain vehicles but also footfall sensors, infrared cameras, night-vision equipment, and Predator Drones. Perhaps the most iconic upshot of this infusion of funding has been the construction of some 720 linear miles of border fencing. Altogether, the barrier is estimated to comprise roughly 680,000 tons of steel and 970,000 cubic yards of concrete and stretches from the hearts of once-vulnerable twin cities into the wilderness. In his 2017 monograph, *Borderwall as Architecture*, Ronald Rael estimates that, by just 2007, the total expense of constructing and maintaining the wall stood at a staggering $49 billion.[34] At no small cost, the United States has fortified its boundary. However, it has not

---

30   Doris Meissner, *Border Patrol Strategic Plan: 1994 and Beyond* (Washington, D.C.: United States Border Patrol, 1994), 7.

31   American Immigration Council, "Fact Sheet: The Cost of Immigration Enforcement and Border Security" (January 2021).

32   United States Border Patrol, "United States Border Patrol Fiscal Year Staffing Statistics" (Washington D.C.: United States Border Patrol, 2020)

33   Ibid.

34   Ronald Rael, *Borderwall as Architecture: A Manifesto for the US–Mexico Boundary* (Berkeley: University of California Press, 2017). Rael notes that this price tag makes the border fence roughly as expensive per linear mile as New York's highline park. With different priorities, he proposes, the US government might have used the money to create one of the longest gardens in the world. The bulk of Rael's book is dedicated to proposing similar ideas. Though many of Rael's proposals verge on the comical (e.g. 720-mile-long burrito stand or an absurdly long series of see-saws), these jokes convey the truth that the border could be conceived otherwise than it is, as a place of friendship rather than fratricide, of encounter rather than alienation.

FIGURE 8   Map of extant (black) and planned (red) border fencing as of July 2023.
SOURCE: US CUSTOMS AND BORDER PROTECTION. BORDERWALL SYSTEM
[MAP]. "USCUSTOMS AND BORDER PROTECTION." LAST UPDATED JULY 24,
2023. HTTPS://WWW.CBP.GOV/BORDER-SECURITY/ALONG-US-BORDERS/
BORDER-WALL-SYSTEM

constructed this bulwark against a hostile state proportionately armed with advanced tanks or fighter jets. The United States' multi-billion-dollar border infrastructure has been built to hold off migrants, the majority of whom are unarmed, traveling on foot, and equipped for their crossing with no more than the meager resources they can carry on their backs. There is a dark irony to border enforcement.

This irony is acutely visible in San Diego, where the border fence cuts directly through Friendship Park. This park was created in the nineteenth century, following the end of the Mexican-American War, as a statement of goodwill. For more than a century, it was a place where citizens from both countries could gather together in peace. In 2006, however, the federal government suspended a host of laws, seized the land as eminent domain, and constructed a stretch of border fencing that divides the United States from Mexico and stretches for hundreds of feet into the waters of the Pacific Ocean. Such irony is common on the borderline and belies a more profound and still more troubling contradiction. Both in urban areas like San Diego and in wilderness regions like Organ Pipe National Monument, the construction of border fortifications has required myriad legal exceptions and emergency measures. The construction of border fences has required the government to suspend laws such as the Clean Air Act, the Safe Drinking Water Act, the Endangered Species Act, the Native American Graves Protection and Reparation Act, and dozens of others. While the Secretary of Homeland Security derives the authority to waive these laws from the REAL ID Act of 2005, the suspensions nevertheless reveal a tendency to enforce the law in the borderlands through extralegal means. Border enforcement initiatives enacted through legal exceptions evince that its procedures are less acts of law enforcement as assertions of sovereign power beyond the law. Nowhere is this point more paradigmatically demonstrated than on the 'hostile terrain' onto which border fencing has diverted the bulk of migrant traffic.

At first blush, a reader of the *Strategic Plan* that laid out the doctrine of PTD might judge that the terrain between ports of entry is 'less suited for crossing and more suited for enforcement' irrespective of its 'hostility.' Such a judgment is not wholly without merit. Here, the transportation resources that make twin cities attractive points of entry grow scarce and eventually vanish. Moreover, this terrain might also be suited to enforcement because it shifts the work of border policing away from populated areas where its most disruptive elements obstruct citizens' abilities to live their everyday lives. Before PTD, border enforcement followed a reactive model. After a migrant crossed the line, law enforcement would scramble to find and apprehend them. However, in predominantly Latinx neighborhoods near the borderline, citizens were frequently detained on the suspicion that they were migrants unlawfully present in the country. Such problems were so common in El Paso that they made the Border Patrol exceedingly unpopular with its residents. These troubles came to a head when, in 1992, five students and two staff members at El Paso's Bowie High School won a judgment in district court against the Border Patrol for violating their civil liberties.[35]

In the case's aftermath, new Sector Chief Silvestre Reyes was determined to repair the Border Patrol's reputation and end the reactive border enforcement model. To this end, he instituted 'Operation Hold the Line,' a forerunner to PTD. This initiative was designed to push migrant traffic away from the city by posting border patrol officers directly along the international line—sometimes no more than 100 feet apart.[36] With the banks of the Rio Grande effectively sealed, migrants could no longer wade from one side to the other. To avoid these officers, they would have to avoid urban crossings entirely. Meanwhile, enforcement efforts in sparsely populated areas would be far less likely to lead to debacles like the Bowie case. This history supports the judgment that the Sonoran is more suited to enforcement because it allows law enforcement officials to pursue their work without impinging on civil liberties. Nevertheless, even as this interpretation bears some merit, it pays insufficient attention

---

35   Murillo v. Musegades, 809 F Supp 487 (WD Tex 1992)
36   On the connection between Operation Hold the Line and California's Operation Gatekeeper, see Nevins, *Operation Gatekeeper and Beyond*, 111ff.

to the Border Patrol's determination to leverage the 'mortal danger' that the Sonoran's unforgiving landscape poses to human life.

In the Sonoran, the terrain's distinct suitability for enforcement derives from the convergence it facilitates between the state's sovereign power to exclude and the natural landscape's violent indifference to migrants' bodies. The *Border Patrol Strategic Plan: 1994 and Beyond* sets out from the awareness that "illegal entrants crossing through remote, uninhabited expanses of land ... can find themselves in mortal danger."[37] It is precisely this danger that the strategy's logic depends upon to deter crossings. If the decision to cross is supposed to be motivated by an economic calculus of costs and benefits, then no possible benefit could outweigh the loss of one's life. As Jason De León observes, the Department of Homeland Security actively leverages this fact, having gone so far as to publish and distribute fliers that warn migrants that they may "end up victims of the desert."[38] Moreover, although the *Border Patrol Strategic Plan* identified a decrease in migrant mortalities as an indicator of the strategy's success, decades of escalating mortalities have done little to change the strategy's logic or the federal government's commitment to implementing it.[39] To the contrary, as human rights observers have reported, the Border Patrol continues to use brazen interdiction tactics that amplify the danger that the environment poses.

In a series of reports titled "Disappeared" and published in cooperation with La Coalición de Derechos Humanos, the Arizona-based humanitarian aid group No More Deaths has sought to chronicle the Border Patrol's tactical utilization of the hostile terrain. The first report focused on a widely used tactic termed 'chase and scatter.' This tactic, aimed at splitting up groups of migrants who are traveling together, involves pursuing migrants at high speeds through wilderness corridors between ports of entry.[40] Crossing in the desert, migrants seldom travel alone. Making the journey in a group can mitigate

---

37   Meissner, *Border Patrol Strategic Plan*, 2.

38   Jason De León, *The Land of Open Graves: Living and Dying on the Migrant Trails* (Oakland: University of California Press, 2015), 29–30.

39   Meissner, *Border Patrol Strategic Plan*, 9–14. C.f. Doris Meissner, et al, "Immigration Enforcement in the United States: The Rise of a Formidable Machinery," (Washington, D.C.: The Migration Policy Institute, 2013). Now a senior member at the Migration Policy Institute, Doris Meissner, in this report, does not propose that the United States must revise PTD's strategy, but rather better deploy the 'formidable machinery' that it helped to produce.

40   See No More Deaths & La Coalición de Derechos Humanos, "Disappeared: The Consequences of Chase & Scatter in the Wilderness" (Tucson, 2021) (http://www.thedisappearedreport.org/reports.html) (accessed July 25, 2023)

the environment's dangers, especially when the group is led by a professional guide (frequently referred to as a 'coyote').[41] Further, to minimize the risk of exposure, these groups often rest during the hottest parts of the day and travel during the cool of night. Consequently, it is often at night that migrants encounter border enforcement personnel. Under these circumstances, chase and scatter tactics do not guarantee the whole group's interdiction. Nevertheless, they are effective for breaking up groups of migrants, isolating them from one another, and pressing them deeper into uninhabited stretches of the Sonoran's terrain.

As the "Disappeared" Report's authors point out, these pursuits are markedly more dangerous for border crossers than for enforcement personnel. While border crossers are left with little more than the clothes on their backs, the pursuing officials enjoy the benefits of GPS, night vision goggles, and other technologies designed to help them traverse the terrain with minimal risk. In interviews with migrants, No More Deaths found that 40.9% of such pursuits were reported to have resulted in at least one migrant being injured.[42] However, even those who escape uninjured do not thereby evade danger. Separated from their guides, these migrants find themselves at a dramatically greater risk of becoming disoriented and lost. Thus, the migrants whom enforcement personnel fail to interdict directly are handed over to the Sonoran. In subsequent reports, No More Deaths found that in 63% of cases where distress calls were made to the Border Patrol's Search and Rescue Division, no confirmed search took place, and in 27% of cases where searches did occur, neither the person nor their remains were recovered.[43] Taken together with the use of 'chase and

---

41   This practice, as it occurs today, does not appear to have pre-dated PTD. Prior to 1994, migrants might have relied on a guide from their town, but this was typically someone they knew. After 1994, as border crossings became more strenuous, the increasing difficulty of crossing created a lucrative black market for 'professionals.' Thus, the securitization of the border had the curious side-effect of drawing black-market organizations, including drug cartels, into the 'business' of illegal immigration. On the relationship between border securitization and black-markets in the borderlands, see Peter Andreas, *Border Games: Policing the U.S.-Mexico Divide* (Ithaca: Cornell University Press, 2009).

42   No More Deaths & la Coalición de Derechos Humanos, "Disappeared," 7. No More Deaths' data was collected from several sources including a voluntary survey of 58 migrants in the Arizona backcountry and in Nogales and the missing persons cases collected by the Missing Migrant Crisis Line. No More Deaths reports that their requests to obtain official government records through a filing under the Freedom of Information Act were ignored by the Border Patrol (See p. 5).

43   No More Deaths & La Coalición de Derechos Humanos, "Left to Die: Border Patrol, Search and Rescue, & the Crisis of Disappearance" (http://www.thedisappearedreport.org/) (accessed 21 November 2023)

scatter' tactics, the failure to respond to distress calls reveals PTD's willingness to leverage the mortal danger that the environment poses.

The Sonoran Desert is immense. Its rugged landscape is a maze of jagged mountains and sweltering valleys. In the summer, daytime temperatures can crest at just over 120 º F. Meanwhile, water is scarce. Even after crossing the border, migrants may have to travel for days in the wilderness before reaching a populated area. Migrants who lose their bearings in this maze—or who have been made to lose their bearings—must find their way through a desert that is greater in size than the entire United Kingdom. In the mountains, migrants face the challenge of scrabbling through natural obstacles while avoiding pit-falls and abandoned mineshafts. In the valleys, they must reckon with blister-ing heat, an arid environment, and, in the rare instances of rainfall, the danger of flash flooding. In the cases where a cause of death can be identified, the vast majority of migrant mortalities are the consequence of exposure or blunt force injury from the environment. This is the 'hostility' that suits the Sonoran Desert to the work of border enforcement, and this is the 'hostility' that, in thousands of cases, PTD has leveraged for lethal effect.

Whereas alienage strips a migrant of whatever dignity they might claim as legal subjects, PTD uses the Sonoran to drive a partition between them and the social body. Left to the desert, it is as if their sanctity is neither approved nor denied. It is merely met with nature's indifference. PTD's assertion of sov-ereign power is not expressed in malicious acts of killing. Rather, it takes the form of cruel indifference, a willingness to let die those whom the polity will not dignify. In the provision of this partition, PTD offers its practical solution to the problem that haunts our projects of collective self-determination. Our political associations come to be haunted only as they are confronted with the lingering presence of the good incarnate in the lives denied. The pain of break-ing faith with this good, in turn, supplies the motivational energy necessary to inspire political change. However, where this pain is not felt, political change is stymied in a situation of motivational deficit. That is, the emergence of ethical subjectivity depends on a form of ethical experience that occurs in embod-ied encounters with the other. However, if the other is never encountered because she has been cast from our view, the prospect of ethical experience is effectively pre-empted. With it, any concomitant tension that might emerge between our ethical subjectivity and our political subjectivity is canceled.

5   Fatal Contradictions

However, in its flight from responsibility, PTD produces a cascade of contra-dictions that render it fatal not only to migrants but to the law and the polity in whose name it kills. As anthropologist Jason De León has observed, PTD turns the Sonoran Desert into what Michael Callon and John Law term a 'hybrid collectif,' a nexus of actants wherein power does not issue from discrete, intentional centers of will but rather a complex nexus of relationships binding together human and non-human actors.[44] On the one hand, this transforma-tion of the natural environment furthers the fratricidal effort to deny that any ethical demand has taken place by mystifying the conceptions of agency that undergird our thinking about responsibility. On the other hand, it achieves this effect at the cost of undermining the possibility of collective self-determina-tion, the very good that PTD is ostensibly meant to uphold.

Central to the concept of the hybrid collectif is a refutation of the notion that our concepts of agency should refer fundamentally to an actor's capacity for free outward action according to internal mental states or intentions. Call this the 'standard view.'[45] According to the standard view, the actor's deter-mination to act makes her act her own. In turn, identifying the actor and act provides the basis for judgments regarding her responsibility. However, con-ceiving agency on these terms allows PTD to conceal and deny state respon-sibility for migrant mortalities. To call migrant mortalities 'fratricides' is to suggest that these deaths were the consequence of some unjustifiable inten-tion to kill. However, in the vast majority of cases, migrant mortalities are not the consequence of border enforcement officials running down or shooting migrants.[46] In most cases, no border patrol officer is even present at the scene of the death. If responsibility lies with anyone, it seems that it must be with the one whose intention it was to enter this harsh landscape. That is, it appears that the fault must belong to the migrants themselves. How can one expect

---

44   See De León, *The Land of Open Grave*; c.f. Michael Callon and John Law, "Agency and the Hybrid Collectif," *Mathematics, Science, and Postclassical Theory*, ed. Barbara Herrnstein Smith & Arkady Plotnitsky (Durham: Duke University Press, 1997), 95–117.

45   This general view of agency, which distinguishes voluntary and non-voluntary acts owing to the antecedent states that produce them, enjoys a deep philosophical heritage that traces at least as far back as Aristotle (see Aristotle, *Nicomachean Ethics*, Book III). For a recent articulation (and criticism) of this conception see Berent Enç, *How We Act: Causes, Reasons, and Intentions* (New York: Oxford University Press, 2003)

46   This is not to say that no such instances occur. According to the Southern Borders Com-munities Coalition's aggregate of USCBP statements and reports, the use of force by Border Patrol agents has resulted in at least 64 fatalities. While the majority of victims involved in fatal shootings were not US nationals, this number also includes some US Cit-izens killed in confrontations with enforcement personnel. (See "Fatal Encounters with CBP Since 2010," southernborder.org, Southern Border Communities Coalition, Decem-ber 20, 2022, last accessed January 26, 2023, https://www.southernborder.org/deaths_by_border_patrol)

to survive multiple days of hiking in an environment defined by searing heat and extreme water scarcity? Even if the intention to enter the United States through the Sonoran Desert is not indicative of *mens rea*, it is foolhardy at the very least. On what grounds could the state be judged to bear responsibility for the foolish wagers of non-members? De León helps us appreciate that PTD's distinctive cunning is to encourage us to believe that the answers to such questions are foregone conclusions. I wish to add that PTD achieves this end only as it freights the law with natural violence, confounds the boundary between city and wilderness, and erodes the very notion of freedom essential to collective self-determination.

By resisting the standard view of agency, De León helps us see that agency is never as simple a phenomenon as the standard conception might suggest. "People [and] objects don't act in isolation," De León counters, "but instead have complex relationships at different moments across time and space that sometimes create things or make things happen."[47] "It is these *relationships*," he continues, "that 'perform agency,' and not isolated humans or solitary objects."[48] 'Agency,' that is, is the expression of a 'hybrid collectif,' best understood as a constellation of actors and actants, some human, others not, some capable of intentions and others incapable of it, yet all joined together in the relationships that make them the causes of some effect. By shifting its focus from individual actors to complex relationships, this mode of conceptualizing agency decenters the concept of 'intention.' With this shift in perspective, ascribing responsibility to the state does not necessitate that one supposes each migrant mortality is the outcome of a discrete determination to kill. Neither must one imagine that the sun, terrain, or wildlife bear some ill-intent toward these sojourners. Nor even must one presume that the migrants who find themselves in the Sonoran do not intend to go there. One need only acknowledge that the border environment, in which all of these (human and non-human) actors encounter one another, is a nexus of relationships that has been shaped in significant ways by law enforcement policies designed to make suffering and death more likely. If we can do this much, then we can assert the state's share of responsibility for these deaths. We can see them as fratricides.

To this end, thinking of the migrant actor as an unlucky gambler provides a valuable analogy for understanding her place in the complex of relationships that constitute PTD's hybrid collectif. Think, for a moment, of a game of blackjack. The game occurs between a player and a dealer and sets the context for each one's expression of agency. Each human actor enters the game

---

47   De León, *The Land of Open Graves*, 39.
48   Ibid, 40.

with a distinct purpose. The player hopes to win a sum from the house. Conversely, the dealer wishes to preserve the house's money. Yet, even as the player and the dealer's respective purposes place them in opposition to one another, their relationship does not consist in a direct opposition of wills. In addition to their decisions, the game's outcome will depend on a group of causes that are independent of them and intend no effect at all. What occurs in a game of blackjack, that is, depends on the probabilities established by the makeup of the deck with which the participants play. The element of chance built into this system of probability ensures that, for both the player and the dealer, the interaction is a gamble.

Viewed from without, the player is the only one who appears to intend anything at all. Her agency is expressed in her decisions to hit or to stay. The cards, for their part, intend nothing. Yet, as they are dealt, they set the context in which the gambler makes her decisions and, ultimately, in concert with her choices determine the outcome of the game. Of course, a dishonest dealer determined not to suffer loss is not without her own measure of agency. A deck of cards is not immune to tampering, and the dealer might seek to improve her odds by stacking the deck in her favor. Importantly, however, if we imagine a game of blackjack in which the dealer has engaged in this sort of dishonesty, her agency would not be visible to someone who was merely observing the game. The observer would only see the player's decisions to hit or stay. The game's outcome, for her, would either appear to be the consequence of bad luck or poor calculation on the player's part. Nevertheless, despite the observer's inability to see it, the dealer's agency would have had a tangible impact on the probable outcomes of the game. By stacking the deck, she would not have decided the game's outcome. The element of chance would still remain. Nevertheless, her intention to alter the deck would have changed the game sufficiently to increase the likelihood of the player's loss. For this, we would rightly judge the dealer responsible.

To return to the case of PTD, if we are to think of deceased migrants as 'unlucky gamblers,' we must also understand that their 'bad luck' is the consequence of a law enforcement policy that stacks the deck against them and encourages them to make foolhardy wagers. Again, it is not an accident that so many migrants cross in remote stretches of wilderness. From the beginning, the Border Patrol identified urban areas with safe access to roads, rail, and airports as most vulnerable to illicit entries.[49] Thus, PTD sought to harden these

---

49   Meissner, *Border Patrol Strategic Plan*, 7.

points of entry. The strategy was built on the express assumption that as some areas of approach became more heavily policed, migrants would make their crossings elsewhere. Gradually, their journeys would bring them further and further from other people and onto increasingly hostile terrain. Since 1994, a near-constant aggregation of enforcement personnel and assets has produced a border topography comprising natural and human-made obstacles that work in concert to intensify the dangers associated with the crossing.

At first blush, we may not be able to identify in any single instance a discrete intention to kill this or that migrant. However, as with the dealer who stacks the deck against the player, we can see an exercise of agency whose purpose is to increase the probability of loss. The Sonoran's complex maze of mountains, valleys, and arroyos provides a forbidding challenge in its own right. Injuries and deaths resulting from falls and drowning compound the ever-present dangers of dehydration and heat stroke, and migrants are driven toward these dangers by the border topography itself. The movement of migrant traffic is never determined by the decisions of migrants alone but by the constellation of barriers, natural and constructed, that make some areas of approach appear more viable than others. Indeed, migrants may determine for themselves to make their crossings in remote wilderness areas that will expose them to mortal danger. Still, they practice their agency within the constraints of an enforcement apparatus that encourages them to risk death over detection and apprehension. In this landscape, migrant mortalities cannot be judged to result from unlucky gambles disconnected from state agency. To the contrary, the state has gone to great expense to produce the context that makes these gambles so extraordinarily hazardous. In this way, it kills. In this way, it perpetrates fratricide.

However, just as PTD's hybrid collectif complicates its critics' efforts to blame the state for migrant mortalities, it also undermines the very things that the strategy sets out to preserve. For many Western political philosophers, the city is distinguished from the wilderness as a place of laws from a place of violence. Thomas Hobbes, perhaps, stated the distinction most dramatically when he likened the state of nature to a perpetual state of war and the commonwealth to an order of laws. Perhaps less dramatically, Arendt (as already discussed in the last chapter) distinguishes the polity, ruled by freedom, from nature, ruled by necessity, further identifying the law as the assertion of the boundary between the two. As Arendt puts it, law makes equal those whom nature makes unequal. Thus, the law acts as a wall that keeps the violence of nature out while protecting freedom within. Arendt's view is not far afield from classical thinking. The Greek term *polis* initially denoted a place with a ringed wall, and Heraclitus declares that "the people must fight for the law as for the city wall."[50] To make natural violence law's inheritance is nothing less than to raze this wall to the ground.

Moreover, the state's monopoly on violence, at least ideally, is not meant to terrorize people by subjecting them to a capricious entity that holds unchecked power over their lives. Rather, it is intended to deliver them from the chaos of anomie by defining the *legitimate* uses of physical force and, thereby, establishing bounds by which to articulate the rightful justifications for and extent to which physical force may be enacted. At a minimum, the rule of law should replace caprice with cause and excessive force with proportionality. However, if this is to be the case, then it is necessary that those entrusted with enforcing the law, whether in the courts or the city streets, would practice sound judgment. Statute, on the one hand, is meant to support this judgment by defining crimes and stipulating proportionate responses. Title 8 of the US Code offers just such a provision, making the charge of unlawful entry applicable to any alien entering the United States by crossing between designated ports of entry or using fraudulent identifying documents.[51] Regarding unlawful entry, the statute permits penalties in the form of fines not exceeding $250 and prison sentences not to exceed six months for the first offense.[52] In the case of repeat offenders, the law assigns harsher penalties but relents from assigning maximum prison sentences over two years.[53] On the other hand, express protocols on the use of (potentially) lethal force place additional restraints on the agents of law enforcement whose jobs may entail the direct use of physical coercion. USCBP is no different, stipulating that deadly force is strictly prohibited except in cases where the subject "poses an imminent danger of death or serious physical injury to the agent or another person."[54] Such guidelines do not guarantee that disproportionate or unjustified uses of force will not occur. However, in the instances that they do, they are meant to provide at least a provisional set of criteria for beginning critical conversations on the issue and holding the offending party to account. However, PTD's use of natural violence pre-empts any such form of regulation.

At the point of convergence between sovereign power and natural violence, exclusions are enacted by an agent of law enforcement that exercises lethal

---

50   Heraclitus, Fragment 44

51   8 USC 1325(a)

52   8 USC 1325(a)(3) & 8 US Code 1325(b)

53   8 USC 1326; In some circumstances, this sentence may be increased if the alien guilty of unlawful entry is charged with additional crimes.

54   US Customs and Border Protection, "CBP Use of Force Policy" (Washington, DC: January 2021), 4.

force without intention, discretion, or proportionality, nihilating the law it holds in its hands. The desert does not abide by statutory or regulatory limits and, for many migrants, makes death the *de facto* sentence for the crime of unlawful entry. Moreover, it metes out its retribution indiscriminately. It does not ask whether a migrant's advance poses an imminent threat. Neither does it conduct credible fear interviews. It makes no differentiation between economic migrants and asylum-seekers, between refugees and violent criminals. The desert withholds the rain from both the just and the unjust alike. Thus, in thousands of cases, the Sonoran has delivered its sentence independent of any legal judgment and is invulnerable to scrutiny. The idea of charging the sun or an arroyo with excessive force is ridiculous. Therefore, all that the law can do is follow in violence's wake and offer the semblances of a justification for the deaths that occur. The law can propose to us that the remains we encounter are the remains of someone who entered the United States unlawfully. They are the remains of a person who would have made no claim on our duty to offer refuge. It may suggest that they are the remains of that sort of 'alien,' who would rightly have earned our enmity by virtue of our irreconcilable differences. However, these proposals are tentative at best and deceptive at worse.

Disarticulated bones give us precious little information to confirm or refute any such assertion. As already noted, in many cases, the remains found in the Sonoran cannot be identified. Ironically, then, it is in its moment of crowning success, of ultimate exclusion, that PTD implodes. If the activity of exclusion is an expression of the rule of law, then it is not sufficient that migrants be excluded. Especially in the cases where lethal force is utilized, it is crucial that these exclusions appear to be justified. It is essential, perhaps, that the dead seem to us as 'invaders.' Indeed, at least since the Chinese exclusion cases, we have been encouraged to think as though we live in a world of attackers and defenders, of friends and enemies. However, with the drama of migration and border enforcement pressed out of sight, few of us witness such a conflict directly. Instead, we come to know it only in the remains it produces. Nevertheless, fragmented bones do not display the vicious dispositions we expect in alien enemy combatants. Instead, as they arrest our attention, they create (or rather reveal) a relationship more fundamental than the one made by any political association. Our encounter with the dead is an encounter with a fellow, vulnerable human being. 'Friend' and 'enemy' fade like mirages. What remains are two vulnerable, dependent beings, not quite face to face, one dwelling among the living, the other banished to sojourn among the dead. What is no longer clear is what has made either one deserving of their fate. Whatever exigency may have demanded the migrant's death has lost its force, and the moral demand that they might have posed to us in life returns to the fore. Lingering in the margins between life and death, the bones in the Sonoran attain an afterlife in the indictment they bring against PTD. This indictment is written on their bodies. By entrusting the law to the Sonoran's hands, PTD forces it to wander into the same hostile terrain to which it has subjected thousands of migrants. Here, the law, no less than the migrants it condemns, faces mortal danger.

At last, with the boundaries between city and wilderness and law and violence confounded, collective self-determination too succumbs to the Sonoran's hybrid collectif. This high ideal's realization depends on the people's ability to practice agency according to the standard conception. It holds that the political subject's shape is to be determined by whom the members choose to admit and whom they choose to exclude. Furthermore, these choices should reflect how the community understands membership as a social good. But if this is to obtain, it is crucial that the etiology of any given admission or exclusion can be traced to some free and intentional decision (of some authorized agent of the people, if not the people themselves). However, it is not only the migrants' freedom that becomes entangled in the hybrid collectif. Even as we judge that the state has a share in creating and maintaining this constellation of relationships, we must acknowledge that the state does not act upon it exclusively from without. In the game of blackjack, the dealer, no less than the player, is subject to what the cards decide. Despite the agency she exerts, the outcome of her wager will still depend on chance. Likewise, in the borderlands, the desert decides who is admitted and excluded. It makes this decision without regard for the meaning of membership or the common values the people share. Thus, by handing responsibility over to the hybrid collectif, PTD perpetrates one final and fatal contradiction: it surrenders to the desert precisely that which collective self-determination seeks to reserve for the people. The fratricide, meant to release political freedom from ethical necessity, chains it instead to natural necessity and falls afoul of both.

6   Can These Bones Live? a Provisional Answer to the Question

"Law," Robert Cover writes, "may be viewed as a system of tension or a bridge linking a concept of a reality to an imagined alternative."[55] "A nomos, as a world of law," he continues, "entails the application of human will to an extant state of affairs as well as toward our visions of alternative futures."[56] In these

---

55   Robert Cover, "Nomos and Narrative," *Harvard Law Review* 97 (Nov 1983), 9.
56   Ibid.

lines, Cover resists the idea that the law could function if reduced to a mere instrument of coercive state power.[57] This is because if the law is to be worthy of our commitment, it must do significantly more than restrain destructive or unwanted behavior. It must express purpose no less than prohibition. "Our visions," Cover writes, "hold our reality up to us as unredeemed."[58] Each of us, Cover contends, long for a future that sets aright the disorders of the present state of affairs (whatever we may believe them to be). We imagine worlds where the lion lies down with the lamb, the creditor forgives her debtor, and estranged siblings are reconciled. However, such visions, on their own, do not dictate actions. They do little to clarify how we move from the unredeemed present to future redemption. The law inspires our commitment as it fills this gap, giving our vision "depth of field, by placing one part of it in the highlight of insistent and immediate demand while casting another part in the shadow of the millennium."[59] The law that fails to do this, the law that is no more than the expression of force, might restrain behavior, but the 'alternative future' promised in its action would be fundamentally nihilistic. It would not be a bridge to redemption but a barricade against it. Consequently, such a law would do little to inspire our commitment.

Conceiving the law in this way, as that which simultaneously interposes and bridges the space between the present and the eschaton, reveals it as a field for negotiating the tensions of our riven human condition. The problem of fratricide that recurs in the borderlands is the painful revelation of a deep-seated contradiction in our humanity. The bones in the Sonoran are not the bones of strangers. They are the bones of estranged siblings. A human being is both an *animal socialis* and a *zōon politikon*. On the one hand, we are vulnerable, interdependent creatures. Our ethical subjectivity emerges from the approval of the demands this interdependence places upon us. With this approval, we hold our interdependence as our common trust. On the other hand, we are also rational beings, capable of self-legislation and determining the course of our lives if only we can shed the lash of necessity's chains. This freedom is the basis of our political subjectivity. However, we are never merely one or the other. We are free, even as we are subject to necessity, and vulnerable, even as we are capable of self-determination. These aspects of our being sow a tension

---

57   Of course, he does not deny that, at certain times and places, this has been and continues to be the case. He refers to law reduced to coercive force of the state as the 'imperial' pattern of law but warns against the "price paid in the often coercive constraints imposed on the autonomous realization of normative meaning." (Ibid, 13, n. 36)

58   Ibid, 9.

59   Ibid.

within us and our political histories. This tension is ossified in the simulacra of self-determination's remainder. In the language of rights, however, the law seems to promise a means of mediating between the ethical demands of vulnerable, interdependent creatures and the free pursuits of collectively self-determining persons. In the law, we find an institution that appears to bear the potential for reconciling us with our humanity. If there is to be redemption, if there is to be reconciliation, perhaps it can be reached through the law. Indeed, this was the aim of the Holiness Code—"do this, and you will live."

However, under PTD, law enforcement foregoes any effort to reconcile our riven condition and, instead, seeks to complete the work of fratricide. Our estranged siblings are named and treated as alien-born creatures from another world. Isolation in the landscape follows alienage in the law. Damning migrants to a lonely demise, severed from the social body and body politic, PTD struggles to resolve the tensions between our ethical and political subjectivity by canceling the preconditions for the former. Like Cain, who rebuffed God when asked where his brother was to be found, PTD refuses vainly to allow the body politic to be defined in relation to the sibling it denies. However, Genesis 4 is not a story about Cain's emancipation from responsibility for his brother. Cain is a character haunted. He may indeed succeed in founding Enoch, but in his itineracy, he keeps his brother with him. "Listen!" This is the imperative that the divine issues to the first city's founder. This imperative is Genesis 4's theological bequest to our political thought. The ethical and political must be held in tension. Thus, by refusing the imperative, PTD makes the law an instrument for alienating us from our humanity rather than reconciling us with it. 'Sin,' for heirs to Augustine's theological inheritance, stems from *superbia*, an inordinate pride that denies our creaturely nature. It is, in Kierkegaard's later language, a 'mutiny' against not only God but the very meaning of our humanity. By enlisting the law in this mutiny, PTD makes the law itself an expression of sin that defiantly refuses correction. In the borderlands, no less than in scripture, the wages of sin is death. For thirty years, PTD has precipitated the wanton destruction of migrant's lives and the undoing of the very body politic it purports to preserve.

In the borderlands, a great effort is failing. It is failing because PTD, in its attempt to refuse our interdependence, must also refuse our freedom. The vision of redemption that PTD offers is freedom without responsibility and a world without the other. PTD issues an emphatic "no!" to the possibility that the excluded other could be reconciled to the self-determining polity. In its use of the Sonoran, it denies that any other is being excluded at all. Like Cain, who left his brother's body in the field, PTD refuses to dignify the migrant's life and discards her body without ceremony, setting her to wander in the wilderness.

Under PTD, the law is no bridge to redemption. It is set as a bulwark against the alienated other and, with her disavowal, becomes a bulwark against our redemption. Weaponizing the natural environment, it renders the landscape grotesque and our politics terminally inhumane. Can these bones live? If this question is to be answered in the affirmative, it will not be through conceit and artifice that denies the ghosts that haunt our polities. Instead, we must make peace with the ghosts. We must learn to be haunted. Likewise, we must find a way for the law to become haunted by the excluded other's demands. Though we may leave resurrection in the shadow of the millennium, addressing the inhumanity in the borderlands is an insistent and immediate demand.

PART 3

Samaritans and Sojourners

∴

An expert in the law stood up to test Jesus. "Teacher," he said, "what must I do to inherit eternal life?" He said to him, "What is written in the law? What do you read there?" He answered, "You shall love the Lord your God with all your heart and with all your soul and with all your strength and with all your mind and your neighbor as yourself." And he said to him, "You have given the right answer; do this, and you will live."

But wanting to vindicate himself, he asked Jesus, "And who is my neighbor?" Jesus replied, "A man was going down from Jerusalem to Jericho and fell into the hands of robbers, who stripped him, beat him, and took off, leaving him half dead. Now by chance a priest was going down that road, and when he saw him he passed by on the other side. So likewise a Levite, when he came to the place and saw him, passed by on the other side. But a Samaritan while traveling came upon him, and when he saw him he was moved with compassion. He went to him and bandaged his wounds, treating them with oil and wine. Then he put him on his own animal, brought him to an inn, and took care of him. The next day he took out two denarii, gave them to the innkeeper, and said, 'Take care of him, and when I come back I will repay you whatever more you spend.' Which of these three, do you think, was a neighbor to the man who fell into the hands of the robbers?" He said, "The one who showed him mercy." Jesus said to him, "Go and do likewise."

—LUKE 10.25–37

CHAPTER 5

The Samaritan's Virtue

> Because compassion abolishes the distance, the worldly space between men where political matters, the whole realm of human affairs, are located, it remains, politically speaking, irrelevant and without consequence ... it is incapable of establishing 'lasting institutions.'
>
> —HANNAH ARENDT, *On Revolution*

∙ ∙ ∙

> But a Samaritan while traveling came upon him, and when he saw him he was moved with compassion. He went to him and bandaged his wounds, treating them with oil and wine. Then he put him on his own animal, brought him to an inn, and took care of him. The next day he took out two denarii, gave them to the innkeeper, and said, "Take care of him, and when I come back I will repay you whatever more you spend."
>
> —LUKE 10.33–36

∙ ∙
∙

1   From Contempt to Compassion

"Violence was the beginning," Arendt insists, "and, by the same token, no beginning could be made without using violence, without violating."[1] The *zōon politikon* is not born without violating the needs of the *animal socialis*. Of necessity, the body politic extricates itself from the social body by a fratricide—by putting to death the moral sentiment that would drown the activity of politics in the unending labor of tending the needs of vulnerable, interdependent creatures. Compassion opens us up to the suffering of the other and closes the space between us, eliminating the distance that is the space of

---

1   Hannah Arendt, *On Revolution* (New York: Penguin Books, 1963), 20.

political activity. Yet Prevention Through Deterrence (PTD), in its efforts to liberate our political freedom from moral necessity, lashes it instead to natural necessity and, in so doing, brings on its end. It may be, as Arendt thought, that compassion for the vulnerable cannot provide the foundation of lasting institutions. Nevertheless, if our polities are to comprise humane institutions and not just lasting ones, compassion cannot be eliminated from them altogether. PTD's inhumanity suggests that without compassion's drive to bind us one to another, we may be scattered and lost from each other in the wilderness.

The question, then, is whether compassion can make itself felt upon the body politic without both being eradicated. Arendt conceives compassion as a passion that traces to our "innate repugnance at seeing another creature suffer."[2] On the one hand, Arendt supposes that this passion inspires selflessness, "the capacity to lose oneself in the sufferings of others" and to establish and confirm the "'natural bond' between men."[3] However, compassion achieves this bond on the hither side of language. Curiously mute, compassion tethers its subject to a good so elemental as to be unutterable.[4] Law, on the other hand, is a language, and words are its currency.[5] It lends stability to the societies it orders by providing names that allow us to perceive classes and categories by which the indeterminacies of everyday experience may be rendered determinate. From words can be constructed patterns, and from patterns analogies. Through these analogies, the law can vouchsafe the expectation that like circumstances will be treated in like manner. The power of compassion, however, "hinges on the strength of passion itself, which, in contrast to reason, can comprehend only the particular, but has no notion of the general and no capacity for generalization."[6] The moment compassion is mandated, generalized, and attached to an entire class, it passes over into something else.

Compassion, by these lights, cannot be legislated. Nevertheless, to suggest that compassion cannot be made the content of the law is not at once to say that it cannot be made a condition for the right interpretation of the law. Put another way, Arendt's line of reasoning does not rule out immediately the possibility that the law might be read and applied compassionately—that the law might find in compassion's good its unutterable yet indispensable supplement. For her part, Arendt resists this possibility, judging that good, no less than evil,

2   Ibid, 71. For this phrase, Arendt cites Rousseau directly.
3   Ibid, 81.
4   Ibid, 82ff.
5   On the intrinsic connection between law and language see James Boyd White, *The Legal Imagination* (Chicago: University of Chicago Press, 1985)
6   Arendt, *On Revolution*, 85.

is capable of tyranny. However, she constructs her argument with an eye to Robespierre and his Committee on Virtue. Her eye is on the legislator and not the litigator. We may be accustomed to thinking of the former as a creator of the law and, therefore, as the one that determines its meaning. Likewise, we may be inclined to think of the litigator merely as one who applies the law and, therefore, as one who is bound by the system of meanings that the legislator posits. However, philosophers of language have been careful to point out that language acquires its meaning in its use. Similarly, legal scholars concerned with the connection between law and narrative have argued that the same is true of legal speech.[7] Exploring the possibility of legal meaning as a creation not only of the legislator but also of the litigator opens further opportunities for reconceiving the relationship between compassion and law that Arendt does not consider.

To this end, I turn to the parable of the Samaritan, recounted in the Gospel of Luke. Like the story of Cain and Abel, this parable attends to the ties of responsibility that bind vulnerable, interdependent creatures. It asks what is to be done with the experience of compassion and the 'natural bond' it confirms between us. Whereas the story of Cain and Abel locates these ties in a filial relationship within the family, Luke's parable appears to address a relationship between two sojourners who, by chance, meet on the road. Nevertheless, whereas Cain's fratricide indicates the refusal of responsibility by which siblings are estranged, the Samaritan's works of mercy evince that approval by which they are to be reconciled.[8] Moreover, Luke situates the parable within a

---

7   Robert Cover is famous for drawing this connection at the societal level. However, Teresa Godwin Phelps argues compellingly that the same holds true at the micro level, in the context of trial courts. See Robert Cover, "Nomos and Narrative," *Harvard Law Review* 97 (1983): 4–68; & Teresa Godwin Phelps, "No Place to Go, No Story to Tell: The Missing Narratives of the Sanctuary Movement," *Washington and Lee Law Review* 48 (1991): 123–138.

8   Although she does not go so far as to make the parable of the Samaritan the inversion of the primordial fratricide, Rajendra dedicates several pages in *Migrants and Citizens* to refuting interpretations of the parable that portray the encounter between the Samaritan and the sojourner as an encounter between strangers. Rajendra assumes that, based on the direction of the sojourner's travel, Luke's reader would assume that he was a Jew. In the Samaritan, she argues, the reader would have seen a member of the former northern kingdom—a former kinsperson turned enemy. That is, an estranged sibling. The parable's central function, then, as Rajendra sees it, is to provide a narrative that reasserts the kinship between the residents of Judea and their northern neighbors and, thereby, demands a reconciliation between their peoples and brings an end to the history of hostilities between them. See Tisha Rajendra, *Migrants and Citizens* (Grand Rapids: William B. Eerdmans Publishing Company, 2017), 142–146.

legal controversy.[9] Here, compassion is presented as more than a private experience of co-suffering. As a virtue of the good legal hermeneut, it becomes the bridge that connects the law with that good, which is its ground, aim, and limit. Read with an eye to the vital connection between compassion and law, the parable may yet allow us to glimpse the possibility of a politics wherein the excluded other is drawn back into the fold—or, perhaps, wherein she draws us out.

2   "Who is my Neighbor?": the Parable's Context and Stakes

The parable of the Samaritan emerges amid a crisis of legal meaning that makes legal hermeneutics a matter of profound significance. Although some critics have questioned the reasoning or success of locating the parable in this context, Luke situates the parable of the Samaritan in an exchange between Jesus and a character he refers to as a '*nomikos*.'[10] Variously translated as 'lawyer' or 'expert in the law,' commentators doubt whether this term refers to any specific professional or religious class.[11] However, at minimum, it seems to denote a character engaged in the interpretation of Mosaic Law; a character whose concerns with the law, I will argue, are not superficial or rule-mongering, but for whom law articulates a distinctive form of life in relation to God and the other. It is fitting, then, that this character would ask Jesus about the

---

9   C.f. Mt. 22.34–40 & Mk. 12.28–31. While the parable of the Samaritan is unique to Luke's gospel, the legal controversy that prompts it is not. In both Matthew and Mark, Jesus is confronted by authorities asking which is the greatest of the commandments. In these Gospels, Jesus answers them directly, condensing the Levitical Holiness Code in the dual love commands of God and neighbor. Luke differs from the other Synoptics not only in the provision of the parable but also in inverting the dialogue. It is Jesus who asks his interlocutor how they read the law, and the interlocutor who responds with the love commands. Moreover, whereas Matthew and Mark are satisfied to leave the interaction there, Luke alone identifies and elaborates on the ambiguity regarding the second love command's object. It is ostensibly to alleviate this ambiguity that Jesus offers the parable of the Samaritan.

10   See, for instance, John Dominic Crossan, *In Parables: The Problem of the Historical Jesus* (Sonoma: Polebridge Press, 1992), 56–61. I will return to this criticism at greater length below.

11   Luke-Acts uses the name nomikos in only one other episode apart from this controversy. In ch. 11, Luke portrays a group of *nomikoi* associating with the pharisees. Both end up being subjects of Jesus' criticisms, guilty of weighing the people down with burdens and doing nothing to make these burdens any lighter. However, despite this conjunction, the term lacks the same specificity conveyed by the term 'pharisee.' See Birger Gerhardsson, "The Good Samaritan—The Good Shepherd?" *Coniectanea Neotestamentica* 16 (1958): 3–31.

practice constitutive of life under the Reign of God (*tis poiēsas zoēn aiōnion klēronomēsō*). (Lk. 10.25) Jesus, in turn, meets this character on his own terms, asking, "What is in the law? How do you read it?" (*en tō nomō ti gegraptai; pōs anaginōskeis;*). (10.26) The issue is not whether or not the law has any significance under the Reign of God. The issue is how the law must be interpreted if it is to reconcile the interpreter with the life that Jesus preaches and embodies.[12] The answer that the *nomikos* provides is a condensed citation of the *Shema*, from Deuteronomy 6:4–5, and the Levitical love command: "You shall love the Lord your God with all your heart, soul, mind, and strength; and your neighbor as yourself."[13] (Lk. 10.27) This gloss elicits Jesus' approval. What prompts the parable, however, is an apparent ambiguity in the meaning of the term 'neighbor' (*plesion* in the Septuagint's Greek text, or *rea* in the original Hebrew).

All the law's power to reconcile the human being to God is at stake in this name's intelligibility. In the context of the Holiness Code, the injunction to love the neighbor (and the sojourner!) expresses one of the defining responsibilities of God's covenant people. Commentators have noted the apparent implausibility of treating Leviticus 19.18 as though it summed up the Holiness Code's central message (let alone all of the Torah). A more likely summary might be the imperative that begins the holiness code: "Be holy, for I, YHWH, your God, am holy." However, as James Robson proposes in his treatment of the theme of "holiness" in the Hebrew Bible, there is a substantial literary tradition that suggests God's holiness is expressed most consistently in love.[14] Consequently, it would be precisely through the work of love that God's people would participate in the divine holiness to which they were called. The *nomikos* appears to be expressing just this interpretation of the holiness tradition. By joining the love of God with the love of neighbor in a single verbal imperative (*agapēseis kurion ton theon ... kai ton plēsion sou ōs seauton*), the *nomikos* underscores the connection between the two, making this injunction *the* defining characteristic of God's people. To borrow a phrase from Knud Ejler Løgstrup, it is as if "the individual's relation to God is determined wholly at the point of his relation to the neighbor."[15] Thus, were this command to become impracticable, the law

---

12   See, for instance, John J. Kilgallen, "The Plan of the Nomikos," *New Testament Studies* 42 (1996): 615–619 & Joshua Marshall Strahan, "Jesus Teaches Theological Interpretation of the Law: Reading the Good Samaritan in its Literary Context," *Journal of Theological Interpretation* 10 (2016): 71–86.

13   C.f. Lev. 19.18.

14   James Robson, "Forgotten Dimensions of Holiness," *Horizons in Biblical Theology* 33 (2011): 121–146.

15   Knud Ejler Løgstrup, *The Ethical Demand* (Notre Dame: University of Notre Dame Press, 1997), 4. It bears stating that Løgstrup offers this phrase to gloss the work of a German

would cease to be an instrument that reconciled its adherents to the divine life and would become instead a figure that signaled their alienation from its very source. The *nomikos'* desire to be justified to this life prompts him to ask his question: "And who is my neighbor?" (10.29)

Despite the question's extraordinary stakes, it has become an interpretive commonplace to read Jesus' interactions with the *nomikos* as some cunning adversarial contest that differentiates Christianity's universalist ethic of love from Judaism's sectarian one.[16] This interpretive tendency sets out from the assumption that the *nomikos* already has a correct answer to his question in mind. To be fair, we are indeed told that the *nomikos* stands and poses his question 'to tempt' or 'to test' Jesus (*anestē ekpeirazōn auton*). (10.25) Consequently, we might read the two exchanges that precede the parable as the opening rounds of a rhetorical duel, wherein the *nomikos* seeks to reveal some contradiction between Jesus' proclamation and the Mosaic Law. In this reading, the *nomikos* and the reader alike can expect this follow-up question to bring about the controversy's climax. The contradiction will reveal itself in how Jesus defines the neighbor. The lawyer will have succeeded in showing Jesus to be at odds with the Torah, yet, for the reader, this revelation will constitute a moment of dramatic irony wherein Jesus, and not the *nomikos,* is vindicated.

Familiar as this interpretive approach may be, must we assume that the *nomikos* truly has a correct answer already in mind? If not, must we ascribe to him some malintent? How might the term 'neighbor' have been defined in his day? Treated within its Levitical context, the term indeed appears to have a narrower definition than the one implied by the parable. Here, it does not denote the abstract human 'other' of which philosophers speak. Instead, it sits within a lexical web of terms that identifies the neighbor with a member of one's people, while distinguishing the neighbor from the 'resident alien' or 'sojourner' (*ger),* on the one side, and the 'outsider' (*nekri),* on the other.[17] Were this definition the sole one on offer in the first century, the parable's radical expansion of the neighbor's identity might indeed signal love's transcendent

---

theologian, who, for his part, failed to appreciate the radical significance of this very point.

16   R. Allan Culpepper, "Luke," in *The New Interpreter's Bible: A Commentary in Twelve Volumes,* vol. 9, 12 vols. (Nashville: Abingdon Press, 1994), 229. The other synoptic gospels corroborate this interpretive approach by placing the question about the greatest of the commandments in the mouths of parties clearly antagonistic toward Jesus. However, in my reading of the parable and its context, I will take another approach.

17   C.f. Joel Kaminsky, "Loving one's (Israelite) Neighbor: Election and Commandment in Leviticus 19," *Interpretation* 62 (2008):123–132 & Charles A. Kimball, *Jesus' Exposition of the Old Testament in Luke's Gospel* (Sheffield: JSOT Press, 1994).

overcoming of invidious legal distinctions—Christianity's universalist super-session of Judaism.[18] However, by the time of Luke's composition, competing approaches to interpreting the Holiness Code had led interpreters to adopt varied definitions of the term.

Reinhold Neudecker identifies at least three interpretive possibilities already on offer in the first and second-century midrash.[19] The first of these possibilities ties the love command to the prohibition on taking vengeance against one's kin that appears in Leviticus 19.17 and, subsequently, upholds the view that the neighbor is one's fellow Israelite. The second narrows the idea of the neighbor further to include only those fellow Israelites who are 'one's brother' in keeping the commandments. According to this view, even a fellow Israelite might not be considered one's 'neighbor' if they failed to keep the covenant. The third option cuts in the opposite direction. Inspired perhaps by Hillel the Elder's command to love one's fellow creature, it expands the concept of the neighbor beyond the bounds of the Israelite community to include all of humankind (and perhaps even non-human others). According to this view, not only the Israelite who fails to keep the covenant, but conceivably any human being one encounters is a 'neighbor.' By the first century, then, the term 'neighbor,' which was to be the proper object of the Levitical love command, was open to a wide range of potential meanings. In light of this diversity of potentials, the gospel's contemporary readers would possess genuine cause for doubt regarding the neighbor's identity. They would have good reason to read the *nomikos*' questions as critically discerning but genuinely interrogative.

Moreover, Luke's gospel presents a scene wherein the controversy over the neighbor's identity had come to be the cause of considerable political violence. The birth narrative sets Jesus' nativity under Publius Sulpicius Quirinius' reign as legate of Syria. Before Quirinius' installation, Judea was ruled by the ethnarch Herod Archelaus and enjoyed a measure of autonomy vis-à-vis Imperial

---

18   Such conclusions about the parable are not absent from the Christian ethics of migration either. Wilbanks celebrates the parable as love's triumph over legalism and the assertion of an ethical obligation whose scope cannot be contained by national or statist boundaries. See Dana W Wilbanks, *Re-Creating America: The Ethics of U.S. Immigration & Refugee Policy in a Christian Perspective* (Nashville: Abingdon Press, 1996).

19   Reinhard Neudecker, "'And You Shall Love Your Neighbor As Yourself—I am the Lord,' (Lev 19:18) in Jewish Interpretation," *Biblica* 73 (1992): 496–517; c.f. Mark A. Proctor, "'Who is my Neighbor?': Recontextualizing Luke's Good Samaritan (Luke 10:25–37)," *Journal of Biblical Literature* 138 (2019): 203–219. Corroborating the most expansive interpretations of the term proposed by Neudecker's study, Proctor suggests that, for many of Jesus' contemporaries, the term 'neighbor' had come to signify one's fellow member in any relationship of reciprocal responsibility.

governance. Quirinius' installation stripped Judea of this autonomy and placed the territory under direct Imperial control. However, Rome's imposition of imperial power sparked violent resistance from a sect of Jews to which Flavius Josephus refers as 'Zealots' in his *Antiquities of the Jews*. According to Josephus, the Zealots would obey 'no lord but God' and sought to incite a violent uprising against the occupying Romans. Their efforts to spur on an uprising included perpetrating assassination attempts on imperial officials and their Jewish collaborators. However, the willingness to kill fellow Jews in the name of God had either to represent a willing transgression of the injunction to neighbor-love or a bloody narrowing of the term's meaning: the neighbor is that member of the Jewish people who has not been compromised by their complicity in imperial governance. In a word, the neighbor is the one who recognizes 'no lord but God.' Strikingly, Josephus names one of Jesus' fellow Galileans, Judas of Gamala, as the leader of this sect of Judeans.[20]

Situated within this moment of bloody interpretive contest, then, the *nomikos'* question about the neighbor may be read as the *nomikos'* effort to locate Jesus' position within the interpretive field and, perhaps, to rescue the prospect of legal reconciliation within this turbulent landscape. Contrary to supersessionist readings, the parable of the Samaritan does not effect a transition from a narrow Jewish jurisprudence to a universalist Christian ethic. Instead, Jesus' exchange with the *nomikos* locates the parable in a dialogue internal to Judaism and vital to recovering the law's justifying power.[21] The problem is that an ambiguity in the neighbor's identity has divided the members of the Jewish community from one another, even inspiring violence, and, thereby, has made the law an instrument of alienation from rather than reconciliation with divine holiness and the fullness of human life. For our purposes, Jesus' exchange with the *nomikos* provides a literary frame wherein the law's power to reconcile us with our humanity will depend on a compassionate reading of its statutes that grounds and orients them with reference to a good unutterable.

---

20   See Josephus, *Antiquities of the Jews*, XVIII, 1.

21   C.f. Francois Bovon, "The Samaritan or Eternal Life as an Inheritance" in *Luke 2: A Commentary on Luke 9:51–19:27* ed. Francois Bovon, Helmut Koester & Donald S. Deer (Minneapolis: Augsburg Fortress Publishers, 2013): 49–65 & Lenn E. Goodman, *Love Thy Neighbor as Thyself* (New York: Oxford University Press, 2008); Scholars like Bovon and Goodman note that this more universal manner of interpreting the law is by no means alien to Judaism. Bovon proposes that in coming to this hermeneutical perspective, the parable reaches a similar conclusion to one championed by Philo of Alexandria.

3   On the Road from Jerusalem to Jericho: the Neighbor as Object

Whatever its significance, the parable seems to insist that the term 'neighbor' attains its meaning neither within a closed system of names nor in the context of a discrete social, religious, or political community. Although the date of Leviticus' composition remains the topic of some controversy, the current scholarly consensus places its compilation somewhere in the post-exilic period, while the Jewish community yet aspired to return to a land that was to be their own.[22] Consequently, we may reasonably suppose that its laws were meant to have their life amid a landed people in control of their territory. However, this was not the case by the time of Luke's composition (nor had it been for some time before). Instead, its people were residents of a colonized imperial territory.[23] Hence, the parable confounds efforts to define the neighbor with reference to membership in any stable social, religious, or political group. This point is made implicitly by the parable's setting, the names it does (and does not) assign to its characters, and the wordplay by which it describes their actions. More in line with Hillel the Elder than with Judas of Gamala, the parable gives the impression that the word 'neighbor' does not refer to one's fellow member in a narrowly defined ethnic group or moral community; instead, it is the point of contact between the community and the demand of the other who hails from beyond its bounds. It leads us to believe that law's power for reconciliation is coextensive with its potential for approving this outsider's demand.

It is not without significance that this ethical demand emerges outside—or, better, betwixt and between—the walls of two polities. The parable takes place on the road that goes down from Jerusalem to Jericho. Its setting transports Jesus and the *nomikos* from a settled place of dwelling to one of sojourning. The people passing through this space share no necessary antecedent relationships with one another. As Robert Heimburger and Oliver O'Donovan observe,

---

22   See Walter C. Kaiser, "Leviticus," in *The New Interpreter's Bible: A Commentary in Twelve Volumes*, vol. 1, 12 vols. (Nashville: Abingdon Press, 1994), 985–1004.

23   C.f. Emerson Powery, "Under the Gaze of the Empire: Who is My Neighbor?" *Interpretation* 62 (2008): 134–144. Powery notes the peculiarity that Jesus who has much to say about love of neighbor and even the love of the enemy, omits the Levitical charge to love the *ger/proseluto*. Powery proposes that the second Levitical command likely fell from prominence in an imperial context, in which the Jews did not strictly possess the land they occupied. Under the empire, Powery argues, the Israelites were inclined to think of themselves as aliens resident on the land. The interpretation I offer here takes a different tack. The parable intentionally blends Lev. 19.18 and 19.34 together through its presentation of the characters' actions. More on this point below.

the road is a site of 'chance encounter.'[24] The ethical demand, then, is conveyed not in the nearness of kinship (nor, I might add, the nearness of political membership) but in "the nearness of encounter and contingency."[25] For Heimburger and O'Donovan, therefore, this parable gives the love command a universalist inflection. However, this universalism does not attach to some abstract conception of humanity. This is a story about particular characters on a specific road. The universalism it articulates, Heimburger and O'Donovan rightly observe, is one communicated in concrete encounters with particular others. In this setting, one's neighbor is not a member of a determinate class of persons; instead, she is merely the one who 'comes near.' However, I would like to emphasize that to allow the neighbor to be defined in this way is, in effect, to refuse a definition.

This refusal is underscored by the names that the parable ascribes to its characters, a rhetorical exercise that functions to subvert the expectations of Jesus' listeners. The Samaritans' precise historical identity is not entirely clear. Some textual traditions identify them as the Judeans' estranged siblings from the northern kingdom, others as a people planted there by the Assyrians following the northern kingdom's downfall and its inhabitants' expulsion, and still others as a distinct religious community worshipping at Mount Gerizim.[26] Nevertheless, it is well understood that, in the Gospel of Luke, they are presented as outsiders typically excluded from the political and religious community. They are natural objects of suspicion and contempt. Thus, it is readily understandable that the Samaritan's presence (and depiction as an exemplar) would be jarring to Jesus' listeners and, perhaps, even to Luke's readers. What is not immediately apparent is why this outsider should appear in a trio with a priest (*iereus*) and a Levite (*levitēs*). What purpose do these other characters serve?[27] Why not simply use the brigands (*lēstēs*) or some other traveler

---

24   See Robert W. Heimburger, *God and the Illegal Alien: United States Immigration Law and a Theology of Politics* (New York: Cambridge University Press, 2018); & Oliver O'Donovan, *The Ways of Judgment* (Grand Rapids: Eerdmans Publishing Co, 2008).

25   Heimburger, *God and the Illegal Alien*, 195.

26   This ambiguity is reflected in the writings of Luke's contemporary Josephus. C.f. Reinhold Pummer, *The Samaritans in Flavius Josephus* (Tübingen: Mohr Siebeck, 2009). On Pummer's analysis, it is never entirely clear when the name 'Samaritan' refers to a people (for instance, the descendants of the Cutheans) or the religious community convened on Mount Gerizim.

27   Although, of course, many interpreters have made this constellation of characters evidence of an implicit moral critique of alleged Jewish ritual practices. The soundness of such interpretations is a topic of exegetical dispute. As the foregoing argumentation has hopefully made clear, I am suspicious of potentially supersessionist interpretations that premise Christianity's moral superiority to Judaism on the denigration of characters like

(*ekdēmos* or *parepidēmos*) as foils for the Samaritan? As Michael Gourgues keenly observes, this particular trio is the 'echo' of a rhetorical device commonly used in ancient Judaism and the Hebrew Bible:

> Priests, Levites, and all the people," "the priests and the Levites and the people of Israel," the priests, the Levites, and the children of Israel," the exact formulations may vary, but ancient Judaism and the [Hebrew Bible] use this tripartite division in order to give account of the composition of religious society in its diversity.[28]

Familiar with this turn of phrase, Jesus' listeners would have expected some representative of the people to make their way down the road after the Priest and the Levite. Thus, the parable sets its reader up to expect the neighbor to be a fellow member of this people. Instead comes a Samaritan, an outsider, and the parable reproduces rather than resolves the social crisis that necessitated the *nomikos'* question. Instead of providing closure, the names 'priest,' 'Levite,' and 'Samaritan' together blast open the lexical and social web within which the 'neighbor' is to be known. The neighbor is the one who draws near, and the one who draws near could be *anyone*—including the estranged sibling or the reviled outsider.

One additional refusal of definition is worth noting, and this occurs in the parable's highly ambiguous manner of naming the traveler who becomes the center of the story. The person traveling from Jerusalem to Jericho is merely 'a certain person' (*anthrōpos tis katebainen apo Ierousalēm eis Ierixō*). (10.30) Each of the other characters receives some measure of identification from their name. The brigands (*lēstēs*) can, at least, be defined in their relationship to the law as 'law-breakers.' The priest, Levite, and Samaritan can be identified relative to the religious community (*iereus, Levitēs, Samaritēs*). The innkeeper (*pandocheus*) can be defined according to his profession. However, the traveler assaulted by the brigands is described with the most general term on offer for a human being. Based on the direction of the individual's travel, down the road from Jerusalem and to Jericho, Jesus' listeners might have assumed that he was Jewish. However, the text leaves this point in ambiguity. One of Luke's

---

the priest and Levite as rule-mongering or uncompassionate. Regarding the argument of the Priestly or Levitical desire to maintain ritual purity see C.f. Bovon, "The Samaritan or Eternal Life as an Inheritance" & Thomas Kazen, "The Good Samaritan and a Presumptive Corpse," *Svensk Exegetisk Årsbok* 71 (2006): 131–144.

28 See Michel Gourgues, "The Priest, the Levite, and the Samaritan Revisited: A Critical Note on Luke 10:31–35," *Journal of Biblical Literature* 117 (1998): 709–713.

gentile readers may have just as easily imagined the wounded traveler as a fellow gentile. Furthermore, stripped of his clothes and possessions, the traveler is stripped of any other effect by which he might be marked as belonging to any given race, religion, region, or trade.[29] In this way, the parable also disidentifies the presumptive object of neighbor-love with any defining features. The neighbor could be any other human being suspended at the threshold between life and death.

Additionally, it bears stating that the parable confounds narrow definitions of the neighbor not only through processes of disidentification but also through contradictory identifications. Leviticus distinguishes the neighbor (*plesion*) from the sojourner (*prosēlutos*). Although the Holiness code commands the community to love both, they are nevertheless presented as distinct legal figures, differentiated by the sojourner's lack of filial bonds with the community (Lev. 19.33–34). As the parable shifts the name's signification from the object of the Levitical prescription to the subject that enacts it, this distinction breaks down. The neighbor's identification with the sojourner is accomplished through its description of the priest's, Levite's, and Samaritan's actions. In the Septuagint, the Greek term *prosēlutos* is used to render the Hebrew term *ger*. An alternate form of the word *proserxomai*, this term derives from the pronoun *pros*, meaning 'toward,' and *erxomai*, meaning to 'come' or 'go.' The sojourner, then, is, quite literally, the one who 'comes near.' As the parable depicts them, the Priest and Levite do not act as 'sojourners' but instead as the sojourner's antitype. Upon seeing the half-dead traveler, both cross to the other side of the road (*antiparēlthen*, from *antiparerxomai*). (Lk. 10.31–32) The Samaritan, by contrast, acts as the sojourner, seeing the traveler and 'coming near to him' (*proselthōn* from *proserxomai*). (10.33) This depiction invites a series of identifications. The first is the identification of the Samaritan and the *prosēlutos*. The second, however, is the confounding identification of the *prosēlutos* and the *plēsion*—in the world of the parable, the sojourner is the neighbor. With this turn, the term 'neighbor' ceases to function in a binary that distinguishes insiders and outsiders but rather names the point of indistinction between them.

In all these ways, the parable refutes any effort to define the neighbor as the object of a command. The parable's setting suggests that the neighbor does not emerge within the political community but in its interstices. Its use of names and depictions of action serves to confuse rather than to confirm. Instead of determining the neighbor's identity with reference to some other legal name, the language of the parable makes this name a symbol of indistinction where

---

29   Culpepper, "Luke," 229.

the determinacy of the law meets with the indeterminacy of the human. Conceived as the object of a command, the neighbor fails to fit with any general class and, therefore, could be anyone, including and perhaps especially the estranged sibling or reviled outsider. Nevertheless, if the parable does not permit us to define the neighbor as an object, it encourages its reader to think of the neighbor as a distinctive kind of ethical subject and, by extension, an exemplary paradigm for legal interpretation.

4   Moved by Compassion: the Neighbor as Ethical Subject

Consistent with Critchley's theory of ethical subjectivity, the parable of the Samaritan depicts an ethical subject constituted not by freedom unalloyed but by receptivity to the demand of another. Before the Samaritan *moves*—before the Samaritan becomes the neighbor—the Samaritan *is moved*. Verses 31 and 32 set up a pattern wherein a character comes down the road, sees the wounded traveler, and then, after seeing him, crosses away from him:[30]

> By chance, there came a priest + and when he saw him + he passed by on the other side (*kai idōn auton, antiparēlthen*).
>   And, likewise, a Levite + and when he saw him + he passed by on the other side (*kai idōn, antiparēlthen*).

However, when the Samaritan sees the wounded traveler, we read, "he [is] moved with compassion" (*esplagxnisthē*). This word's appearance in v. 33 marks an interruption in the pattern established by the preceding verses:

> But a certain Samaritan came where he was + and when he saw him + *he had compassion on him* + and went to him (*kai idōn auton, esplagnisthē, kai proselthōn*).

The pattern, established by the Priest and Levite, is a moment of vision followed immediately by a movement away from the wounded traveler. In each instance, the injured traveler is the fulcrum on which the action turns. By refusing to come near the wounded traveler, the priest and the Levite became antitypes for the neighbor. However, in the case of the Samaritan, compassion

---

30   Strahan also emphasizes this literary structure in "Jesus Teaches Theological Interpretation of the Law."

intervenes and initiates a different course of events. Instead of crossing away from the wounded one, the Samaritan comes near to him.

With compassion's intervention, the act of vision renders the Samaritan receptive to the wounded sojourner's need. We see that the wounded traveler is not a mere object of vision who can be turned away with indifference, but rather, he is a subject of moral concern who acts on the viewer. That is, the parable's language ascribes to the wounded man a degree of agency to produce an effect on the other travelers coming down the road. English translations of the parable do not always make this point with clarity, often rendering the sentence in the active voice ("and seeing him, the Samaritan took pity on him").[31] However, the term *esplagxnisthē*, which denotes the movement of compassion, appears in the aorist passive. The Samaritan, then, is not the subject of this phrase but the object. Put another way, this verbal formulation suggests that compassion is not something that begins in the will of the Samaritan. Rather, it is a movement within which he and the wounded traveler are caught up. Caught up in this movement, the Samaritan's will is exposed to the wounded one's demand. Of course, we need not suppose that compassion preempts or overrides the Samaritan's freedom. The priest and Levite prove that, even after seeing this mortally wounded traveler, it is still possible to cross away from him. Compassion's effect is to posit a choice: approve the demand and become a neighbor to the wounded traveler or refuse it and be defined by the rejection. Like Critchley's, the ethical subject presented in the parable is formed in the accusative and not in the nominative. It is constituted not through acts of autonomous self-legislation but by an ethical experience that sounds from without and suspends the sovereignty of the I.[32]

---

31   It is standard convention to translate the aorist passive into the English active voice. But this practice is an endeavor to make normal in English that which is strange in the Greek. This endeavor's consequence is to emphasize the familiar and to let slip that which is most foreign and challenging. As Walter Benjamin writes, "translation finds itself not in the center of the language forest but on the outside facing the wooded ridge; it calls into it without entering, aiming at that single spot where the echo is able to give, in its own language, the reverberation of the work in the alien one." See Walter Benjamin, "The Task of the Translator" in *Selected Writings: Volume 1: 1913–1926* ed. Marcus Bullock and Michael W. Jennings (Cambridge: The Belknap Press, 1996), 258–259.

32   This parable is not the only case in which Luke presents us with compassion's movement. He uses the verb *splagxnizomai* on two other occasions: in Jesus' meeting with the widow at Nain (Lk 7.11–17) and in the parable of the prodigal son (Lk. 15.11–32). In both instances, it appears in the passive voice following an act of vision. When Jesus sees the widow leading her son's funeral procession, Jesus is moved with compassion. (Lk. 7.13) When the prodigal's father sees him approaching, he is moved with compassion. (Lk. 15.20) In each case the response that compassion inspires restores someone dead to life. Jesus lit-

Nevertheless, the parable's account of compassion also allows us to amend Critchley's largely formal theory by stressing that ethical experience is an emphatically embodied phenomenon. Just as the parable presses the term 'neighbor' to the point of its indistinction from the term 'sojourner,' it also makes the body the site of indistinction between self and other.[33] The half-dead traveler does not cry out to the Samaritan as he passes him by. No word is uttered between him and the Samaritan at any point in the parable. The claim this traveler makes on the Samaritan is not communicated in the medium of language but in the immediacy of interdependent bodies. *Esplagxnisthē* derives from the word *splegxnon*, a noun literally translated as 'bowels,' but more aptly taken to refer to the *viscera thoracis*.[34] In the wounded traveler, the Samaritan sees a fellow human being suspended at the perilous crossing between life and death. The sight of the suffering body seizes him in heart and lung, making the body the site of an experience wherein the traveler's suffering becomes indistinguishable from the Samaritan's own.

As the heart skips and the lung draws sharp breath, it is as if the Samaritan's fate is bound together with the wounded traveler's. Again, the Samaritan is not coerced by the experience's embodiment. Like the priest and Levite who went down the road before him, he is free to cross away from the wounded traveler and leave him in the dust. However, by focusing our attention on an embodied ethical experience, the parable of the Samaritan also accentuates the pain that would be brought about by refusing the ethical demand. This addition raises

---

erally resuscitates the widow's son. The prodigal's father twice declares, to his servants and then to his eldest son, that the prodigal "was dead and has come to life." Perhaps not coincidentally, this triad of compassion stories describes a widow, an orphan, and a sojourner—the three figures to which the prophetic literature directs God's steadfast love and justice. (N.b., Lk. 15.12, 19, & 21; the prodigal son effectively declares himself an orphan first by demanding from his father that which would be his only upon his father's death and twice more by declaring himself no longer worthy to be called his father's son.)

33   In this respect, the parable articulates a parallel insight about the body to one that Daisy Machado has pointed out. In the intellectual traditions that have been shaped by the borderlands, Machado explains, the body is not a principle of separation. Bodies do not differentiate selves and others. To the contrary, the body is the site of experiences that reveal the interconnections between the self and the other and resist atomizing conceptions of the subject. See Daisy L. Machado, "Borderlife and the Religious Imagination," *Religion and Politics in America's Borderlands,* ed. Sarah Azaransky (Lanham: Lexington Books, 2013), 79–96; c.f. Daisy L. Machado, Bryan S. Turner, and Trygve Wyller, "Traces of a Theo-Borderland," in *Borderland Religion: Ambiguous Practices of Difference, Hope, and Beyond,* ed. Daisy L. Machado, Bryan S. Turner, and Trygve Wyller, Religion, Resistance, Hospitalities (New York: Routledge, 2018).

34   See the entries for *splagxnizomai* and *splagxnon* in *Lidell and Scott's Greek English Lexicon* (New York: Oxford University Press).

the stakes and captures the reflexivity of the cited love command. "You shall love the neighbor *as yourself*" or "*contemn* yourself as you contemn the neighbor." To refuse the other's plight is at once to refuse something about ourselves. It is to deny, or at least hold in contempt, the fact of interconnection and interdependency that knits embodied human animals together. The refusal of our ethical subjectivity is a refusal of one of the very things that makes us human.

The final exchange between Jesus and the *nomikos* confirms that the neighbor, contrary to the one who resists compassion's movement, becomes recognizable as their receptivity to ethical experience is converted into action. "Which of these three," Jesus asks him, "do you think, was a neighbor to the one who fell into the hands of the robbers?" (10.36) "The one who showed him mercy (*eleos*)," replies the *nomikos*. (10.37) The fact of co-suffering, the parable suggests, is not yet virtuous. Compassion is only made complete as it is realized in direct responses to the material needs of the other. The traveler that the Samaritan happens upon is mortally wounded. He is left incapacitated in the dust of the road. He is without shelter and unable to seek it out. In conformity to these needs, the love of neighbor comes to be expressed in the cleaning and binding of wounds. It is expressed in the Samaritan's decision to put the traveler on his animal and to remove him to the shelter of an inn. There, the Samaritan makes arrangements with the inn's proprietor that draw this character into the work of mercy.[35] It is not as if the love of neighbor is directly identifiable with dressing wounds or providing transportation and shelter. Rather, this is the form that love takes in light of this person's specific needs. However, if the needs differed, we might expect compassion to take a different form.

As noted above, many biblical critics doubt whether, in the end, Luke's parable offers any logically consistent answer to the question that prompts it. The breakdown occurs with the transition from neighbor conceived as object

---

35   See Bruce Longenecker, "The Story of the Samaritan and the Innkeeper (Luke 10:30–35): A Study in Character Rehabilitation," *Biblical Interpretation* 17 (2009): 422–447. Longenecker argues that the oft-overlooked innkeeper extends the parable's message to reveal that the work of neighbor love is inevitable. Moreover, the society formed by this love is one formed by relationships of vulnerability and risk. The Samaritan takes a risk, stopping on the road to rehabilitate the wounded traveler. He cannot be sure that the brigands will not return and victimize him as well. The innkeeper, likewise, is placed in a position of risk by the Samaritan. The money that the Samaritan pays him will not be enough, and he has no guarantee that the Samaritan will return the money to pay the debt. Moreover, other travelers may be unwilling to stay at an inn with a person on the brink of death lest they be exposed to the 'evil eye.' Therefore, as he enters into the work of neighbor-love, the innkeeper attends not only to the wounded traveler's vulnerability but is also confronted by distinctive risks concomitant with the task.

to neighbor conceived as subject. John Dominic Crossan put the matter succinctly in the third chapter of his 1992 study, *In Parables*:

> There is a logical inconsistency between the meaning of the term neighbor in 10:27, 29 and 10:36 such that the parable in 10:30–35 which is located between these two frames is pulled in opposite directions. In 10:27, 29 the neighbor is he to whom love must be offered; in 10:36 the neighbor is he who must offer love to another's need. In other word, the prefixing of 10:27–29 would indicate that the neighbor in the parable is the wounded man by the roadside; but the suffixing of 10:36 would indicate that the neighbor is the Good Samaritan himself.[36]

However, Crossan also points out that this logical discrepancy need not be considered fatal. It might be the point. If one is determined to find a moral in the parable, it might reasonably be inferred that Jesus means to indicate that love, mercy, and being a neighbor are all two-way streets that impose responsibilities on the Samaritan and the wounded man alike.[37] However, if all of the preceding is meant to provide us not merely with a tidy moral but with a fundamental insight for the right reading of the law, then the significance of this curious literary conjunction must be traced further. To make this move, Crossan proposes, the reader must seek in the parable more than an example of proper behavior, but the passage's metaphorical figuration. For Crossan, parables function to do more than to provide illustrations of familiar ideas. They are eschatological stories about the advent of the Reign of God that overturn "prior values, closed options, set judgments, and established conclusions."[38] A parable's endeavor is "to utter the unutterable and to admit thereby that other world which was at that very moment placing their own under radical judgment."[39] Completing our reading of the parable and addressing the problem with which this chapter began, requires us to sketch out the connection between compassion and an eschatological legal hermeneutics. It requires understanding why introducing the unutterable is crucial to the right reading of the law.

---

36   Crossan, *In Parables*, 58.
37   Ibid.
38   Ibid, 64.
39   Ibid.

5   Compassion and Law

Jesus' exchange with the *nomikos* sets up the right reading of the law as an answer to the question, "What must I do to inherit eternal life?" Although the phrase 'eternal life' might incline us to think of some heavenly life in the hereafter, biblical critics have proposed that the Greek *zoēn aiōnian* is better understood as referring to the form of life characteristic of the Reign of God whose inbreaking Jesus proclaims.[40] From the very outset, the parable's literary

40   See John Nolland and Bruce Manning Metzger, *Luke 9:21 - 18:34*, ed. David A. Hubbard and Glenn W. Barker, Nachdr., Word Biblical Commentary / [General Ed.: Bruce M. Metzger; David A. Hubbard; Glenn W. Barker. Old Testament Ed.: John D. W. Watts. New Testament Ed.: Ralph P. Martin], Vol. 35, B (Nashville: Nelson, 2008). I prefer this translation to retain the political dimensions of Jesus' proclamation more strongly. As Steve Walton points out, the first and, perhaps, oldest reading of Luke-Acts in modern scholarship considered it an apology to Rome on behalf of the church. A second interpretive approach suggests the converse. Luke-Acts is an apology to the church on behalf of Rome. Common to both interpretive approaches is the assertion that, for the evangelist, there was no ultimate tension between Jesus' proclamations and the *Pax Romana*. However, in more recent years, Lukan scholars, especially those engaging with post-colonial and de-colonial theories, have proposed a spectrum of more resolutely anti-imperial and expressly political interpretations of the text. To name only a portion, this group includes Warren Carter, Amanda C. Miller, C. Kavin Rowe, and Kazuhiko Yamazaki-Ransom. In a rhetorical analysis of the songs in Lk. 1–2, Carter finds the evangelist reframing the situation of oppression in the wake of a benevolent divine intervention that bestows dignity upon the oppressed singers and turns them toward the vision of a better counter-reality. Miller offers a sociological analysis of the Gospel of Luke that finds in the Lukan motif of reversal a demand for status changes that are concrete rather than merely spiritual. While Rowe does not find a clarion call for revolution in Luke-Acts, his narrative analysis does depict the inception of the Christian community as an inversion of Roman values that initiates a culture war that spills into the courts of the Empire, even if they do not readily recognize it. Yamazaki-Ransom, likewise, does not suppose that right reading of Luke-Acts would have led the early church to take up arms and mobilize in the streets. Nevertheless, he contends that the book provides a literary model for analyzing the legitimacy or illegitimacy of Roman governance based on its subordination and obedience or disobedience to divine sovereignty. Perhaps most striking is Yamazaki-Ransom's treatment of the angelic announcement of Jesus' birth, which identifies its parallels and inversions of concepts that first appeared on the Prine Calendar inscription celebrating the birth of Caesar Augustus. By the angels' proclamation, here, in an imperial backwater, is born a new leader who stands in opposition to Caesar, who had already been lauded as a 'savior' and 'prince of peace.' In light of all this scholarship, it is difficult to resist the notion that Luke's eschatological theology is not at once a political theology with immediate implications for this world. Insofar as *zoēn aiōnion* describes the form of life that will predominate under the *basileia theou*, then to translate this term as 'eternal life' loses its imminent political connotations to other-worldly ones. See Steve Walton, "The State They Were in: Luke's View of the Roman Empire" in *Rome in the Bible and the Early Church* ed., Peter Oaks (Grand

setting establishes that the law and its observance are the avenues to attaining the life that Jesus preaches. Put another way, the parable of the Samaritan presupposes for the law a narrative function in the process of human redemption. The parable's musing on the neighbor's identity, then, shows itself to be a musing on the nature of that humanity which is to be redeemed. Among the parable's reversals, however, is a refusal to define this word's meaning and an apparent determination to draw out its indeterminacies. The 'human,' as it appears in the parable, is not the *genera* containing all species, the 'set of all sets.' Instead, it is that which is left when every other name has (literally!) been stripped away. The human is that in us which escapes name or categorization. It is the unutterable ground that at once enables and negates every utterance. The redemption that the Reign of God proclaims is a reconciliation with this ground.

This point is underscored by the linguistic maelstrom that compassion's movement creates in the text. Coming to terms with the love of neighbor initiates the overturning of familiar categories by bringing them to the point of indistinction with their opposites. The parable's eschatological radicality does not merely consist in its application of the category 'neighbor' to the Samaritan, a figure of contempt. Rather, its radicality stems from compassion's undermining of the very epistemic conditions under which insider and outsider, neighbor and sojourner, self and other are to be differentiated in the first place. Compassion conveys an ethical demand that is unspoken and embodied. It transposes the love command from a closed system of names to the site of concrete encounters. Moving in an immediacy that runs behind language's back, it relativizes from the outset whatever names we might interpose to distance ourselves from or identify ourselves with the other. At a minimum, compassion forces the legal interpreter to acknowledge that although we may become known to ourselves and one another by the names the law provides, these

Rapids: Baker Academic, 2002), 1–41; Warren Carter, "Singing in the Reign: Performing Luke's Songs and Negotiating the Roman Empire (Luke 1–2)," in *Luke-Acts and Empire: Essays in Honor of Robert L. Brawley,* ed., David Rhoads, David Esterline, & Jae Won Lee (Eugene: Pickwick Publications, 2011), 23–43; Amanda C. Miller, *Rumors of Resistance: Status Reversals and Hidden Transcripts in the Gospel of Luke* (Minneapolis: Fortress Press, 2014); C. Kavin Rowe, *World Upside Down: Reading Acts in the Graeco-Roman Age* (New York: Oxford University Press, 2009); Kazuhiko Yamazaki-Ransom, *The Roman Empire in Luke's Narrative* (New York: T&T Clark, 2010); & Halvor Moxnes, "Kingdom Takes Place: Transformations of place and power in the Kingdom of God in the Gospel of Luke" in *Social Scientific Models for Interpreting the Bible: Essays by the Context Group in Honor of Bruce J. Malina* ed., John J. Pilch. (Boston: Brill, 2001), 176–209.

names never exhaust or wholly capture our identity. Compassion teaches us that the right reading of the law does not begin in the law itself but in the body.

The right reading of the law is possible only insofar as the law remains bound to its unutterable other. By blasting open the law's system of names, the parable refutes any narrow notion that the law's reconciliatory potentials lie in its ability to achieve closure through some terminable process of nomination. As long as the law remains bound to its other, any imposition of closure would only represent ossified conceit, a dialectic forced to halt before the next moment of negation set it back into motion. Each excluded other's ethical demand, embodied and unspoken, draws the law back to ground and exposes it to the negative principle in its dialectic. If the law is to be read rightly, the parable seems to insist, then the law must be read *for* the other's benefit and *from* the other's subject position. The challenge it puts to the legal interpreter is finding ways to mediate between ethical demand and political right. However, the indeterminacy of the human condition renders this task interminable. Legal names and fictions, novel or otherwise, will always involve a measure of falsification. Consequently, compassion plunges legal interpretation into an unending negotiation and renegotiation of identities. Compassion does not transfigure the law by overcoming its limits but rather by forcing it, again and again, to reckon with them.[41]

With this assertion, we are returned to Arendt's fear that compassion will tire of the slow-moving institutional processes constitutive of the political and opt instead for direct action that does them violence. Given the parable's eschatological freight, we might even consider that it introduces risks that Arendt does not even consider. If the interpreter intends to announce the advent of that other world that places our own under radical judgment,

---

41   C.f. Jacques Rancière, "Ten Theses on Politics," *Theory and Event* 5 (2001). The proposed approach to legal interpretation runs parallel to Rancière's conception of democracy. "The *demos*" Rancière asserts, "designates the category of people who do not count, those who have no qualifications to part-take in *arche*, no qualification for being taken into account." By extension, Rancière judges that democracy "is not a political regime," but rather, "a rupture in the logic of *arche*." It is a break in the system of name's that order and legitimize the polity's common life and this break signals the possibility of another ordering and a common life structured otherwise. The *demos*, then, expresses in the plural for Rancière what the *anthrōpos* appears to express in the singular for Luke. It is the unnamed, the unaccounted for, the other. Therefore, if it pleases the reader, the right reading of the law described above might be termed a 'democratic reading of law'—and a democratic reading of the law that carries with it the curious possibility of an anarchy without anomie. As I will suggest in the next chapter, the law read compassionately, becomes an instrument for the creation of interstitial spaces within the polity wherein we may glimpse the possibility of a world ordered otherwise.

what is to stop compassion's negative potentials from becoming absolute in their reach? Is anything more absolute or ubiquitous than the humanity that the parable makes the negative principle of our dialectics? On the one hand, I do not want to deny compassion's anarchic potential. By exposing us to a good that ruptures the system of names upon which much of our governance is premised, the judgment it issues does press for a radical reordering of our politics.[42] On the other hand, it is of no minor significance that Jesus answers the *nomikos'* questions with a parable rather than, say, a discourse on natural law. Had Jesus instead begun with an abstract definition of the human and then, with the use of this general concept, declared the wholesale inadequacy of the law to do it justice, Jesus might have produced a discourse that would confirm Arendt's worst fears. However, the parable of the Samaritan is a story about particular people traveling down a particular road. Indeed, compassion's ethical force implies some general claim about the human condition. However, by its form, the parable resists the notion that *the* human is ever encountered generally. On the contrary, the general can be known only in the particular—in our encounter with *this* person (*anthrōpos tis*). For the Samaritan, it is announced in the pain accompanying the visage of the wounded traveler, bleeding and abandoned in the dust of a mountain road. Compassion discovers and responds to its good at the site of encounter. It dresses wounds and arranges shelter. To issue an absolute judgment in the name of *the* human would already signify a departure from the parable's interpretive logic, which begins and ends in the particular.

Strikingly, then, what Arendt believes to be compassion's shortcoming, its particularity, is precisely what stops it from bringing everything asunder. Compassion's negations are not absolute. They are determinate negations. The compassionate legal interpreter does not, on account of their limitation, reject every legal name from the outset, renounce the law entirely, and swear herself to silence. Instead, she allows these limitations to be revealed in the midst of the particular. *This* name or *this* law is suspended or challenged only as it excludes the good of *this* life, which it holds in contempt. The ethical subject depicted in the parable is no legislator. She does not relate to the law as a creator to its creation. Rather, like the litigator, she interprets a text that has already been given to her. However, as compassion drives a wedge between name and named, it creates the possibility for the emergence of new names and new legal meanings. True enough, the concrete encounters that inform the compassionate legal subject bind her to particularity and render her

---

42   More on this in the next chapter.

incapable, on her own, of creating lasting political institutions. Nevertheless, without compassion's negations, standing institutions would become, at best, mausoleums for the goods they were once meant to uphold. At worse, they might become bulwarks against our responsibility to this good full stop.

Do we have any reason to believe that such possibilities can be glimpsed in the United States' territory in the twenty-first century? Are there Samaritans to be found in the US–Mexico borderlands? What is compassion's effect on the Samaritan when the other with whom she meets is not suspended at the crossing between life and death but already abandoned to death? What becomes of these Samaritans who arrive too late? Can their ethical experiences nevertheless constitute a form of subjectivity that inspires us to a compassionate reading of the law? Is such a reading capable of resisting PTD's inhumanity? To what extent, that is, can the litigator bring meaningful relief to the humanitarian crisis that has been playing out in the Sonoran for the last three decades? To answer these questions, I turn now to a different Samaritan on a different road and to the case of the United States v. Scott D. Warren.

CHAPTER 6

A Samaritan in the Sonoran

> When I see people who are going to undertake a crossing of the
> desert or who are in the desert or who stumble out of the desert into
> our town ... I see these bones at the same time.
> —SCOTT WARREN, Testimony in District Court of Arizona, 2018

∴

1   What Must We Do to Live?

To what extent can the legal hermeneutics proposed in the parable of the
Samaritan inform legal hermeneutics in the twenty-first century? In this
chapter, I seek to explore this problem by attending the story of another self-
styled 'Samaritan,' Arizona professor and humanitarian Scott D Warren. As a
volunteer for the Ajo Samaritans and No More Deaths, Warren's own ethical
subjectivity was shaped by his encounters with migrant remains. Haunted by
his encounters with the lives PTD denied, his humanitarian aid work reflected
a determined effort to become a neighbor to the sojourners who might yet
share their fate. However, in 2018, after allowing two injured migrants to stay
in a property under his care, Warren was arrested and indicted on two felony
harboring charges. Covered by multiple national media outlets, his case shed
light on the struggles faced by migrants seeking to cross the Sonoran Desert
and the humanitarians seeking to make these crossings less deadly.[1] Following

---

1   Reports on the trial were published in major outlets, including The New Yorker, The New
    York Times, and Time Magazine, as well as independent media, including *The Intercept*
    and *The New Inquiry*. See "Humanitarian Scott Warren Found Not Guilty After Retrial for
    Helping Migrants at Mexican Border," Time, November 21, 2019, https://time.com/5732485/
    scott-warren-trial-not-guilty/; Liz Kinnamon, "United States v. Scott Daniel Warren," *The New
    Inquiry* (blog), June 27, 2019, https://thenewinquiry.com/united-states-v-scott-daniel-war-
    ren/; Miriam Jordan, "An Arizona Teacher Helped Migrants. Jurors Couldn't Decide If It Was a
    Crime.," *The New York Times*, June 11, 2019, sec. U.S., https://www.nytimes.com/2019/06/11/us/
    scott-warren-arizona-deaths.html; Murat Oztaskin, "'USA v Scott' and the Fight to Prove That
    Humanitarian Aid Is Not a Crime," *The New Yorker*, July 8, 2020, https://www.newyorker.com/
    culture/the-new-yorker-documentary/usa-v-scott-and-the-fight-to-prove-that-humanitari-

a successful defense based on appeals to his religious freedoms, Warren was acquitted. I propose that Warren's trial provides a compelling (if imperfect) twenty-first-century analog to Luke's parable. During the trial, his right to religious conscience became the point of contact by which the other's ethical demand made itself felt upon the law. By attending to the defense's legal tactics, we may gain a glimpse of how this point of contact was achieved. Furthermore, by reflecting on the outcome of the case, we gain, on the one hand, a sense of what sorts of victories such tactics can bring about and, on the other hand, what we may lose by winning. Better to anticipate these claims, the points of divergence between contemporary conceptions of law and the one presupposed by the gospel writer bear elucidation.

The priority of compassion forces the twenty-first-century legal interpreter to confront primary questions about the nature and purpose of the law that occur neither to Jesus nor the *nomikos*. We might suppose that Jesus and the *nomikos* differed in their interpretation of the Holiness Code. Nevertheless, we may take for granted that both saw this collection of injunctions and prescriptions as more than a bare aggregate of commands. The parable of the Samaritan does not ask *what* law is or *whether* it serves some greater purpose. It presupposes that law articulates (or at least attains its purpose within) a distinctive vision of human life well lived and that its interpretation and observance are meant to carry us from our present condition toward this ideal vision. That is, the parable presupposes a theory of law in which law is not merely a coercive system but also a normative edifice devised to reconcile us to our humanity. Today, however, the idea of law as a normative edifice has become a topic of considerable controversy.

The erosion of the natural conjunction between the ideas of law as a coercive system and as a normative edifice began as early as the seventeenth century, at which point the law's provision for the common good was increasingly being identified with the law's ability to issue commands. Often identified as a precursor to, if not a founder of modern legal positivism, Thomas Hobbes writes in *The Leviathan* that "law in generall, is not counsel, but command" and that 'Civill Law':

> Is to every subject, those rules which the Common-wealth hath commanded him, by word, writing, or other sufficient sign of the will, to make

---

an-aid-is-not-a-crime; & Ryan Devereaux, "The Unraveling of the Conspiracy Case Against No More Deaths Volunteer Scott Warren," The Intercept, August 10, 2019, https://theintercept.com/2019/08/10/scott-warren-trial/.

> use of, for the distinction of right, and wrong; that is to say, of what is
> contrary and what is not contrary to the rule.[2]

Hobbes' use of the term 'civill law' does not indicate the modern distinction
between civil and criminal law. Instead, it indicates the distinction between
'positive laws,' laws created by human beings for the organization of a commonwealth, and 'natural law,' laws given by God for the governance of the
creation.[3] By focusing on the positive law, Hobbes' legal philosophy effects a
fundamental shift in the meaning of 'right' and 'wrong.' Hobbes' conception of
human law does not require that the law categorizes 'right action' and 'wrong
action' according to what actions estrange or reconcile us to our humanity.
Rather, it propounds a vision wherein 'right' and 'wrong' describe merely what
is or is not 'contrary to the rule' itself. According to this view, one would not
lend their fidelity to the law because they desired to live, not in the robust sense
that Luke's *nomikos* has in mind anyway. Subjects would give their fidelity to
the law only because this rule and its consolidation of rights is what stands
between them and the political association's collapse into a war of all against
all. The good of the command, in a word, is its capacity to restrain anarchic violence through the threat of superior violence. Thus, a century later, John Austin
would elaborate Hobbes' conception of law in his *Lectures on Jurisprudence*,
adding to its definition the explicit threat of sanction.[4]

By the twentieth century, the idea of law as a coercive system had come to
predominate in anglophone legal philosophy and practice under the (at times
contested) heading of 'legal positivism.'[5] As British philosopher HLA Hart
describes 'legal positivism' in his landmark study, *The Concept of Law*, 'legal

---

2 Thomas Hobbes, *The Leviathan*, Part 1, Chapter XXVI. On Hobbes' complex legacy in the
   tradition of legal positivism, see James Boyle, "Thomas Hobbes and the Invented Tradition
   of Positivism: Reflections on Language, Power, and Essentialism," *University of Pennsylvania
   Law Review* 135 (1987):383–426.

3 The Natural Law theory, on the other hand, found one of its most iconic expressions in
   Thomas Aquinas, *Summa Theologiae I–II*, qq. 90–108. Here, Thomas defines law as "an ordi-
   nance of reason for the common good, made by one who is in charge of the community, and
   promulgated." (q, 90, a. 4, trans. Alfred J. Freddoso). Thomas would ultimately distinguish
   between eternal law, which exists in the reason of God, natural law, which is eternal law's
   imprint on the natural world, divine law, which was given to guide human beings toward
   their supernatural end, and human law, which is derived to guide human conduct toward the
   good. (q. 91)

4 See John Austin, *Lectures on Jurisprudence, or, the Philosophy of Positive Law* (London: John
   Murray, 1885).

5 On the challenges of defining 'legal positivism' as a discrete school or theory see, for instance,
   Keekok Lee, *The Positivist Science of Law* (Brookfield: Avebury, 1989).

positivism' does not so much describe a discrete school or set of doctrines but a tradition whose members share certain family resemblances.[6] Among these resemblances, Hart grants, may be a command theory of law like the one introduced by Hobbes and further developed by John Austin.[7] However, twentieth-century positivism, as Hart articulates it, appeals less to the command theory of law itself and emphasizes instead two theses to which the command theory opened the door. First, as 'right' and 'wrong' come to be defined relative to the rule rather than some higher moral law, this manner of definition reveals a separation between law and morals. Second, and by extension, legal rules and decisions do not rely for their coherence or motivational force upon appeals to specifically moral justifications. Hart, for his part, conceded that there might be instances in which law and ethics intersected. However, he rejected the notion that ethics could or should supply the law's indispensable foundation.[8]

Instead, Hart argues, the law finds its ground in a set of customs and social facts. In relatively simple legal societies, such as the ones imagined by some command theorists, the law may find its necessary and sufficient conditions in the mere situation that "the majority of a social group habitually obey the orders backed by the threats of the sovereign person or persons, who themselves habitually obey no one."[9] However, Hart doubts whether most modern legal orders emerge from a sovereign whose power emanates from a single source. Instead, the fact that law has *multiple* sources (e.g. the constitution, the common law, the statutes, and the rulings of courts in the United States) indicates that in the place of a system of authority wherein power emanates from a singular sovereign, most contemporary legal orders disperse sovereign power into various political organs. Nevertheless, Hart does not suppose this dispersal is justified vis-à-vis some transcendent moral norm. Rather, what grounds the legal order is nothing other than a collection of social consensuses regarding (1) the sources of law, (2) who has the authority to decide disputes, (3) what sorts of reasons count as binding, and (4) in what matter the law may

---

6   HLA Hart, *The Concept of Law* (New York: Oxford University Press, 1994); C.f. HLA Hart, "Positivism and the Separation of Law and Morals," *Harvard Law Review* 71 (1958): 593–629.

7   Hart would ultimately judge this theory insufficient for failing to account for the productive types of laws which function less to restrain violence and more essentially to facilitate creative collaboration. Hence, he supposed that a positivist might ascribe to a command theory of law, but that such ascriptions were not essential to positivism.

8   This topic would draw the attention of American legal philosopher Lon Fuller in "Positivism and Fidelity to Law: A Reply to Professor Hart," *Harvard Law Review* 71 (1958): 630–672.

9   Hart, *The Concept of Law*, 100.

be changed.[10] On this view, law and morality may intersect insofar as those internal to the legal society may adduce moral justifications in defense of the legal order. Nevertheless, according to Hart's theory of law, the relationships between law and ethics that such statements might produce are only contingent. If the good of a legal system lies in its validity and not its correspondence to some substantive theory of justice, then the standards of internal coherence applied to the legal system are like to and, of necessity, need be no more ethical in nature than the standards of internal coherence posited in the rules that govern a game of baseball or ice hockey.

In the wake of this history, the *nomikos'* central question, "What must I do to live?" no longer generally informs the predominating view of the law. Only a minority of legal scholars and professionals see their role as though it were caught up in a larger project aimed at reconciling us to our humanity.[11] Therefore, those seeking to apply the parable's recommended mode of legal interpretation face several obstacles. First, at the level of theory, they must unsettle our satisfaction with legal validity and demand more of the legal system. In Part Two of this book, I have sought, if only implicitly, to make this case. Like Abel's ghost, the good to which our ethical subjectivity is bound lingers, haunting the polity and its laws. We may judge that PTD operates on a valid system of rules, but the bones in the Sonoran render this validity grotesque. However, even if this theoretical hurdle is overcome, there remains a challenge at the level of actual practice. Legal arguments are not straightforwardly ethical ones, and ethical arguments are not straightforwardly legal ones. Therefore, those who would make the ethical demand heard in the courtroom must adopt an approach that translates the demand into language and reason that the court recognizes as valid. Thus, the compassionate interpreter must become a savvy tactician, pursuing her objectives based on the resources and constraints

---

10   Ibid, n.b. Hart's discussion of 'primary' and 'secondary' rules on pp. 79–99.

11   According to the American Bar Association's Model Rules of Professional Conduct, for instance, the lawyer's purpose does not lie in the advancement of substantive justice, but in the providing access to procedural justice through zealous advocacy for their clients' interests. Legal scholars like Daniel Markovits propose that this work may find moral justification in the feelings of democratic legitimacy that zealous advocacy seems to produce in clients. Nevertheless, most legal ethics that seek to provide moral justifications for the work of advocacy set out from the assumption that there is a distinction between law and ethics and, perhaps, even an opposition. See Daniel Markovits, *A Modern Legal Ethics: Adversary Advocacy in a Democratic Age* (Princeton: Princeton University Press, 2008); & Stephen Pepper, "Lawyers' Ethics in the Gap Between Law and Justice," *South Texas Law Review* 40 (1999): 181–207.

imposed on her by the juridical field.[12] The language of rights proposes itself as such a resource. However, the translation that this language affords is not achieved without meaningful loss. Thus, if compassion is to retain its negative dialectical force, the compassionate interpreter of the law must take care, even as she seeks to utilize the court's language, never wholly to be submerged in it. She must find ways, that is, to ensure that the law continues to be confronted with the good's haunting excess, lest compassion should lose its eschatological force.

2   Encounters on a Different Road

On January 14, 2018, Kristian Perez-Villanueva, a national of Honduras, and Jose Arnoldo Sacaria-Goday of El Salvador arrived in Ajo, Arizona, a small town some forty miles from the US–Mexico line.[13] Two days prior, they had crossed the border without submitting themselves to immigration authorities for inspection. To avoid detection, they had made their crossing in the wilderness, between ports of entry. The gambit was a marginal success. They had made it into US territory, after all. However, a run-in with Border Patrol officers in the desert led to a pursuit that cost them most of their supplies. Moreover, multiple days of hiking in the Sonoran's rugged terrain had left them dehydrated,

---

12   On the distinction between 'strategy' and 'tactics' as it regards the exercise of agency under constraint, see Michel De Certeau, *The Practice of Everyday Life*, trans. Steven Rendall (Berkely: University of California Press, 1984), n.b., 34–39. De Certeau calls "a strategy the calculation (or manipulation) of power relationships that becomes possible as soon as a subject with will and power (a business, an army, a city, a scientific institution) can be isolated." (pp. 35–36) A strategy, he continues, "postulates a place that can be delimited as its own and serve as the base from which relations with an exteriority composed of targets or threats (consumers or competitors, enemies, the country surrounding the city, objectives and objects of research, etc.) ca be managed." (p. 36) De Certeau's parenthetical remarks reveal that he has in mind more than literal battlefield strategy. Instead, the idea of 'strategy,' or rather, the figure of the 'strategist,' indicates a distinctive kind of subject that occupies a strong position capable of defining the space into which its action will proceed. They act on their field of influence as if from above or from without. The tactician, on the other hand, is an agent who must practice her agency in the landscape that the strategist produces. Operating from the comparatively weak position, a tactic "takes advantage of 'opportunities' and depends on them, being without any base where it could stockpile its winnings, build up its own position, and plan raids... It must vigilantly make use of the cracks that particular conjunctions open in the surveillance of the proprietary powers. It poaches in them. It creates surprises in them." (p. 37)
13   "Criminal Complaint," Document 1, *The United States v. Scott Daniel Warren* (District of Arizona, 2018).

malnourished, and with severe blistering and swelling in their feet. Perez-Villanueva also showed symptoms of a cold, while Sacaria-Goday complained of severe pain in his torso from falling onto a rock. Plagued by dehydration and blunt-force injuries from the environment, the migrants' physical conditions were consistent with the effects of exposure suffered by many who have lost their lives in the Sonoran. Fortunately for them, they remained among the living and, upon reaching Ajo, made their way to a gas station, where they were able to find food and directions to a building known to local humanitarian aid activists as 'the Barn.'

Like most migrants who find themselves in Ajo, Perez-Villanueva and Sacaria-Goday did not see this little town as their final destination. Lying relatively close to the international line and with a dwindling population of fewer than 3,000 people, Ajo is a pit-stop at most. The nearest cities are Phoenix to the north and Tucson to the east. Both are over 100 miles away. Reaching either one by car would only take a matter of hours. However, hiking there on foot would take days. North of Ajo is the uninhabited Barry Goldwater Bombing Range. To its East is the sparsely populated reserve of the Tohono O'odham Nation. Although it is difficult to say how many mortalities have occurred in the Goldwater range, local journalists report that no fewer than 1,400 migrants have died on the O'odham reserve since 2000.[14] By no means, then, does arrival in Ajo signal one's escape from the Sonoran's hostile terrain or the mortal danger upon which PTD relies. Blistered feet make for slower movement and prolong the time migrants must spend on parched ground under a beating sun, exacerbating the dangers of dehydration and exposure.[15] Faced with another 100 miles of hiking in the desert, the seemingly minor injuries affecting Perez-Villanueva and Sacaria-Goday posed a genuine threat to their chances of survival.[16] At the Barn, however, they had heard that they would be able to

---

14   Uncertainty regarding migrant mortalities in the Goldwater Range is a consequence of aid groups' inability to look for remains there. The Goldwater Range is among the largest active bombing ranges on US territory and the danger posed by military exercises and unexploded munitions keeps this stretch of land closed to the public. On the mortalities that have taken place on O'odham land, see Curt Prendergast Devoid Alex, "Arizona Daily Star Investigation: Death in the Desert," Arizona Daily Star, December 2, 2021, https://tucson.com/news/local/subscriber/arizona-daily-star-investigation-death-in-the-desert/collection_c013265c-4896-11ec-afe5-eb4b401c87df.html.

15   This point was repeated in defense attorney Greg Kuykendall's argumentation and underscored by the witness testimonies of No More Deaths volunteers including Isabella Reis-Newsom and former EMT Flannery Shay-Nemirow.

16   See testimonies of Reis-Newsom and Shay-Nemirow in United States v. Scott Daniel Warren, Transcript, 4–88, Jun. 5, 2019

find shelter, food, water, and, perhaps, a chance to recover from their injuries before continuing their journey.[17]

A wood and sheet metal structure exposed to the desert on its northern, western, and southern sides, the Barn served as a makeshift staging area for humanitarian aid organizations operating in the western Sonoran Desert. Within, a kitchen and living area were partitioned from a small bedroom, bath, and one additional space that could function as a clinic. Though the Barn's living area and bedroom could accommodate sleeping arrangements for a few volunteers, when large groups came to the property, many would stay outside the building in tents. So, the property had to be prepared whenever such a group was expected. For this purpose, Warren went to the Barn on January 14, 2018. Volunteers from a group called Los Armadillos, organized to recover migrant remains from the desert, would be staying at the Barn while conducting their work. Warren meant to get the property ready to host them. However, upon arriving at the Barn, he discovered Perez-Villanueva and Sacaria-Goday on the premises. Yet, he did not turn them away or report them to law enforcement. To their relief, he offered them food, water, clean clothes, and beds on which to sleep while they recovered from their injuries. In all, Perez-Villanueva and Sacaria-Goday would spend three nights at the Barn. However, the two men would not successfully make it from Ajo to the next stop on their journey.

While staying at the Barn, they came under the surveillance of one of the Border Patrol's 'Disrupt' or 'Target Enforcement' units. As explained in court by Agent John Marquez, this was a plain-clothes investigative unit tasked with identifying, disrupting, and dismantling alien smuggling and drug trafficking organizations.[18] On January 17, Marquez and his partner, Brendan Burns, parked their vehicle in a concealed position roughly one-tenth of a mile from the Barn. After watching the property for several hours through a spotting scope, Marquez saw Warren, Perez-Villanueva, and Sacaria-Goday emerge from the building. According to Marquez's witness testimony, Warren was speaking with one of them and gesturing toward the north, perhaps giving them direction on how they could avoid detection at a border patrol checkpoint along the highway. Whatever their intended meaning or purpose, Warren's gestures were enough to arouse Marquez's suspicions. After Warren, Perez-Villanueva, and Sacaria-Goday went back inside the Barn, Marquez and Burns called

---

17   Reports on the video depositions can be found in Devereaux, "The Unraveling of the Conspiracy Case Against No More Deaths Volunteer Scott Warren," & Kinnamon, "United States v. Scott Daniel Warren."
18   United States v. Scott Daniel Warren, Tr., 12ff, November 13, 2019.

for backup. Once the property's perimeter was secured, Marquez and Burns performed a 'knock-and-talk' to ascertain the men's immigration statuses. Upon seeing Marquez and Burns, Sacaria-Goday tried to flee on foot. This time, however, he and Perez-Villanueva would not successfully elude the Border Patrol. When Perez-Villanueva admitted that he had entered the country unlawfully, Marquez and Burns arrested him. Sacaria-Goday and Warren were subsequently arrested. After videotaped depositions, in which they served as material witnesses to Warren's crimes, Perez-Villanueva and Sacaria-Goday's journeys ended. After being placed in the expedited removal process, both men were swiftly deported from US territory.

Warren's arrest was met with suspicion by many Arizona humanitarians, who saw it as an effort to intimidate anyone seeking to mitigate PTD's deadly effects. In his witness testimony, Marquez noted that Border Patrol was aware of the Barn and its uses. Marquez also testified to having researched Warren beforehand, believing him to be the "de facto leader" of No More Deaths. In fact, Warren was only a volunteer for the organization. Nevertheless, fellow volunteers could not help but notice the timing of the arrest. It coincided with No More Death's release of the first edition of their "Disappeared" report, which criticized the Border Patrol's enforcement tactics and charged detention facilities with perpetrating a culture of abuse. Along with the report, No More Deaths also released a video of US Border Patrol agents intentionally destroying water reserves that were left on migrant trails in the desert.[19] In his testimony, Marquez initially denied any knowledge of the report, suggesting instead that his decision to surveil the Barn on that day was purely serendipitous. He and his partner had discovered Warren, Perez-Villanueva, and Sacaria-Goday by chance.[20] He would later admit to having seen the videos. In any event, as one journalist would put it, Warren's legal controversies seemed to take on the character of a 'referendum' on both the present political moment and the decades-long policy of PTD.

In Warren, by all appearances, the United States government had indicted a sympathetic character for showing compassion to two men lost in a deadly environment. Strikingly, the criminal complaint filed after Warren's arrest based the state's charges on Warren's decision to "[take] care of [Perez-Villanueva and Sacaria-Goday] in 'the barn' by giving them food, water, beds,

---

19   These videos circulated widely, even being shared by international publications like *The Guardian*. See Rory Carroll, "US Border Patrol Routinely Sabotages Water Left for Migrants, Report Says," *The Guardian*, January 17, 2018, sec. US news, https://www.theguardian.com/us-news/2018/jan/17/us-border-patrol-sabotage-aid-migrants-mexico-arizona.

20   United States v. Scott Daniel Warren, Tr., 21ff, November 13, 2019.

and clean clothes."[21] Doubtless, the criminalization of mercy runs counter to the vision of law articulated in the parable of the Samaritan. However, coming to terms with the trial's ethical and political significance requires a little more clarity regarding the legal issues that would occupy the court over the course of what would ultimately become two trials.[22] The legal issue in the case was not the provision of care *per se*. Regarding the law, the court would have to answer two questions. First, it had to determine whether Warren had acted with a criminal intention to shield Perez-Villanueva and Sacaria-Goday from detection or if he had acted based on a sincerely held religious belief. Second, if Warren's motivations were religious, it had to determine whether the state's charges constituted the 'least restrictive means' of advancing its own compelling interest in regulating the nation's borders.

On one level, then, what was at stake in these trials was a question regarding Warren's character and how it was to be made legible under the law.[23] The prosecution endeavored to portray Warren as a smuggler. According to the defense, however, Warren was "nothing more nor less than a Good Samaritan."[24] The trial's significance, however, did not stop with the naming of this particular individual. More fundamentally, by revealing the law's ambivalent potential to characterize Warren under radically divergent names, the trial also demonstrated the law's ambivalent potential to serve two divergent normative regimes. As deployed by the state, the law would serve as a sword for striking out at actors undermining the self-determining polity's ability to regulate the boundaries of its territory and membership. As deployed by the defense, on the other hand, the law provided a shield for moral actors determined to respond to outsiders' ethical demands, regardless of their membership status. From this perspective, the trial's stakes extended beyond the particular issues that would determine Warren's guilt or innocence, soliciting, if only implicitly, deeper judgments regarding the law's fundamental nature and purpose.[25]

---

21   United States v. Scott Daniel Warren, Compl, January 18, 2018.

22   Warren's first trial began in May of 2018 and, in addition to two counts of harboring, included 1 count of conspiracy. This trial, however, ended in a mistrial. His second trial, from which much of the material cited in this chapter is drawn, began in November of 2019, with the prosecution abandoning the conspiracy charge and focusing instead on the two counts of harboring.

23   On the construction of character types in modern legal proceedings, see Lindsay Farmer, "Trials," in *Law and the Humanities: An Introduction*, ed. Austin Sarat et al (New York: Cambridge University Press, 2009), 455–477.

24   United States v. Scott Daniel Warren, Tr., 10, November 12, 2019.

25   Farmer, "Trials," n.b., 455–457. Regarding high-profile trials like Warren's, Farmer proposes that our fascination owes to the sense that these trials "are always about more than one particular case; they reveal something about the time and culture in which they take

3   What is in the Law? How Do You Read It?

Whether, in the eyes of the law, one becomes a 'smuggler' or a 'Samaritan' depends on the outcome of a kind of high-stakes narrative contest. Moreover, this narrative contest does not indicate a perversion of the legal process but rather the necessary means by which the judgment of cases takes place. Legal rules are formulated to express general norms of behavior potentially applicable to various situations and actors. Applying them in context requires determining their connections to the facts of the case. However, the meaning of a given fact (legal or otherwise) is never self-evident. Rather, facts attain their meaning as they are combined to form patterns. These combinations do not occur without the fictive activity of a narrator. As such, in their efforts to apply statutes, litigators inevitably find themselves engaged in constructing and reconstructing legal fictions.

Nevertheless, narrative's necessity does not give lawyers carte blanche to tell whatever story they please in whatever manner they please. Since these narratives are aimed at eliciting specific judgments, they are oriented, on the one hand, by the elements of the relevant statutes. The litigator's task is not merely to tell a story whose details prove dramatically compelling but also a story whose details reproduce the elements of the law in question. Whether an act of killing, for instance, is judged to be manslaughter, first-degree murder, or self-defense will depend on the specific details of the story in which the act is inscribed. A story that differentiates murder from manslaughter will address the presence or absence of a defendant's deliberate intention to take life. One that differentiates murder from self-defense will include subplots about extenuating circumstances or a desperate situation that necessitated an extreme act which we would otherwise prohibit. The upshot of all these plots and subplots will be a story that guides us to apply the statute such that the character depicted is judged accordingly.

Further, the narrative contests playing out in one courtroom never unfold in isolation. Except in unprecedented cases, lawyers are also informed by previous applications of the law, and these previous applications provide narrative conventions of their own. Likewise, Teresa Godwin Phelps points out that the

---

place." (p. 456) This sense, Farmer argues, is promoted by the 'staging' of modern trials themselves. Today, that is, we have grown accustomed to the idea of the 'reconstructive trial.' According to this idea, the courtroom becomes a stage wherein actors and acts are reconstructed before our eyes through the litigators' provision of evidence and narrative context. Moreover, in trials such as Warren's, which counterpose a sympathetic character against their criminal charges, it is not only the character of the defendant who becomes visible on the court's stage, but the character of the law itself.

legal fictions that guide statutory interpretation also refer to the conventions of dominant social narratives.[26] "For example," Godwin Phelps explains, "if a battered woman kills her abuser and tries to plead self-defense, she may well find that the rules governing that plea are embedded in a male narrative, a story of two men of equal size confronting each other in an alley."[27] This presumptive fiction will impose distinct conventions on the story she tells. She will not only be challenged with narrating the circumstance that justified her action, but she will also have to do so with reference to issues of immanence, equal force, and attempted retreat. Insofar as legal controversies are situated within broader social narratives, litigators must grapple not only with the law itself but also with prevailing assumptions that may influence the degree to which their stories appear plausible or credible to jurors.

To return to Warren's case, the applicable statute was Title 8 USC §1324, which charges with harboring any person who:

> knowing or in reckless disregard of the fact that an alien has come to, entered, or remains in the United States in violation of law, conceals, harbors, or shields from detection, or attempts to conceal, harbor, or shield from detection, such alien in any place, including any building or any means of transportation[.][28]

However, as would be the case with any other criminal charge, the state would need to demonstrate both *actus rea*, the commission of an illicit act, and *mens rea*, the presence of a 'guilty mind.' It would not be sufficient to demonstrate that Warren had attempted to shield Perez-Villanueva and Sacaria-Goday from Border Patrol's detection by hiding them in the Barn. The state would also have to show that Warren did this 'knowingly' or 'in reckless disregard of the fact' that they had entered the United States surreptitiously.

Nevertheless, precedent favored the prosecution on both fronts. Although the statute does not define 'harboring' explicitly, the Ninth Circuit defines the term such that it would include any conduct that 'affords shelter to' undocumented individuals.[29] The considerable latitude that the circuit ascribes to the term favors criminal liability concerning *actus rea*. Regarding *mens rea*, defendants in the Ninth Circuit can be judged to have acted with 'reckless

---

26   Teresa Godwin Phelps, "No Where to Go, No Story to Tell: The Lost Narratives of the Sanctuary Movement," *Washington & Lee Law Review* 48 (1991): 123–137.

27   Ibid, 124.

28   8 USC § 1324 (a)(1)(A)(iii)

29   Valle del Sol Inc. v. Whiting, 732 F.3d 1006, 1017 n.9 (9th Circuit 2013)

disregard' if "(1) the person is aware of facts from which a reasonable inference could be drawn that the alleged alien was, in fact, an alien in the United States unlawfully; and (2) the person actually draws that inference."[30] When it came to demonstrating that a client had, in fact, drawn the inference, other courts before Warren's trial had judged circumstantial evidence sufficient to establish it.[31] The most significant source of resistance facing the prosecutors would come with the defense's invocation of another statute.

Warren's defense was premised on the claim that his humanitarian intervention was an expression of his religious convictions. According to the Religious Freedom Restoration Act (RFRA), this meant that to produce a conviction, the case would have to be tried on standards of strict scrutiny. That is, if jurors determined that Warren's illicit actions followed from a 'sincerely held' religious belief, and if they judged that the law substantially burdened his ability to exercise these beliefs, then it would fall to the state to prove that convicting Warren would advance a 'compelling interest of state,' and that it would do so by the 'least restrictive means' available.[32] Put another way, the state would need to demonstrate that it would be unable to pursue its interest in regulating the border without criminalizing religiously inspired acts of humanitarian aid like Warren's. Given this legal backdrop, the ensuing contest between the State and Warren's defense team would turn almost entirely on the matter of intent.

Thus, the prosecution, led by Anna Wright, relied heavily on the testimony of the arresting officers to support a narrative about alien smuggling that downplayed the plausibility of religious explanations. As Wright put it to the jurors in her opening statement, "This case [was] about what the defendant Scott Warren did to help two men, Kristian and Jose, continue their illegal journey north into the United States."[33] After crossing over the US–Mexico line without permission from the proper authorities, the two men had "lost their camouflage" and were at risk of detection by Border Patrol. After eventually making their way to Ajo, they conveyed this point to Warren, and he sheltered them for four days and three nights. While making their case, the prosecution took care to share selfies and other photographic evidence meant to cast doubt on the claim that they were in poor health and in need of humanitarian aid. This extenuating circumstance denied, it would have to be judged that

30   "9.3 Alien—Harboring or Attempted Harboring | Model Jury Instructions," accessed December 1, 2023, https://www.ce9.uscourts.gov/jury-instructions/node/409.

31   United States v. De Jesus Batres, 410 F.3d 154, 161 (5th Circuit 2005); & United States v. Rubio-Gonzalez, 674 F.2d 1067 (5th Circuit 1982).

32   United States v. Scott Daniel Warren, Affirmative Defense Mem., June 15, 2019

33   United States v. Scott Daniel Warren, Tr., 3, November 13, 2019.

Warren's intention was nothing other than to aid these men in staying hidden from "the watchful eye of the Border Patrol." Warren's crime was presented as a matter of material fact, perpetrated with full knowledge that Perez-Villanueva and Sacaria-Goday were aliens unlawfully present in the United States. Warren might have harbored the pair longer had his operation not been disrupted by a Border Patrol unit expressly tasked with combatting criminal human smuggling. Whatever other details or stories the defense might raise, Wright insisted to the jurors, were nothing more than distractions.[34]

Whereas the prosecutors sought to tell a tightly framed story about what Warren *did* at the Barn over four days and three nights, Warren's defense attorney, Greg Kuykendall, sought to recast these actions by inscribing them in a larger story about humanitarian crisis and aid. The four days and three nights spent at the Barn were not the whole story, only a chapter in a larger one; one that had been unfolding for years on the Sonoran's exceptionally hazardous terrain. In his own opening statements, Kuykendall took care to set this scene for the jurors:

> What surrounds Ajo is no ordinary desert. It's a multimillion-acre desert, bigger than some states, owned by, almost exclusively, owned almost entirely, by the federal government, with virtually nothing, no towns, no farm houses, no help, anywhere except Ajo.[35]

In this vast expanse, Kuykendall went on, Perez-Villanueva and Sacaria-Goday's seemingly minor injuries could have mortal consequences. Here, getting hurt, slowing down, and being left behind meant falling into a common cycle that all too often ends in death. Indeed, at the time of the trial, this had already been the case for more than 3,000 migrants in Pima County alone.[36] By the time they had arrived in Ajo, Perez-Villanueva and Sacaria-Goday had already begun to slip into this cycle. Warren understood this cycle, Kuykendall explained, and he knew first-hand the mortal danger that Perez-Villanueva and Sacaria-Goday faced. Confronted with two men suspended at the crossing between life and death, Warren could not act otherwise than he did. Kuykendall meant to prove that his client's intent was not to break or disregard the law. It was to interrupt the "lethal sequence of slowing down, getting abandoned, being lost, and dying."[37] "That lethal sequence," Kuykendall urged the jurors, "is

---

34   Ibid.
35   United States v. Scott Warren, Tr., 13, November 12, 2019
36   Ibid, 16.
37   Ibid, 15.

what explains [Warren's] intent."[38] To prove it, he would rely, in no small part, on the eloquence of his client's testimony.

4   The Samaritan Moved with Compassion

As Warren's defense team put it, their client was a 'good Samaritan,' "morally, ethically, and spiritually *bound* to offer assistance to human beings in need of basic necessities."[39] Whatever the tactics that informed their strategy, I do not want to suggest that Warren's likeness to the biblical Samaritan is the mere artifice of courtroom procedure. On the contrary, the very same witness testimony that helped establish the sincerity of Warren's religious belief also reveals an ethical subject constituted by an experience of demand analogous to the biblical Samaritan's. Much is caught up in the recognition that Warren was *bound* to act as he did. It reveals that, for him, turning Sacaria-Goday and Perez-Villanueva away would have meant breaking faith not only with them but with himself. Consequently, attending to Warren's testimony allows us to glimpse the point of contact between compassion and law in the context of a twenty-first-century courtroom. Further, as we consider what this testimony allowed his defense team to accomplish, it will enable us to assess compassion's efficacy in yielding a more humane reading of the law.

As Warren explains, he did not move to Ajo to join the Samaritans or become an organizer for No More Deaths. A PhD candidate in Cultural and Environmental Geography at Arizona State University, Warren initially moved to Ajo to find "a quiet place to write [his] dissertation."[40] However, he did carry with him the conviction that "to live ethically in a place," one must "be engaged with that place, and ... with the ways that people in ... that place are shaped and suffering."[41] Thus, despite his intentions, he quickly found himself drawn into the stories of migration and border defense playing out in the local community. Throughout its history, Ajo has always been an industry town. In its early days, that industry was copper mining. In more recent history, however, it has become a company town for Border Patrol officers assigned to the southwestern border. This transition is what occupies Warren's dissertation. Predictably,

---

38   Ibid.
39   United States v. Scott Daniel Warren, Tr., November 13, 2019.
40   United States v. Scott Daniel Warren, Tr., June 5, 2019, at p. 163.
41   Ibid, 191.

his research interests led him to register for a Border Patrol Citizen's Academy.[42] This program comprised a six-week course designed to showcase the Border Patrol's facilities and help community members understand the agency's mission and work. However, as Warren got to know several Ajo Samaritans who were also enrolled in the Citizen's Academy, his academic interests gradually gave way to deeper ethical concerns.

Warren explains that after the Samaritans at the Citizens Academy invited him to attend one of the organization's meetings, he obliged. As he became increasingly involved with the Samaritans and other local organizations, his eyes began to open to the gravity of the humanitarian crisis on their doorstep. He came to understand the borderlands as a theater of 'low-intensity conflict,' where the state was arraying its power in opposition to outsiders it believed to be a destabilizing threat to its security.[43] Unpersuaded that the putative threat justified the inhumane tactics being deployed against migrants in the desert surrounding his town, Warren began going on 'water drops,' hikes into the desert organized to leave jugs of water on the migrant trails. The hope behind these endeavors was that migrants in need would happen upon this water and, in turn, stand a better chance of surviving their journeys. This volunteer work was consistent with Warren's general ethical commitments regarding a person's responsibility to the place in which they live. As Warren explained, it would also become the setting for a life-changing encounter in which the crisis truly 'became real' to him.

In his testimony, Warren recounts the events of an evening several years before the trial. Warren was at a Samaritans meeting when two men arrived unannounced and visibly shaken. After volunteers managed to settle them down, the men explained that they had been hiking in the western desert and had stumbled across the remains of a deceased migrant. Although they did not know the man or his story, it must have seemed to them wrong to leave the body where it lay. Thus, they went to the Samaritans to seek help recovering his remains. Though Warren had yet to be on such a trip with the Samaritans, the

---

42   C.f. Scott D Warren, "Across Papaguería: Copper, Conservation, and Boundary Security in the Arizona-Mexico Borderlands" (Doctoral Dissertation, Arizona State University, 2015).
43   C.f. Departments of the Army and the Air Force, "Military Operations in Low Intensity Conflict," (Washington, DC, December 5, 1990). Indeed, PTD was developed in a strategic partnership between the Border Patrol and the US Army's Center for Low-Intensity Conflict. Although this center has since closed, and although the term 'low-Intensity Conflict' is no longer widely used, it is a military doctrine meant to describe "protracted struggles of competing principles and ideologies" that lead to "political-military confrontation between contending states or groups below conventional war and above the routine, peaceful competition among states." (p. 1–1)

organization did more than organize water drops. They also organized 'search and recovery' trips, in which they sought to locate and assist in the recovery of human remains reported in the desert. This trip would be Warren's first, and it would bring him face to face with PTD's deadly effects. In so doing, it would precipitate an ethical experience that would forever change how he understood his moral relationship to himself, his neighbor, and the divine. Unlike the biblical Samaritan, who found the wounded traveler at the threshold between life and death, Warren would arrive too late to bring relief. Nevertheless, death did not efface the good of the life denied. Warren later reflected in his testimony that he believed "that an essence of a person, their soul or whatever … you want to call it, is absolutely in that place, and if they die there, their soul is there in a way."[44] This fact was one that Warren could not meet with indifference. It imposed a duty. He felt a defining obligation to respond—to bear witness and to join this disavowed spirit in its isolation. In this way, he hoped, he could bring this estranged sibling some measure of peace.

Like the biblical Samaritan, whose compassionate action conformed to the site of his encounter, Warren developed his own distinctive way of responding to the reality of suffering with which he was confronted. If the life could not be saved, it needed to be mourned. Over subsequent 'search and recovery' trips, Warren explains, he developed a distinctive mourning ritual aimed at collapsing the space between his own embodied experience and the deceased migrant's:

> If we find a body or bones, I will acknowledge the person by facing them, and then I will turn away and look out onto the desert, onto the land, and the significance of that, for me, is seeing with my own eyes what this person saw right before they died or what I imagine they would have seen from that particular place. That offers a … spiritual connection for me immediately.
>
> And then the other piece of that is I'll sit down or kneel down and grab a handful of the desert, of dirt, of sand, whatever is there, and slowly … release that from my hands, breathe deeply, offer … a moment of meditation for this person and acknowledgment of what they felt, in addition to what they saw[.]
>
> And the significance of that to me is, when I've let go of the desert from my hands, that that's sort of the moment of completion and a way of bringing some rest to that person.[45]

---

44   United States v. Scott Daniel Warren, Tr., June 5, 2019, 191–192.
45   Ibid, 193–194.

Warren's testimony suggests that this pattern of acts affords rest for the migrants but not release for him. Warren's mourning ritual resembles a form of practiced compassion, a somatic determination to see and feel the good of this life and, in so doing, not to leave it behind but to bind himself to it and bear it along with him.

The ritual, that is, is the expression of a demand approved, a willingness to live with the ghosts that haunt the borderlands and to be initiated into a distinctive form of ethical subjectivity that allows the dead to inform his responsibilities to the living. As Warren explains in what is, perhaps, the most striking line in all his testimony, the bones that he saw on that first search and recovery trip would never leave him:

> When I see people who are going to undertake a crossing of the desert or who are in the desert or who stumble out of the desert into our town, I see these bones at the same time. It's almost like a split screen or something. Not that I see them as bones, but I see that disturbing, disturbing reality of how people who are living can become lost and disappeared to the desert.[46]

This is why Warren was *bound*—"morally, ethically, and spiritually"—to act as he did when he discovered Sacaria-Goday and Perez-Villanueva in the Barn. He had become a neighbor to the dead and, in so doing, had become a neighbor to the presumptive strangers who stumbled into his town. He could not meet them with cool indifference. He could only encounter them as subjects of intense moral concern, vulnerable travelers ever at the threshold between life and death. Perez-Villanueva and Sacaria-Goday were no different from the others. He could surmise what they had been through and the mortal dangers they were likely to face. They, too, might disappear into the Sonoran, never to be heard from again. Thus, when he encountered them, his decision to respond to their need, to provide them with food, water, clothes, and shelter, felt 'choiceless.'[47] To have chosen otherwise would have meant not only to abandon them to death but to stand at odds with the very form of life that had come to define him. He could not abandon them without breaking faith with the dead, without breaking faith with the ritual he had practiced so many times before, without denying the person that he had become. For this 'good Samaritan,' it would have been both fratricide and ethical suicide.

---

46   Ibid, 175.
47   Ibid, 186.

According to the parable, if the law is to become an instrument of mercy and reconcile us to our humanity (and to the divine), it must be reconciled with that good it cannot name. Compassion is the Samaritan's virtue and in compassion's movement, he is confronted by this good. The Samaritan's is not an ecstatic encounter with some abstract transcendence nor a secret rendez-vous with some moral gnosis; instead, it is an embodied experience that brings before him the demand of an embodied other. It does not, that is to say, orient him toward some general conception of humanity but *this* concrete human before his eyes. Thus, compassion does not vivify the law by placing it under the sacralizing tutelage of some higher law. Rather, it calls in for judgment the law's system of names by drawing them into the rich indeterminacy of the par-ticular. The law, read rightly, must be read at the site of the encounter and, at this site, discover its meaning ever anew. Rather than the elements of a closed system, the names the law provides must become the point of contact between the named and the unnamed, the familiar and the strange, the self and the other.

Delivered on the witness stand amid a criminal trial, Warren's eloquent narration of his ethical and spiritual awakening puts a profound issue to the court. US Courts have long recognized the state's sovereign duty and right to determine who should be permitted to cross its borders. This recognition can be traced to the legal fiction established by Chae Chan Ping v. United States, which sees in the alien the specter of threat and vests her exclusion with exis-tential import. Where this fiction comes up short, the state's plenary power in matters of exclusion and removal can be justified according to that right of closure, without which the people's capacity for collective self-determination would be overrun. The result is a reading of the law that makes it a bulwark against the alienated other's ethical demand. Yet, in Warren's testimony, Sacar-ia-Goday and Perez-Villanueva are not presented as figures of enmity whose alienage necessitates their repulsion. Instead, they are presented as fellow con-tingent human animals whose survival depends upon our willingness to hold their lives in common trust. By presenting two 'aliens' in this way, Warren's testimony challenges operative understandings of the alien and invests it with new meaning. By extension, it also reconfigures the responsibilities that per-sist between aliens and citizens. Stranded in forbidding wilderness, the alien is not to be met with violence but with the practices of care necessary to sustain them.

Thus, Warren's testimony allows the other's ethical demand to spill into the courtroom and, by presenting the jurors with the haunting that shapes Warren's own ethical and religious self-understanding, forces a reckoning between the law and the good of the lives it would deny. To return to the language of Luke's parable, the testimony beckons the court to consider the law from within the context of compassion's movement. It achieves its persuasive force only as it draws the law into the rich indeterminacy of the particular, only as it replaces flat stories about illegal aliens, subterfuge, and smuggling with narratives about complex characters with deep-seated motivations. It invites the listener to join Warren in the Barn and to see Sacaria-Goday and Perez-Villanueva's need for potentially life-saving humanitarian aid through his eyes. It invites the listener to see what would become of these men were their needs neglected. After they had seen the bones, after they had felt the desert sand slipping through their fingers, after they had joined migrants in their lonely isolation, could they act differently than Warren? Could they, in good faith, turn these men away without denying something about themselves? By confronting the jurors with these questions, Warren's testimony also invites them to judge whether the law must prioritize the state's compelling interest or create space for actors like Warren to approve the ethical demands before them. To acknowledge this way of seeing and responding to the alienated other as a protected form of religious conscience would be to find in this right of conscience a point whereupon the approval of the other's demand supervenes over the state's interest in regulating its borders and, thereby, interrupts the normal operations of collective self-determination. It would be to acknowledge, however indirectly, that the law needn't function as a bulwark against the other's demand. It might also provide a shield for politically transformative social action that achieves reconciliation across lines of political division. And thus they ruled, acquitting Warren of both harboring charges.

5   The Works of the *Nomikos*

Warren's acquittal on both harboring charges suggests that Kuykendall's effort to cast him as a 'good Samaritan' was a success. Further, it appears to indicate the legal potency of the ethical demand. However, one would err by drawing from this trial the conclusion that the federal government's legally sanctioned powers for exclusion must yield before the excluded other's ethical demand. The matter is still more complex. Whereas Warren's ethical subjectivity is constituted by his response to that good revealed to him in ethical experience, the court's legal decision redounds not to the law's recognition of this same good but its respect for the sincerity of his response to this experience. Put another way, while we might distill from Warren's testimony an account of approval and demand, Warren's religious freedom defense does not turn on the strength of this demand but on his right of conscience for responding to it. To put the matter bluntly, Warren's acquittal did not necessitate Perez-Villanueva and Sacaria-Goday's admission into the United States, nor did it prohibit their exclusion. Their need may have compelled Warren to act. It may even have given rise to a religious conviction that the state could not transgress, but it did not halt the expedited removal process. Consequently, even after Warren's ethical subjectivity has been articulated, there is yet more to be said about his legal subjectivity and about how these two relate to one another.

The issue before the court was not whether or not the other's ethical demand should override the state's power to exclude. Rather, the issue before the court was whether the state's compelling interest in controlling its borders could justify incursions on Warren's sincerely held religious beliefs. This framing of the issue places it squarely within the rubric of autonomy. In the case of criminal harboring, the state's compelling interest is to preserve its authority to regulate the movement of persons across its territorial borders. Although the Constitution does not explicitly assign any such power to the State, as discussed in previous chapters, a series of judicial decisions have given rise to the plenary power doctrine.[48] Simply put, this doctrine assigns the legislative branch the power to determine the terms of admission, exclusion, and removal and charges the executive branch with administering and enforcing them. The federal government's plenary power in matters of admission and exclusion derives, then, from the sovereign state's right and responsibility to define its territory and its membership. It derives its normative significance from the part the state is assigned to facilitate the process of collective self-determination. The state's plenary power, then, is not supposed to be an instance of blind coercive force but of collective autonomy.

Likewise, the defendant's First Amendment rights fit within this process. However, they are distinguished by their regulative function. Legally acknowledged rights articulate that set of entitlements that halt the advance of government power in critical instances that this power threatens to trample over the very convictions by which a member of the polity understands her life's meaning. The notion of 'religious freedom' that traffics in popular discourse derives from the First Amendment's establishment and free exercise clauses, which state that "Congress shall make no law respecting an establishment of religion, or prohibiting the free exercise thereof."[49] Underlying these limitations on

---

48   See Chae Chan Ping v. United States, 130 U.S. 581 (1889) & Fong Yue Ting v. United States, 149 U.S. 698 (1893). The court's refusal to intervene in the federal government's enforcement of the Chinese Exclusion Act of 1882 served to consolidate the federal government's plenary power for purposes of both exclusion and removal.

49   U.S. Const. Amend. I.

state power is a deeper commitment to the 'freedom of conscience.' Commitments to this freedom pre-date the United States Constitution, tracing a tradition from Roger Williams and William Penn to Thomas Jefferson. Jefferson laid the groundwork for the establishment and free exercise clauses enshrined in the Bill of Rights in an earlier piece of Virginia legislation that forbade the establishment of state religion on the grounds that "Almighty God hath created the mind free, and manifested his supreme will that free it shall remain by making it altogether insusceptible of restraint."[50] To be human, that is, is to possess freedom in matters of belief. Laws that would compel or (unduly) constrain belief, then, represent incursions on our humanity. Consequently, if collective self-determination is to be autonomy's expression at the social level, it cannot dispense with individual rights except on pain of self-contradiction. Nevertheless, the polity cannot accommodate every conviction and certainly not every conviction's *exercise*. What convictions can be accommodated and to what extent is the thing left to the courts to determine.

By their nature, jury trials do not afford a direct view of the deliberation that brings about conviction or acquittal. However, the jurors in Warren's trial did receive instructions for adjudicating his case on the grounds of a First Amendment defense. They had to rule based on their beliefs regarding the sincerity of his religious convictions, the government's interest in enforcing the statute, and whether or not the state's enforcement exceeded the least restrictive means of advancing its interest. Whatever they may have believed about the plenary power doctrine, Warren's acquittal suggests that they judged Warren's testimony sincere and the government's action excessively restrictive. This is not to say that the jurors, too, found themselves compelled by Perez-Villanueva and Sacaria-Goday's ethical demands. That issue, after all, was not up for consideration. However, they appear to have been convinced that Warren was convicted of his duty to help them. Concerning the abridgment of Warren's religious exercise, it is conceivable, then, that the jurors ruled that the Government's successful exclusion and removal of Perez-Villanueva and Sacaria-Goday did not require criminalizing Warren. Therefore, a harboring conviction did not appear to the jurors the least restrictive means of pursuing the government's interest. Thus, the case's paradoxical outcome was that as the ethical demand was rendered legible to the court, its unruly heteronomy was recaptured under the principle of autonomy. What, then, can Warren's trial be said to have achieved?

---

50   Thomas Jefferson, "A Bill for Establishing Religious Freedom," June 12, 1779.

Despite taking place in the apparent isolation of a courtroom on the polity's territorial margins, Warren's trial has not failed to capture the attention of theologians and legal scholars interested in its broader significance. Ulrich Schmiedel and Rose Cuison-Villazor suggest that Warren's testimony confronts the law with religion's performative, non-doctrinal elements, opening the way for a novel form of public theology that supports religious freedoms not directly tied to one familiar confession or another.[51] Taking a different tack, Jason A Cade has suggested that Warren's acquittal provides the precedent for something like a 'right of rescue.' Already recognized by some European Courts, 'rights of rescue' protect an individual's right to provide life-saving aid to another, regardless of her citizenship status, as long as the one extending the aid is not remunerated in return.[52] While Warren's trial yielded no such explicit recognition, Cade contends that the jurors' initial failure to convict and their ultimate decision to acquit Warren proposes that many Americans are reticent to brand humanitarian aid as a crime. For Cade, when taken together with No More Deaths' endeavor to cast light on the deadly consequences of border militarization, Warren's acquittal, at the very least, presses Americans to consider that a humane border enforcement policy must include some legal right to rescue.

While a legally recognized right of rescue would fall far short of re-writing US immigration policy or ending PTD, Warren's trial does propose at least one modern strategy for making the law an instrument of compassion. Warren's indictment occurred as part of a broader initiative to crack down on humanitarians in the borderlands.[53] Scholars in the growing field of 'crimmigration' have noted the striking parallels between immigration and criminal law.[54]

---

51   Ulrich Schmiedel & Rose Cuison Villazor, "'No More Deaths': Religious Liberty as a Defense for Providing Sanctuary for Immigrants," in *Christianity and the Law of Migration*, ed. Silas W. Allard, Kristin E. Heyer, & Raj Nadella (New York: Routledge, 2021), 251–275.

52   Jason A. Cade, "'Water is Life!' (and Speech!): Death, Dissent, and Democracy in the Borderlands," *Indiana Law Journal* 96 (Fall 2020): 261–311.

53   Then President Trump's determination to 'unleash' the power of the Border Patrol included a crackdown on the citizens it perceived to be aiding and abetting in human smuggling. To support this work, Attorney General Jeff Sessions, in a 2017 statement, called for every US Attorney's Office, both on the border and in the interior, to designate one Assistant United States Attorney as the Border Security Coordinator for their district. (See "Office of Public Affairs | Attorney General Jeff Sessions Announces the Department of Justice's Renewed Commitment to Criminal Immigration Enforcement | United States Department of Justice," April 11, 2017, https://www.justice.gov/opa/pr/attorney-general-jeff-sessions-announces-department-justice-s-renewed-commitment-criminal.)

54   See César Cuauhtémoc García Hernández, *Crimmigration Law* (Chicago: American Bar Association, 2015)

Among these similarities are their common political function. Criminal convictions achieve a separation between the criminal and the other members of the polity. While the criminal does not lose her citizenship *per se*, she is excluded from many of the practices definitive of full citizenship. Thus, the analogy between criminal and immigration law lies in the application of state power to produce subjects set apart from the normal members of the polity. The criminalization of humanitarians in the borderlands, then, is a legal project with direct political consequences. A right of rescue that disrupts this project represents an instance of agency wherein defendants may utilize the law to press back against the state's power to define who is or is not a member of the polity.

Like a shield, the right of rescue creates a protected legal space within which humanitarians may act without being overwhelmed by a debilitating fear of punishment. In the right of rescue, the law promises to create an interstitial space between the humanitarian and the state. In this interstitial space, the humanitarian is afforded the opportunity to extend relationships of care that acknowledge the vulnerability and mutual interdependency that citizens and migrants, members and non-members, share in common. As for the biblical Samaritan, the movement of compassion reveals the unutterable side of our humanity that these names do not contain. In so doing, it exposes citizens and migrants to the common ground on which new political coalitions may be formed. The other need not be rejected. Migrants need not be abandoned to the Sonoran. Fratricide need not be repeated. Where the migrant's ethical demand is met with approval, the law yet supplies some measure of protection.

However, it bears restating that this shield does not provide perfect cover. It does not extend its protection to the migrants on whose behalf these humanitarians act. As the right of rescue translates the heteronomy of the ethical relationship into an idiom legible to the autonomy of the political relationship, it loses grip of the good that the defendant wills to hold tight. Ultimately, the right of conscience marks the other's simultaneous presence and absence to the law. Her demand thrusts the defendant into the courtroom, yet the courtroom cannot fully make sense of it. Indeed, a witness, like Warren, may speak at length about their sense of duty to another. They may make overtures to the sanctity of the other's life. In this way, they may become the point of contact between the legal and the extra-legal. Their compassion may, as Warren's did, bring those who are meant to stay outside the law inside the law, even if only indirectly. However, the law is not obliged to dignify this life—only the citizen's. The ethical demand does not compel the law any more than the individual. By extension, the politics enacted in the relationships of care between members and non-members prove unstable and fleeting. They are glimpses of a world ordered otherwise.

But a glimpse is not nothing. As it presses us to consider the law's ambivalent service to contending normative regimes, Warren's trial recalls Cover's insight that the law is not merely that which interposes the space between the present and our visions of redemption, it is also a bridge between them. Further, it reveals that the determination of legal meaning does not belong to the organs of state alone. Civil societies, as they contest the ethical and political significance of legal names also play a role in confirming, resisting, and transforming their signification. What occurs in trial courts on the margins of US territory is not a matter of political indifference. To the contrary, it is a politics. In Warren's case, it is a politics that allows the excluded other's ethical demand to become the negative principle in a political dialectics that strains for a more compassionate future. A fleeting victory, therefore, is still a victory. The force of such witness is to reveal that another world is nascently present within our own. Further, it is to reveal that we are not yet wholly bereft of resources for acting in this world's name. This world, driven by compassion and not contempt, can be witnessed in tired old shacks like the Barn. The hostility with which this witness is met testifies that this world ordered otherwise to our own is not yet fully present. Even so, it beckons us forward, revealing the insufficiency of names like 'citizen' and 'alien,' 'member' and 'non-member,' 'insider' and 'outsider' as it calls us to a future where these names have passed away, and we are reconciled to one another and the fullness of our humanity, in all its tension and complexity.

Political Theology in the US–Mexico Borderlands

> He said to me, "Mortal, can these bones live?" I answered, "O Lord
> God, you know." Then he said to me, "Prophesy to these bones and
> say to them: O dry bones, hear the word of the Lord. Thus says the
> Lord God to these bones: I will cause breath to enter you, and you
> shall live. I will lay sinews on you and will cause flesh to come upon
> you and cover you with skin and put breath in you, and you shall
> live, and you shall know that I am the Lord."
>
> —EZEKIEL 37.3–6

∙ ∙ ∙

> The Past carries with it a temporal index by which it is referred to
> redemption. There is a secret agreement between past generations
> and the present one. Our coming was expected on Earth. Like every
> generation that preceded us, we have been endowed with a weak
> messianic power, a power to which the past has a claim. That claim
> cannot be settled cheaply.
>
> —WALTER BENJAMIN

∙ ∙

1   In Failure's Wake

In the United States-Mexico borderlands, we are confronted with the realization that a great effort is failing. During its period of Westward expansion,
American intellectuals endowed the United States' political project with Messianic purpose. "In its magnificent domains of space and time," John L O'Sullivan
prophesied, "the nation of many nations is destined to manifest to mankind
the excellence of divine principles; to establish on earth the noblest temple
ever dedicated to the worship of the Most High—the Sacred and the True."[1]

---

1 John L. O'Sullivan, "The Great Nation of Futurity," *The United States Democratic Review* 6
   (1839): 427.

However, the nation of many nations has not managed to establish this temple without also creating valleys of dry bones. In the Sonoran Desert, under the indifference of a blazing sun, are withered the 'divine principles' that the polity meant to manifest. This nation, which believed it would outbid the people of Israel as God's witness on the earth, has instead reproduced the desolation that was laid out before the prophet Ezekiel.

The bones in the valleys reveal an unwelcome truth about the human condition. We are tempted to think of ourselves as free, creative beings, dignified, and essentially defined by our capacity for self-determination. The great moments of our political histories attest to the truth in this claim. However, we are not just free, creative beings. We are, at the same time, contingent, interdependent animals, defined no less by our vulnerability than by our capacity for self-determination. This is the truth disclosed to us in our encounter with the other. Our refusal to acknowledge the sanctity of this interdependence, and our struggle to wrest ourselves free from the demand it makes upon us, are the shadows cast in our political histories. In all, our history is not a story of our self-overcoming. Instead, it is a story of our reckoning (and, at times, our refusal to reckon) with our condition's riven nature. This reckoning becomes painfully visible in the borderlands. In a crucial sense, the bones in the valleys are not only the migrants' but our own. We cannot send these people to their deaths without, at the same moment, denying our own humanity. Our fates are no less bound to one another's than are bound our creativity and our embodiment, our freedom and our responsibility.

Can these bones live? To ask this question is to face down our riven condition and the perhaps irreconcilable tension it sows between our ethical and political subjectivity. It is to be driven to consider the possibilities and the limits of our politics and ethics and, in meeting with these limits, to hand these domains of life over to that discourse which, from the beginning, has offered us language for articulating them. In the US–Mexico borderlands, theology should not resolve our riven condition. It should ensure that we are haunted by it. This is not to say that political theologies like Manifest Destiny are not theologies, but it is to make the normative assertion that they are pernicious theologies. The gods that such theologies preach and the futures they envision are premised on our alienation from ourselves and one another. Such gods are not worthy of our worship, and such redemption is not worthy of our hopeful longing. To conclude, I aim to draw out the theological import of the preceding chapters and to find in them a case for hope in a region that, for many scholars, has become a place of hopelessness.

2   Sin, Redemption, and the Collectively Self-Determining State

In the first of the preliminary essays with which I began this book, I argued that the political theology that provides the backdrop for most contemporary Christian ethics of migration resembles the political theology articulated in Reinhold Niebuhr's 'Christian Realism.' Niebuhr's realism, in turn, reflected an effort to rethink our politics and our ethics such that they would incorporate a more rigorous understanding of the doctrine of sin. Niebuhr judged that American and European Liberal Protestantism had failed fully to account for this doctrine's anthropological and sociological significance. Consequently, they had adopted a pollyannish theology and historiography that would come to be smashed in the calamity of the world wars. For Niebuhr, the consequence of sin was that there was no natural continuity between our political history and redemption history. The strength of Niebuhr's political theology, then, was the skepticism it brought to bear on theological visions that saw the progressive advances of human society as the vehicle of human redemption.[2] This skepticism is productive not only for identifying the excesses of Liberal Protestantism but also for theologies like Manifest Destiny. Where O'Sullivan encourages us to see in Westward expansion the manifestation of God's Kingdom on earth, Niebuhr's thought challenges us to see a history shot through with irony.[3]

However, by rereading the doctrine of sin from the perspective of the borderlands, specifically as PTD transforms them into a landscape of death, I want to amend Niebuhr's definition of sin. In Niebuhr's view, the "essence" of the human being is "self-determination."[4] This freedom to direct our lives makes us what we are. Sin, by extension, is the perversion of this freedom that follows from the willfully mistaken presumption that we are the center and end of all things. With this presumption, self-determination is reduced to self-assertion. In our self-assertion, we revolt against our creaturely nature, insisting instead to be as gods. The humanitarian crisis in the borderlands makes explicit a critical point that Niebuhr leaves implicit: our self-determination is inseparable from our embodiment, and sin consists no less in a form of axiological egoism than in a violent contempt for this embodiment. As Hannah Arendt identifies in her reading of the story of Cain and Abel, self-determination—the freedom necessary for politics' *vita activa*—is only ever secured by a fratricide.

---

2   This is a species of skepticism similar to the one Ignacio Ellacuría articulates in his writings on 'the pueblo crucificado.'

3   On the fundamental irony of American history see Reinhold Niebuhr, *The Irony of American History* (Chicago: University of Chicago Press, 1952).

4   Reinhold Niebuhr, *The Nature and Destiny of Man: A Christian Interpretation, Vol I: Human Nature* (London: Nisbet & Co LTD, 1941).

By extension, this fratricide, which attempts to extricate the political from the social, pursues its end by denying the social ties that bind embodied animals in common trust.

Read in its totality, however, the story of Cain and Abel encourages us to carry the point further. Cain's violative act is indeed an effort to liberate freedom from responsibility. It gives violent expression to Cain's disdain at the thought of being his brother's keeper. By killing his brother and leaving his bloodied body in the field, Cain puts to death his responsibility and asserts that his essence lies in nothing other than self-determination. Or, at least, this responsibility is what Cain attempts to put to death alongside his brother. Confronted by God and asked about his brother's whereabouts, Cain spits the question back at God, "Am I my brother's keeper?" (Gen. 4.9) Cain's sneering question implies that 'keeping,' and the 'keeping' of the dead especially, are God's responsibilities—not the human being's. The divine imperative that meets Cain, however, is the command to listen, to hear his brother's blood crying out from the ground. With this command, the divine robs the fratricide of any semblance of efficacy. The living are not rid of the dead, and Cain is not rid of his brother. Set to wander the face of the earth like his brother, Abel, who led the itinerant life of the shepherd, Cain is haunted by his brother's ghost. To deny our embodiment, interdependence, and responsibility is not, in fact, to overcome it. The insight to be drawn from this story concerning our conception of sin, then, is that our riven condition may be a necessary condition for the possibility of sin, but it is not its consequence. On the contrary, sin consists of the futile effort to overcome this condition by imagining ourselves, in essence, to be nothing other than self-determining beings.[5] This sin recurs throughout our history with each successive fratricide and each successive effort to exorcise the slain sibling's ghost.

Moreover, Genesis 4 suggests that the violence that follows in sin's wake cannot be separated from the effort to deny our own creatureliness by destroying our neighbor's.[6] To leave Abel's body in the field is to be rid of the

---

5   We might imagine that this dialectic can be inverted, that there is a sin that emerges from the denial of our self-determination. In some respects, PTD's willingness to lash itself to natural necessity may illustrate such a sin. To conceptualize the doctrine of sin in all its dialectical complexity is no mean feat. Arguably, few thinkers in the western tradition have offered so thorough an accounting of this complexity as does Anti-Climacus in Søren Kierkegaard, *The Sickness Unto Death: A Christian Psychological Exposition for Upbuilding and Awakening*, trans. Howard V. Hong & Edna H. Hong (Princeton: Princeton University Press, 1980).

6   Timothy P. Jackson has also suggested that sin might be understood in these terms, see his treatment of *schadenfreude* in Timothy P. Jackson, *Mordecai Would Not Bow Down: Anti-Semitism, the Holocaust, and Christian Supersessionism* (New York: Oxford University Press, 2021).

obligations that the body enjoins upon us. This sort of violence is all too familiar to those dwelling in and sojourning through the borderlands. By leveraging the Sonoran's hostility to human life to enforce a territorial boundary, PTD
weaponizes the fact of embodiment against the migrants who must traverse its
hostile terrain. Further, as thirst, disorientation, and exposure set in, PTD sews
an enmity between migrants and their bodies, forcing them to pursue their
self-determination through reckless gambits that, for thousands, have cost
their lives. Thus, in the Sonoran Desert, where the bodies of members are protected, and the bodies of non-members disappear in the landscape, the fact of
embodiment becomes the thing that separates insiders from outsiders rather
than that which binds them together. Migrants are reduced to their embodiment, and members are permitted to forget their own. Thus, the violence upon
which PTD relies comes to identify the body politic's capacity for self-determination with its willingness to terminate the body of the outsider.

Moreover, PTD's weaponization of the landscape operationalizes this identification in a system of law enforcement that gives sin an objective reality that
consists of more than the bare aggregation of vicious acts. Without a doubt,
PTD was the creation of individual choices. Its organizing logic was the express
product of a partnership between strategists from the Border Patrol and the
Department of Defense's Center for Low-Intensity Conflict. This logic, in turn,
is enacted through a range of other intentional decisions, including collective
decisions to construct border fencing, strategic choices about where personnel should be accumulated, and tactical decisions that individual enforcement
officers make when pursuing migrants through dangerous terrain. Nevertheless, as the desert takes on a central role in executing PTD's cunning logic, it
attains an agency of its own that outstrips that of the Border Patrol or any of its
officers. The sun, the mountains and the valleys, the desert weather systems,
the flora and fauna, these have no knowledge of and no respect for a federal
agency's jurisdiction. They pay no mind to matters of proportionality or the
differing protections owed to refugees or asylum-seekers. Yet, in thousands of
cases, it is the desert that decides who will live and who will die. In PTD, as
Jason De León puts it, the United States government has thrown the switch on
a perpetual motion device that it no longer has the power to stop. Thus, PTD
has become more than the sum of vicious decisions that brought it about and
serve its maintenance. It has become an objective structure of dehumanization, poised in defiant opposition to the coming Reign of God.[7]

---

7   In this respect, the argument advanced in these pages lends further support to Kristin Hey-
    er's claims that a doctrine of sin fixated on the voluntary actions of individual's is inadequate
    for capturing the realities of the present moment. Drawing on a blend of sources from the

However, if God's response to fratricide is to reassert, in opposition to the crime, the ethical relationship that binds the living brother and the slain, then the divine imperative to listen also bears implications for our understanding of the state's role in salvation history. For his part, Niebuhr only affords the state the modest role of restraining the violence brought on by the fall. In his own theology of politics, Robert Heimburger adopts a similar stance, arguing that states are to act as 'humble guards.' In both instances, the state's legitimacy derives from a God-given mandate. Divine sovereignty, then, functions positively in providing grounds for legitimate authority. Whatever glimpse of redemption history affords, by extension, lies in the (admittedly imperfect) peace that the polity secures through coercive force. However, in enforcement strategies like PTD, we glimpse a form of guarding that entrenches violence rather than restraining it. If, as Genesis 4 suggests, God's side is with the brother denied, then what must come to predominate in the borderlands will be a form of negative sovereignty, God's judgment on the fratricidal acts which demarcate the polity's temporal, identarian, and territorial bounds. Those confronted with the dead's ethical demand do not receive new grounds for justifying political sovereignty. On the contrary, as self-determination comes in for judgment, they experience the revocation of any such grounds. The very concept that today justifies the creation and guarding of borders is rendered vicious (and eventually unmade) by PTD. Given our responsibility to the dead, it appears that whatever redemption may be glimpsed in our history does not reveal itself in the state's power to restrain violence but in those moments that declare this violative power to be unnecessary.

Catholic Magisterium and Latin American Liberation Theology, Heyer develops an account of social sin that consists in at least four things. First, to speak of 'social sin' is to speak of the injustices and dehumanizing trends built into the institutions that structure our common life. Second, it is to speak of the operative cultural ideologies and symbols that lend these structures their legitimacy. Third, social sin entails these symbolic system's blinding of the conscience such that it can no longer differentiate between just and unjust. Fourth, then, and following from this blindness, social sin precipitates individual acts that increase injustice and intensify dehumanizing ends. Each of these forms of social sin can be found, Heyer argues, in contemporary migration systems. Indeed, each can be illustrated in the logics, policies, aesthetics, and acts that together constitute PTD. On Heyer's doctrine of social sin, see Kristin Heyer, "Social Sin and Immigration: Good Fences Make Bad Neighbors," *Theological Studies* 71 (2010): 410—36; Kristin Heyer, *Kinship Across Borders: A Christian Ethics of Immigration* (Washington, DC: Georgetown University Press, 2012); & Kristin Heyer, "Migrants Feared and Forsaken: A Catholic Ethic of Social Responsibility," *Interdisciplinary Journal for Religion and Transformation in Contemporary Societies* 6 (2020): 158—70.

3   Weak Messianic Force and the Law

This idea of sovereign negation finds influential expression in the works of Walter Benjamin. "The Kingdom of God," as he puts it in the "Theologico-Political Fragment," "is not the *telos* of the historical dynamic; it cannot be set as a goal." "From the standpoint of history," he continues, "it is not the goal, but the end."[8] This concept's function—this reality's disclosure—in material history is not, first of all, positive but negative. It takes, as Benjamin seems to propose in the "Critique of Violence," the form of a revocation. Here, this revocation is conceived under the name 'divine violence' and counterposed to 'mythical' accounts of violence meant to legitimize the force, power, and control exerted by extant political orders:

> Just as God is opposed to myth in all spheres, so divine violence runs counter to mythic violence. Indeed, divine violence designates in all respects an antithesis to mythic violence. If mythic violence is law-positing, divine violence is law-annihilating; if the former establishes boundaries, the latter boundlessly annihilates them; if mythic violence inculpates and expiates at the same time, divine violence de-expiates; if the former threatens, the latter strikes; if the former is bloody, the latter is lethal in a bloodless manner.[9]

His language verging on the oracular, Benjamin suggests that divine sovereignty's appearance in the historical dialectic imposes a moment of negation. Given his descriptions of 'divine violence's' 'boundlessly' 'law-annihilating' nature, not to mention its 'lethality,' Benjamin's critics have raised concerns that this moment of negation would amount to an all-consuming nihilism.[10]

Hence, Ted A. Smith has argued that if appeals to negative sovereignty are not to be the death of *phronesis*, then the negations effected by divine sovereignty must be determinate rather than general.[11] For Smith, such is the case in the story of Cain and Abel. Here, divine sovereignty is enacted in God's mark on Cain. On the one hand, this mark serves to delegitimize the crime of fratricide. On the other, however, it also serves to delegitimize that violence, which would

---

8   Walter Benjamin, "Theologico-Political Fragment," in *Reflections: Essays, Aphorisms, and Autobiographical Writings*, ed. Peter Demetz (New York: Schocken, 1986), 312.

9   Walter Benjamin, *Toward the Critique of Violence* (Stanford: Stanford University Press, 2021), 57.

10   C.f. Gillian Rose, *Judaism and Modernity: Philosophical Essays* (New York: Verso, 2017).

11   See Ted Smith, "The Mark of Cain: Sovereign Negation and the Politics of God," *Modern Theology* 36 (2020): 56–73.

avenge the crime and allow its effects to spiral out into history. Crucially, however, the sovereign negation enacted by the divine is articulated and shaped in its relation to *this* crime:

> Cain may not be a historical figure, but he is particular. God marks this particular individual to negate the power of his particular sin to shape the theater of political life. The mark is not a negation of all sin, let alone of all human action. It rather says "No" specifically to reiterations of Cain's violence and the violence of vengeance in Abel's name. The determinate quality of negation—not *this*—gives it a distinctive shape that a more generic disenchantment does not offer.[12]

Negative sovereignty, then, may be 'law-destroying.' It may even be 'boundless' in its capacity continually to confront laws with their fratricidal character. However, Smith's reading of Genesis 4 helps us to appreciate that this 'boundlessness' does not follow from a generic rejection of law but a confrontation that occurs within a particular context and which may occur again and again until history's end. Rather than foreclosing on the possibility of meaningful human action, Smith helps us see the divine's act of negative sovereignty as "a shaped invitation to perform the work of politics rather than simply build according to the blueprint supplied by some sovereign power."[13]

In my readings of Genesis 4, I have sought to clarify the 'shaped invitation' being offered to us in the borderlands. The dead's demand confronts us not only with the fratricide that lies at the originating moment of our political order but also with the fratricides that continue to recur into the present. The dead attain their political afterlife by revealing the sinfulness of the border security regime that has enforced US territory for nearly three decades. Nevertheless, the dead do not condemn law *tout court,* and whatever they say about the guarding of borders more generally may only be drawn by way of implication. Moreover, this implication will have to be drawn based on the determinate crime that is being repeated again and again in the Sonoran Desert. Moreover, in my reading of Genesis 4, I have sought to emphasize, in addition to the mark that occupies Smith, the divine imperative to listen. Although *phronesis,* as it is traditionally conceived, presupposes a situation of ambiguity regarding what is to be done, it nevertheless requires some account of the good or goods that occupy the practically wise actor's attention. Even if sovereign negation issues a shaped invitation to perform the work of politics, undertaking this work responsibly

12   Ibid, 72.
13   Ibid, 72–73.

necessitates that the invitation involve some account of the good that is to orient our judgment. It is in the provision of this good, albeit in the moment of its suspension, that the divine command attains its significance. Cain's form of life is shaped by the good of the life he denies. As it sounds in the borderlands today, the divine command to listen asserts that any emergent notion of political responsibility must be constituted by the demand of the excluded outsider. Our body politic must seek out practices by which to settle the debt it accrues in the ever-growing ledger of the dead.

Whereas Genesis 4 presents us with a story of responsibility refused, I have turned to Luke 10 and the parable of the Samaritan for an account of what it looks like to see this good approved. On the road between Jerusalem and Jericho, the Samaritan is met with the ethical demand put to him by a wounded traveler. Like the story of Cain and Abel, the story of the Samaritan and the sojourner is about particular travelers on a specific road. Where it differs is in the Samaritan's response to the good of the life with which he is confronted. This response, in turn, illustrates an ideal vision of law in which its language supplies the field for mediating between freedom and responsibility. On the one hand, the other's demand may have a negative effect. It may challenge our tacit understanding of legal names and demand new interpretations of legal rules. Nevertheless, it does not issue this challenge in the interest of an interminable nihilism but rather to reorient us to that unutterable good, which is the law's ground and limit. Only insofar as the law equips us to grapple with this good does it reconcile us to our humanity. In the borderlands, such a reading of the law is not without difficulty. Contemporary legal scholars, professionals, and judges may no longer generally assume that law and morality share a common foundation or end. Nevertheless, in the language of rights and in these rights' assertion, the ethical demand makes itself felt upon the court. It supplies the impetus for uses of the law that, at least, create interstitial spaces between persons and the state. In this interstitial space, actors retain a measure of agency to resist the state's power to bind, separate, admit, and exclude. The victories such a reading of the law would achieve are fleeting, nevertheless, the space they open, for however long, is one wherein we may glimpse the possibility of a world ordered otherwise than our own.

In this respect, a political theology developed in the borderlands allows us to rethink law's eschatological significance. It permits us to think of the law as more than a mere expression of coercive force, a violent impediment to be overcome. As Robert Cover suggests, the law may indeed be that which, in one moment, interposes and bridges the space between our unredeemed present and our visions of redemption. Yet, by interposing this space, it provides us with a field for mediating between ethical demand and political right.[14] It furnishes us with a language and procedure for confronting the tension between our ethical and political subjectivity and the riven condition to which this tension attests. In the skirmishes that play out in the space that law creates, we may witness the live contests playing out between countervailing visions of redemption. Where legal language is deployed to create a bulwark between the polity and the outsider's demand, we may intimate a vision of redemption premised on a world without the other. We may intimate a vision of redemption where the fratricide's success is finally realized. However, where the law's language is deployed to create defenses for humanitarian interventions, where it serves as a defense for those who would act in responsive solidarity with the outsider, it strains for a glimpse of a world where names like 'citizen' and 'alien' no longer determine what lives are to be dignified and what lives may be discarded with indifference. The law so used, to borrow another expression from Benjamin, does more than to assert boundaries; it becomes an instrument of 'weak messianic force,' a language for expressing, in word and act, the conviction that, for those who PTD has killed, things could and should have been otherwise.[15]

4   A Case for Hope

If the besetting danger that faces us in the borderlands is an acosmic nihilism, a despair that the grave injustices of our world cannot be overcome, then what does such a political theology as the one sketched in this book accomplish? Would we not, as Miguel De La Torre suggests, be wiser, if not more responsible, if we were to embrace hopelessness? Perhaps, as De La Torre suggests, we would be foolhardy to imagine that, with enough careful argumentation or

---

14   Jayne Svenungsson captures a similar insight in her treatments of the antinomianism that shows itself in much continental political theology. Whereas notable figures like Alain Badiou and Giorgio Agamben see the law as little more than codified coercive force deployed in the service of the state, Svenungsson recovers Judaism's conviction that the law is not merely an assemblage of prohibitions and prescriptions but an instrument for reconciliation with the divine. That is, whereas Badiou and Agamben present law as sin, Svenungsson presents the 'law as grace.' See Jayne Svenungsson, *Divining History: Prophetism, Messianism, and the Divining of the Spirit*, trans. Steven Donovan (New York: Berghahn, 2016), n.b., 151–202; & Jayne Svenungsson, "Law and Liberation: Critical Notes on Agamben's Political Messianism," *European Judaism* 50, no. 1 (2017), 68–77.

15   Walter Benjamin, "On the Concept of History," in *Illuminations: Essays and Reflections*, ed. Hannah Arendt (New York: Schocken, 2007), 254.

civil resistance, we would succeed in changing a United States policy that has done so much to enrich the United States' neo-colonial empire. The time that has passed since PTD's implementation doubtless suggests that such change is improbable. Little substantive change has been made to the United States' immigration laws since the early 1990s. Whatever promises principled candidates might make on the campaign trail, these reforms consistently seem to be the first ones given up at the bargaining table. At the time of this writing, the fate of President Joe Biden's promised US Citizenship Act, an act aimed at "restoring humanity and American values to our immigration system," provides a disappointing confirmation of this trend. For years now, the act has remained stuck in committees. California Representative Linda Sánchez's 2023 effort to revive it has also met with failure. Meanwhile, the Biden Administration has remained in line with the administrations of the four preceding presidents, continuing to pour federal dollars into border security efforts, including dollars that have supported the construction of border fencing designed to press migrant traffic into the wilderness. To call legislative change improbable seems to be a grave understatement. However, if there is one more thing to learn from Ezekiel's prophecy, it is that hope does not bear on the category of the probable and the improbable, but on that of the possible and the impossible. On this point, we may yet provide a response to the feeling of hopelessness that confronts us in the Sonoran.

Admittedly, to meet the charge that change is improbable with the claim that it is, perhaps, impossible, is a deeply counterintuitive rejoinder. However, even where human agency runs up against its limits, the grounds for hope endure as long as theology can resist the temptation of believing that it is all up to us. This temptation is not so easy to resist. Its immediate plausibility is a mark that we are living in a 'secular age.' As Charles Taylor observes, we need not think of secularization, today, as though it must consist in the disappearance of God-talk or the gradual extinction of religious institutions. Rather, we might do well to think of secularization in terms of practical reason, as the growing assumption that our lives are lived in an immanent order disconnected from its transcendent frame.[16] This disconnection means, on the one hand, that it is up to us to determine the nature of the good independent of appeals to a higher authority or order. On the other, however, the disconnection suggests that whatever degree of realization is possible for the ideals we may identify extends only so far as our agency's limit. This assumption's potency is displayed in the seemingly obvious statement that history is a story of human endeavor. However, it is also reproduced in the assumptions that

---

16   Charles Taylor, *A Secular Age* (Cambridge: The Belknap Press of Harvard University, 2007).

theology is a purely normative discourse that can only speak about what *ought* to be. Throughout this book, I have asserted that, in the borderlands, the 'real' itself is a contested thing. Moreover, whether we acknowledge them or not, theological claims have always played roles not only in providing norms for our reality, but for describing reality itself. Ezekiel's thirty-seventh chapter reasserts emphatically theology's role in constituting our idea of what is real and what is possible.

Read from within our immanent frame, Ezekiel's prophecy may indeed come to us as a missive from another world. The prophet's vision is a dogged proclamation that, in the valley of dry bones, redemption will ultimately depend upon divine agency rather than human agency:

> Thus says the Lord God to these bones: I will cause breath to enter you, and you shall live. I will lay sinews on you and will cause flesh to come upon you and cover you with skin and put breath in you, and you shall live, and you shall know that I am the Lord. (Ezek. 37.5–6)

However, this divine declaration does not describe an act that will be withheld for some setting that belongs to the hereafter. Ezekiel's prophetic mission is launched amid a decidedly this-worldly political calamity and demands a redemption to match it. Confronted with the question, "Mortal, can these bones live?" he replies, "O Lord, you know." (37.3) The reply is a direct appeal to divine agency. In the valley of dry bones, God meets this appeal with action. God breathes life into death. God lays flesh to bone. God sets right history's calamities and ushers in redemption. Ezekiel's prophetic mission, for its part, practices the conviction that the possibility of redemption is premised neither on the strength of human will nor the breadth of human imagination. The hope that Ezekiel's prophecy calls for is not an optimistic expectation based on a clear-eyed assessment of the probability of some outcome. Hope, here, has nothing to do with what is probable. In the valley of dry bones, Ezekiel stands after the end of his own history. "Our bones are dried up, and our hope is lost; we are utterly cut off." (37.11) Amidst this desolation, the problem is not that it is *improbable* that the bones laid out around him will be returned to life. It is *impossible for them to* be returned to life. Yet the hope that Ezekiel preaches finds its ground in the agency of a God for whom nothing is impossible.

When the prophet's speech concludes, silence returns to the valley. But this silence does not endure. Suddenly there is a noise, a rattling, quiet at first, but quickly growing. As the sound begins to echo through the valley, the scattered bones are drawn together, re-membered. Just as quickly, they are covered in sinew, flesh, and skin. Ezekiel no longer stands in a valley of bones, but amid a vast multitude of bodies. "Prophesy to the breath," God speaks to Ezekiel, "prophesy, mortal, and say to the breath: Thus says the Lord God: Come from the four winds, O breath, and breathe upon these slain, that they may live." (37.9) Ezekiel speaks once more. Once more, the prophecy is fulfilled. The breath comes into them, and they live. In Ezekiel's thirty-seventh chapter, we encounter hope as a divine imperative and a human impossibility. Nevertheless, the prophet's central task is to anticipate redemption by declaring it—even though its possibility has already been foreclosed upon. It is this radical form of hope, this hope that appeals to the divine to reconstitute our assumptions about the real and the unreal, the possible and the impossible, that we are called to practice in the borderlands.

A world between worlds, the borderlands themselves press us to take up this form of hope. Here, the real is unsettled and uncertain. The very activity of border enforcement underscores the contingency and insecurities of the present international order. The system of nation-states portrayed on political maps is not a brute fact. It is a contingent reality that must continually be asserted and reasserted. The visions of redemption glimpsed in the borderlands, however, are not only visions of what should be but of what could be. Humanitarian interventions and tactical uses of the law point to the possibility of a world that redeems the sins deemed necessary by the present order. I have argued that we may catch glimpses of this world if we turn our focus away from the legislators at the national center and attend instead to humanitarians, artists, and litigators working tirelessly at the margins of American territory. The despair that threatens our hope for the borderlands, especially as De La Torre articulates it, stems from a failure to fully consider the prophetic impact of these actors' works. However, if, on the other hand, we can see these actors as exercising a form of agency on the political, then we can see in them the reassertion of an eschatologically freighted vision of law such as Cover describes. We can see in the Sonoran Desert twenty-first-century Samaritans, who find in the law a language for grappling with the excluded other's demand and, in so doing, attest to the Lukan parable's contemporary legacy. As long as we can imagine forms of political agency that do not rely for their efficacy on legislative policy change, then the possibility of redemption endures, and, against all improbability, so too does our cause for hope.

5   The Bones in the Valley

For decades, American politicians have used the US–Mexico Borderlands as a stage for political theater. Some have staged productions about a border out of control and a nation on the brink of collapse. Others have used this stage to present themselves as strong men, capable of preserving the United States by dint of will. Such dramas naturally require the construction of accompanying set-pieces, towering walls, and flooded detention centers. Still, others have used this stage to pitch themselves as compassionate characters prepared to extend their hospitality to the huddled masses they discover there. Whatever adjustments these characters have made to the stage remain underdeveloped. Perhaps because they, too, benefit from the stage pieces developed by their counterparts. The stage, so dressed, provides a striking opportunity for juxtaposition. However, this theater belongs to a cast of actors far more extensive than the ensemble of politicians hailing from the national center.

There is an old superstition among actors that every theater is haunted and that when the theater is emptied, the ghosts put on performances of their own. The borderlands are no exception. The Sonoran Desert is a haunted place. Here, the dead, no less than the living, have things to show us. They ironize the notion that our essence lies in our capacity for self-determination. They reveal to us that sin which lies in our contempt for our embodiment and the violence that this contempt breeds at the boundaries of the body politic. Of course, this violence is not limited to the borderlands but extends into the interior. In many ways, the dead hold up a mirror that allows us to see the vices of callousness, dominion, avarice, and racism that corrode American life at the borderline, in the interior, and abroad. If these vices are to be resisted and if our politics are to account for the fullness of our humanity, then those willing to see and to hear the ghosts must become haunted as well. A political theology responsive to the United States-Mexico borderlands should serve to enforce this haunting.

There are bones in the valleys. There are thousands of them. For all its beauty, the Sonoran is an extreme environment. Despite its beauty, PTD has rendered this environment horrific, both for those whose lives it takes and for those who are met with their demand. Can these bones live? Can this ground and those who walk it be redeemed? If the outsider's demand is met as a contemptuous encumbrance upon our freedom, if it is seen as a threat to our capacity for self-determination, then these questions must be answered in the negative. However, as PTD's failures reveal, denying our responsibility for the excluded other and attempting to exorcise her ghost is a futile and self-destructive endeavor. The body abandoned in the wilderness is a declaration of the sickness consuming the body politic. Therefore, we must find a way to be haunted, to grant the dead their political afterlife. Their demand must come to shape our ethical subjectivity. It must inspire action on behalf of those who are now living yet might nevertheless come to share their fate. As it makes its way into the political, this demand must saturate our laws, making our courtrooms theaters for the expression of our eschatological longing. And where our striving's end leaves our longings unfulfilled, we must sound the question back to heaven, "Son of Man, can these bones live?"

References

Adorno, Theodor W. "On Kierkegaard's Doctrine of Love." *Studies in Philosophy and Social Science* 8, no. 3 (1939): 413–29.

Agamben, Giorgio. *Pilate and Jesus*. Translated by Adam Kotsko. Cultural Memory in the Present. Stanford: Stanford University Press, 2015.

Agamben, Giorgio. *The Time That Remains: A Commentary on the Letter to the Romans*. Translated by Patricia Dailey. Cultural Memory in the Present. Stanford: Stanford University Press, 2005.

Ahn, Ilsup. "Christian Realism, Human Vulnerability, and the US Immigration Crisis." *CrossCurrents* 71, no. 2 (2021): 115–36. https://www.jstor.org/stable/27090292.

Ahn, Ilsup. *Religious Ethics and Migration: Doing Justice to Undocumented Workers*. Routledge Studies in Religion 34. New York: Routledge, 2014.

Alito, Samuel. Department of Homeland Security et al v. Thuraissigiam, 591 (U.S. Supreme Court 2020).

Allard, Silas W. "Asylum: The Constraint of a Definition and the Agency of a Claim." Moral Agency Under Constraint, August 3, 2020. https://scholarblogs.emory.edu/moralagency2019/2020/08/03/claiming-asylum-as-moral-agency/.

Alonso, Alexandra Délano, and Benjamin Nienass. "Deaths, Visibility, and Responsibility: The Politics of Mourning at the US–Mexico Border." *Social Research* 83, no. 2 (2016): 421–51. https://www.jstor.org/stable/44282194.

American Immigration Council. "Fact Sheet: The Cost of Immigration Enforcement and Border Security." Washington, DC: American Immigration Council, January 2021.

American Immigration Council. "The Cost of Immigration Enforcement and Border Security," September 23, 2013. https://www.americanimmigrationcouncil.org/research/the-cost-of-immigration-enforcement-and-border-security.

Amstutz, Mark R. *Just Immigration: American Policy in Christian Perspective*. Grand Rapids: William B. Eerdmans Publishing Company, 2017.

Andersen, Matthew. "The Myth of Reinhold Niebuhr's Political Realism." University of Oxford: Centre for Intellectual History. Accessed September 19, 2023. https://intellectualhistory.web.ox.ac.uk/article/the-myth-of-reinhold-niebuhrs-political-realism.

Andreas, Peter. *Border Games: Policing the US–Mexico Divide*. Ithaca: Cornell University Press, 2009.

Anzaldúa, Gloria. *Light in the Dark / Luz En Lo Oscuro: Rewriting Identity, Spirituality, Reality*. Edited by Analouise Keating. Latin America Otherwise: Languages, Empires, Nations. Durham: Duke University Press, 2015.

Anzaldúa, Gloria. *Borderlands / La Frontera: The New Mestiza*. San Francisco: Aunt Lute Books, 1999.

Arendt, Hannah. *The Human Condition*. Chicago: The University of Chicago Press, 1998.

Arendt, Hannah. *On Revolution*. New York: Penguin Books, 1990.

Aristotle. "Politics." In *Writings from the Complete Works: Politics, Economics, Constitution of Athens*, edited by Johnathan Barnes, translated by Melissa Lane. Princeton: Princeton University Press, 2017.

Aristotle, Jonathan Barnes, and Anthony Kenny. *Aristotle's Ethics: Writings from the Complete Works*. Princeton: Princeton University Press, 2014.

"Arizona OpenGIS for Deceased Migrants." Accessed December 7, 2023. https://humaneborders.info/.

Associated Press. "Border Officials Warn of Heat Dangers in South Arizona." AP News, June 11, 2021. https://apnews.com/article/az-state-wire-arizona-immigration-environment-and-nature-cda9efe39c45b1f5cdd2187390c2d730.

Auchter, Jessica. *The Politics of Haunting and Memory in International Relations*. New York: Routledge, 2017.

Austin, John. *Lectures on Jurisprudence, or, the Philosophy of Positive Law*. London: John Murray, 1885.

Badiou, Alain. *The Rebirth of History: Times of Riots and Uprisings*. Translated by Gregory Elliott. New York: Verso, 2013.

Badiou, Alain. *Saint Paul: The Foundation of Universalism*. Translated by Ray Brassier. Cultural Memory in the Present. Stanford: Stanford University Press, 2003.

Balmer, Crispian. "Italy Impounds Three Rescue Ships as Migrant Numbers Soar." *Reuters*, August 23, 2023, sec. Europe. https://www.reuters.com/world/europe/italy-impounds-three-rescue-ships-migrant-numbers-soar-2023-08-23/.

Bauböck, Rainer. "Mobility and Migration: Physical, Contextual, and Perspectival Interpretations." In *Contested Concepts in Migration Studies*, by Ricard Zapata-Barrero, Dirk Jacobs, and Riva Kastoryano. Routledge Series on Global Order Studies. New York: Routledge Press, 2022.

Benhabib, Seyla. *Another Cosmopolitanism*. Edited by Robert Post. The Berkeley Tanner Lectures. New York: Oxford University Press, 2006.

Benjamin, Walter. *Toward the Critique of Violence*. Edited by Peter Fenves and Julia Ng. Stanford: Stanford University Press, 2021.

Benjamin, Walter. "Theses on the Philosophy of History." In *Illuminations: Essays and Reflections*, by Walter Benjamin, 253–64. edited by Hannah Arendt. New York: Schocken books, 2007.

Benjamin, Walter. "The Task of the Translator." In *Selected Writings: Volume 1: 1913–1926*, edited by Marcus Bullock and Michael W. Jennings, 253–63. Cambridge: The Belknap Press, 1996.

Benjamin, Walter. "Theologico-Political Fragment." In *Reflections: Essays, Aphorisms, and Autobiographical Writings*, edited by Peter Demetz, 312–13. New York: Schocken, 1986.

Benjamin, Walter. *Reflections: Essays, Aphorisms, and Autobiographical Writings*, edited by Peter Demetz. New York: Harcourt Press, 1978.

Bensaïd, Daniel. "Alain Badiou and the Miracle of the Event." In *Think Again, Alain Badiou and the Future of Philosophy*, edited by Peter Hallward, 94–105. New York: Continuum, 2004.

Blackstone, William. *Commentaries on the Laws of England in Four Books*, 1753.

Blake, Michael. *Justice, Migration, and Mercy*. New York: Oxford University Press, 2022.

Bock, Melissa. "Strict Border Policies Contribute to Rising Immigrant Deaths." National Public Radio, July 2, 2022. https://www.npr.org/2022/07/02/1109557989/strict-border-policies-contribute-to-rising-immigrant-deaths#:~:text=Immigration%20advocates%20warn%20that%20strict,immigration%20for%20the%20Houston%20Chronicle.

Bosman, Hendrik L. "Loving the Neighbour and the Resident Alien in Leviticus 19 as Ethical Redefinition of Holiness." *Old Testament Essays* 31, no. 3 (2018): 571–90.

Bosniak, Linda. *The Citizen and the Alien: Dilemmas of Contemporary Membership*. 2. printing, 1. paperback printing. Princeton, NJ: Princeton University Press, 2008.

Bovon, Francois. "The Samaritan or Eternal Life as an Inheritance." In *Luke 2: A Commentary on Luke 9:51–19:27*, edited by Francois Bovon, Helmut Koester, and Donald S. Deer, 49–65. Minneapolis: Augsburg Fortress Press, 2013.

Boyle, James. "Thomas Hobbes and the Invented Tradition of Positivism: Reflections on Language, Power, and Essentialism." *University of Pennsylvania Law Review* 135 (1987): 383–426.

Brown, Wendy. *Walled States, Waning Sovereignty*. Princeton: Princeton University Press, 2017.

Burggraeve, Roger. "'Am I My Brother's Keeper': On the Meaning and Depth of Our Responsibility." *Ephemeredies Theologicae Lovanienses* 84 (2008): 341–61.

Butler, Judith. *Frames of War: When Is Life Grievable?* New York: Verso Press, 2009.

Cade, Jason A. "'Water Is Life!' (And Speech!): Death, Dissent, and Democracy in the Borderlands." *Indiana Law Journal* 96 (Fall 2020): 261–311.

Callon, Michael, and John Law. "Agency and the Hybrid Collectif." In *Mathematics, Science, and Postclassical Theory*, edited by Barbara Hernstein Smith and Arkady Plotnitsky, 95–117. Durham: Duke University Press, 1997.

Carroll, Rory. "US Border Patrol Routinely Sabotages Water Left for Migrants, Report Says." *The Guardian*, January 17, 2018, sec. US news. https://www.theguardian.com/us-news/2018/jan/17/us-border-patrol-sabotage-aid-migrants-mexico-arizona.

Carter, Warren. "Singing in the Reign: Performing Luke's Songs and Negotiating the Roman Empire (Luke 1–2)." In *Luke-Acts and Empire: Essays in Honor of Robert L. Brawley*, edited by David Rhoads, David Esterline, and Jae Won Lee, 23–43. Eugene: Pickwick Publications, 2011.

Center, Colibri. "About Us—Colibrí Center." Accessed December 7, 2023. https://colibricenter.org/about/.

Cocks, Joan. "On Commonality, Nationalism, and Violence: Hannah Arendt, Rosa Lux-
    embug, and Frantz Fanon." *Women in German Yearbook* 12 (1996): 39–51.
Collins, Rainer C. United States v. Scott Daniel Warren (United States District Court for
    the District of Arizona 2019).
Committee on Homeland Security and Government Affairs. "Southwest Border: Border
    Patrol's Missing Migrant Program." Government Accountability Office, 2022.
Cornelius, Wayne A. "Death at the Border: Efficacy and Unintended Consequences
    of US Immigration Control Policy." *Population and Development Review* 27 (2001):
    661–85.
Court of Justice of the European Union. "Ships of Humanitarian Organisations System-
    atically Carrying out Activities Relating to the Search for and Rescue of Persons at
    Sea May Be Subject to Controls by the Port State." Press Release. Luxembourg: Court
    of Justice of the European Union, August 1, 2022.
Cover, Robert. "Nomos and Narative." *Harvard Law Review* 97 (November 1983): 4–68.
Critchley, Simon. *Infinitely Demanding: Ethics of Commitment, Politics of Resistance.*
    New York: Verso, 2012.
Crossan, John Dominic. *In Parables: The Problem of the Historical Jesus.* Sonoma: Pole-
    bridge Press, 1992.
Cuauhtémoc García Hernández, César. *Crimmigration Law.* Chicago: American Bar
    Association, 2015.
Cuéllar, Gregory. *Resacralizing the Other at the US–Mexico Border.* New York: Rout-
    ledge, 2020.
Cuéllar, Gregory. "Contesting State Violence: The Bible, The Public Good, and Divinely
    Sanctioned Violence in the Borderlands." In *La Violencía and the Hebrew Bible: The
    Politics and Histories of Biblical Hermeneutics on the American Continent,* edited by
    Pablo R. Andiñach and Susanne Scholz, 39–58. Atlanta: Society of Biblical Litera-
    ture, 2016.
Culpepper, R. Allen. "Luke." In *The New Interpreter's Bible: A Commentary in Twelve Vol-
    umes,* Vol. 9. Nashville: Abingdon Press, 1994.
Davis, Andrew R. "A Near Eastern Treaty Parallel to Ezekiel's Dry Bones." *Vetus Testa-
    mentum* 68, no. 2 (2018): 337–45. https://doi.org/https://doi.org/10.1163/15685330-
    12341315.
De Certeau, Michel. *The Practice of Everyday Life.* Translated by Steven Rendall. Berkely:
    University of California Press, 1984.
De Genova, Nicholas. "Spectacles of Migrant 'Illegality': The Scene of Exclusion, the
    Obscene of Inclusion." *Ethnic and Racial Studies* 36, no. 7 (2013): 1180–98. https://
    doi.org/10.1080/01419870.2013.783710.
De La Torre, Miguel A. *Embracing Hopelessness.* Minneapolis: Fortress Press, 2017.
De La Torre, Miguel A. *The US Immigration Crisis: Toward an Ethics of Place.* Eugene:
    Cascade Press, 2016.

De León, Jason. *The Land of Open Graves: Living and Dying on the Migrant Trail*. Oakland: University of California Press, 2015.

Department of Homeland Security. "Vision and Strategy 2020: U.S. Customs and Border Protection Strategic Plan." Washington, DC: Department of Homeland Security, 2020.

Departments of the Army and the Air Force. "Military Operations in Low Intensity Conflict." Washington, DC, December 5, 1990.

Devereaux, Ryan. "The Unraveling of the Conspiracy Case Against No More Deaths Volunteer Scott Warren." The Intercept, August 10, 2019. https://theintercept.com/2019/08/10/scott-warren-trial/.

Devoid, Curt Prendergast, Alex. "Arizona Daily Star Investigation: Death in the Desert." Arizona Daily Star, December 2, 2021. https://tucson.com/news/local/subscriber/arizona-daily-star-investigation-death-in-the-desert/collection_c013265c-4896-11ec-afe5-eb4b401c87df.html.

Dionysius of Halicarnassus. *Antiquities of Rome*. Translated by Earnest Cary. Vol. 1. 7 vols. Cambridge: Harvard University Press, 1937.

Dobbins, James, Miriam Jordan, and J. David Goodman. "Texas Migrant Deaths: 51 Migrants Dead After Overheated Truck Is Abandoned in Texas." *The New York Times*, June 28, 2022, sec. U.S. https://www.nytimes.com/live/2022/06/28/us/texas-migrants-dead.

Doss, Erika. *Memorial Mania: Public Feeling in America*. Chicago: University of Chicago Press, 2010.

Dunn, Timothy J. *Militarization of the U.S.-Mexico Border, 1978–1992: Low Intensity Conflict Doctrine Comes Home*. Austin: CMAS Books, 1996.

Ellacuría, Ignacio. "The Crucified People: An Essay in Historical Soteriology." In *Ignacio Ellacuría: Essays on History, Liberation, and Salvation*, edited by Michael E. Lee. Maryknoll: Orbis Books, 2013.

Ellrod, Bryan M. "The Remembrance of Dismembered Bodies: The Promise and Challenge of Mourning in the Southwestern Borderlands." *Body and Religion* 5, no. 2 (2021): 204–21. https://doi.org/10.1558/bar.22145.

Ellrod, Bryan M. ""God and the Illegal Alien: United States Immigration Law and a Theology of Politics. By Robert W. Heimburger. Cambridge: Cambridge University Press, 2018. Pp 258 $110.00 (Cloth). ISBN: 9781107176621." *Journal of Law and Religion* 35, no. 2 (2020): 331–34.

Enç, Berent. *How We Act: Causes, Reasons, and Intentions*. New York: Oxford University Press, 2003.

Ettinger, Patrick W. *Imaginary Lines: Border Enforcement and the Origins of Undocumented Immigration, 1882–1930*. Austin: University of Texas Press, 2009.

Farmer, Lindsay. "Trials." In *Law and the Humanities: An Introduction*, edited by Austin Sarat, Matthew Anderson, and Catherine O. Frank, 455–77. New York: Cambridge University Press, 2010.

Feinberg, Joel. "The Nature and Value of Rights." *The Journal of Value Inquiry* 4 (1970): 245–57.

Fields, Stephen J. Chae Chan Ping v. United States, 130 581 (U.S. Supreme Court 1889).

Fisch, Jörg. *The Right of Self-Determination of Peoples: The Domestication of an Illusion.* New York: Cambridge University Press, 2015.

Frick, Peter. *Paul in the Grips of the Philosophers: The Apostle and Contemporary Continental Philosophy.* Minneapolis: Fortress Press, 2013.

Fuller, Lon. "Positivism and Fidelity to Law: A Reply to Professor Hart." *Harvard Law Review* 71 (1958): 630–72.

García-Rivera, Alex. *The Community of the Beautiful: A Theological Aesthetics.* Collegeville: The Liturgical Press, 1999.

Gerhardsson, Birger. "The Good Samaritan—The Good Shepherd?" *Coniectanea Neotestamentica* 16 (1958): 3–31.

Gignac, Alain. "Taubes, Badiou, Agamben: Contemporary Receptions of Paul by Non-Christian Philosophers." In *Reading Romans with Contemporary Philosophers and Theologians,* edited by David Odell-Scott, 155–211. New York: T&T Clark, 2007.

Godwin Phelps, Teresa. "No Place to Go, No Story to Tell: The Missing Narratives of the Sanctuary Movement." *Washington and Lee Law Review* 48 (1991): 123–38.

Gomez, Adam. "Deus Vult: John L. O'Sullivan, Manifest Destiny, and American Democratic Messianism." *American Political Thought* 1 (September 2012): 236–62.

Goodman, Lenn E. *Love Thy Neighbor as Thyself.* New York: Oxford University Press, 2008.

Gourgues, Michel. "The Priest, the Levite, and the Samaritan Revisited: A Critical Note on Luke 10:31–35." *Journal of Biblical Literature* 117 (1998): 709–13.

Greenberg, Moshe. *Ezekiel 21–37: A New Translation with Introduction and Commentary.* Vol. 22A. The Anchor Bible. New York: Bantam Doubleday Dell Publishing Group, 1997.

Hart, HLA. *The Concept of Law.* New York: Oxford University Press, 1994.

Hart, HLA. "Positivism and the Separation of Law and Morals." *Harvard Law Review* 71 (1958): 593–629.

Hartman, Sadiya. *Scenes of Subjection: Terror, Slavery, and Self-Making in Nineteenth Century America.* New York: Oxford University Press, 1997.

Heimburger, Robert W. *God and the Illegal Alien: United States Immigration Law and a Theology of Politics.* Cambridge Studies in Law and Christianity. New York: Cambridge University Press, 2018.

Hernández, Arelis R., Nick Miroff, and Maria Sacchetti. "46 Migrants Found Dead in Texas inside Sweltering Tractor-Trailer." *Washington Post,* June 28, 2022. https:// www.washingtonpost.com/nation/2022/06/27/migrants-dead-texas/.

Heyer, Kristin. "Migrants Feared and Forsaken: A Catholic Ethic of Social Responsibility." *Interdisciplinary Journal for Religion and Transformation in Contemporary Societies* 6 (2020): 158–70.

Heyer, Kristin. "A Catholic Ethic for Immigration." *Health Progress* 98 (2017): 31–34.

Heyer, Kristin. *Kinship Across Borders: A Christian Ethics of Immigration*. Washington, DC: Georgetown University Press, 2012.

Heyer, Kristin. "Social Sin and Immigration: Good Fences Make Bad Neighbors." *Theological Studies* 71 (2010): 410–36.

Hitler, Adolf. *Mein Kompf*. Boston: Mariner Books, 1999.

Hobbes, Thomas, and Christopher Brooke. *Leviathan*. Penguin Classics. Harmondsworth, Meddlesex: Penguin Books, 2017.

Jackson, Timothy P. *Mordecai Would Not Bow Down: Anti-Semitism, the Holocaust and Christian Supersessionism*. New York: Oxford University Press, 2021.

Jackson, Timothy P. *Political Agape: Christian Love and Liberal Democracy*. Emory University Studies in Law and Religion. Grand Rapids, Michigan: William B. Eerdmans Publishing Company, 2015.

Jeanrond, Werner G. *Reasons to Hope*. New York: T&T Clark, 2020.

Jefferson, Thomas. A Bill For Establishing Religious Freedom (1779).

Jenson, Robert W. *Ezekiel*. The Brazos Theological Commentary on the Bible. Grand Rapids: Brazos Press, 2009.

Jordan, Miriam. "An Arizona Teacher Helped Migrants. Jurors Couldn't Decide If It Was a Crime." *The New York Times*, June 11, 2019, sec. U.S. https://www.nytimes.com/2019/06/11/us/scott-warren-arizona-deaths.html.

Kai, Lauri. "Embracing the Chinese Exclusion Case: An International Law Approach to Racial Exclusions." *William & Mary Law Review* 59 (2018): 2617–62.

Kaiser, Walter C. "Leviticus." In *The New Interpreter's Bible: A Commentary in Twelve Volumes*, 1:985–1004. Nashville: Abingdon Press, 1994.

Kaminsky, Joel. "Loving One's (Israelite) Neighbor: Election and Commandment in Leviticus 19." *Interpretation* 62 (2008): 123–32.

Kant, Immanuel. *Critique of Practical Wisdom*. Translated by Mary Gregor. New York: Cambridge University Press, 2005.

Kazen, Thomas. "The Good Samaritan and a Presumptive Corpse." *Svensk Exegetisk Årsbok* 71 (2006): 131–44.

Kierkegaard, Søren. *Works of Love*. Translated by Howard V. Hong and Edna H. Hong. Princeton: Princeton University Press, 1998.

Kierkegaard, Søren. *The Sickness Unto Death: A Christian Psychological Exposition for Upbuilding and Awakening*. Translated by Howard V. Hong and Edna H. Hong. Princeton: Princeton University Press, 1980.

Kilgallen, John J. "The Plan of the Nomikos." *New Testament Studies* 42 (1996): 615–19.

Kimball, Charles A. *Jesus' Exposition of the Old Testament in Luke's Gospel*. Sheffield: JSOT Press, 1994.

Kinnamon, Liz. "United States v. Scott Daniel Warren." *The New Inquiry* (blog), June 27, 2019. https://thenewinquiry.com/united-states-v-scott-daniel-warren/.

Lambelet, Kyle BT. ¡Presente! Nonviolent Politics and the Resurrection of the Dead. Washington, DC: Georgetown University Press, 2019.

Lear, Jonathan. Radical Hope: Ethics in the Face of Cultural Devastation. Cambridge: Harvard University Press, 2006.

Lebacqz, Karen. Justice in an Unjust World. Minneapolis: Fortress Press, 1987.

Lee, Keekok. The Positivist Science of Law. Brookfield: Avebury, 1989.

Liebermann, Roseanne. "Justice, Righteousness, and the Davidic Dispute in Jeremiah and Ezekiel." Vetus Testamentum 73, no. 1 (2022): 62–81. https://doi.org/https://doi.org/10.1163/15685330-bja10091.

Lindsey, Matthew J. "The Perpetual 'Invasion': Past as Prologue in Constitutional Immigration Law." Roger Williams University Law Review 23 (2018): 369–92.

Lindsey, Matthew J. "Immigration as Invasion: Sovereignty, Security, and the Origins of the Federal Immigration Power." Immigration and Nationality Review 31 (2010): 591–648.

Livius, Titus. History of Rome. Vol. 1. 14 vols. Livy in Fourteen Volumes. Cambridge: Harvard University Press, 1976.

Lloyd, Vincent. "For What Are Whites to Hope." Political Theology 17 (2016): 161–81.

Løgstrup, Knud Ejlers. The Ethical Demand. Notre Dame: University of Notre Dame Press, 1997.

Longenecker, Bruce. "The Story of the Samaritan and the Innkeeper (Luke 10:30–35): A Study in Character Rehabilitation." Biblical Interpretation 17 (2009): 422–47.

Machado, Daisy L. "Borderlife and the Religious Imagination." In Religion and Politics in America's Borderlands, edited by Sarah Azaransky, 79–96. Lanham: Lexington Books, 2013.

Machado, Daisy L., Bryan S. Turner, and Trygve Wyller. "Traces of a Theo-Borderland." In Borderland Religion: Ambiguous Practices of Difference, Hope, and Beyond, edited by Daisy L. Machado, Bryan S. Turner, and Trygve Wyller. Religion, Resistance, Hospitalities. New York: Routledge, 2018.

Markovits, Daniel. A Modern Legal Ethics: Adversary Advocacy in a Democratic Age. Princeton: Princeton University Press, 2008.

Martinez-Beltrán, Sergio. "Biden's New Executive Order Denies Asylum Claims to Most Migrants Crossing the Border Unlawfully." NPR, June 4, 2024, sec. National. https://www.npr.org/2024/06/04/nx-s1-4991917/biden-executive-order-asylum-migration-border.

Mbembe, Achille. Necropolitics. Translated by Libby Meintjes. Durham: Duke University Press, 2019.

Mein, Andrew. Ezekiel and the Ethics of Exile. New York: Oxford University Press, 2001.

Meissner, Doris. "Border Patrol Strategic Plan: 1994 and Beyond." Washington, DC: United States Border Patrol, 1994.

Meissner, Doris, Donald M. Kerwin, Muzaffar Chishti, and Claire Bergeron. "Immigration Enforcement in the United States: The Rise of a Formidable Machinery." Washington, DC: Migration Policy Institute, 2013.

Miller, Amanda C. *Rumors of Resistance: Status Reversals and Hidden Transcripts in the Gospel of Luke*. Minneapolis: Fortress Press, 2014.

Mitchell, David Forrest. "Ezekiel's Presentation of Divine Sovereignty and Human Responsibility." *The Reformed Theological Review* 76, no. 2 (2017): 73–100.

Moxnes, Halvor. "Kingdom Takes Place: Transformations of Place and Power in the Kingdom of God in the Gospel of Luke." In *Social Scientific Models for Interpreting the Bible: Essays by the Context Group in Honor of Bruce J. Malina*, edited by John J. Pilch, 176–209. Boston: Brill, 2001.

Müntzer, Thomas. *Sermon to the Princes*. New York: Verso, 2010.

Murillo v. Musegades, Supplement 809 407 (Western District of Texas 1992).

National Park Service. "Sonoran Desert Network Ecosystems,." Sonoran Desert Inventory & Monitoring Network. Accessed July 10, 2021. https://nps.gov/im/sodn/ecosystems.htm.

Neudecker, Reinhold. "And You Shall Love Your Neighbor as Yourself - I Am the Lord" (Lev 19,18) in Jewish Interpretation." *Biblica* 73, no. 4 (1992): 496–517. https://www.jstor.org/stable/42611285.

Nevins, Joseph. *Operation Gatekeeper and Beyond: The War on "Illegals" and the Remaking of the U.S.-Mexico Boundary*. New York: Routledge, 2010.

Niebuhr, H Richard. "On the Grace of Doing Nothing." In *The Christian Century Reader: Representative Articles, Editorials, and Poems Selected from More than Fifty Years of The Christian Century*, by Harold E Fey and Margaret Frakes. New York: Association Press, 1962.

Niebuhr, H Richard. "The Only Way into the Kingdom of God." In *The Christian Century: Representative Articles, Editorials, and Poems Selected from More than Fifty Years of The Christian Century*, 228–30. New York: Association Press, 1962.

Niebuhr, Reinhold. *The Irony of American History*. Chicago: University of Chicago Press, 2008.

Niebuhr, Reinhold. "Must We Do Nothing?" In *The Christian Century: Representative Articles, Editorials, and Poems Selected from More than Fifty Years of The Christian Century*, 222–27. New York: Association Press, 1962.

Niebuhr, Reinhold. *Faith and History: A Comparison of Christian and Modern Views of History*. New York: Charles Scribner's Sons, 1949.

Niebuhr, Reinhold. *The Nature and Destiny of Man: A Christian Interpretation*. Vol. I. II vols. London: Nisbet & Co LTD, 1941.

Niebuhr, Reinhold. *Moral Man and Immoral Society: A Study in Ethics and Politics*. New York: Charles Scribner and Sons, 1936.

No More Deaths. "A Culture of Cruelty: Abuse and Impunity in Short-Term US Border Patrol Custody," 2011. https://nomoredeaths.org/wp-content/uploads/2014/10/CultureOfCruelty-full.compressed.pdf.

No More Deaths, and La Coalición de Derechos Humanos. "The Disappeared Report." Accessed November 30, 2023. http://www.thedisappearedreport.org/.

No More Deaths, and La Coalición de Derechos Humanos. "Disappeared: The Consequences of Chase & Scatter in the Wilderness." Tucson: No More Deaths & La Coalición de Derechos Humanos, 2021. http://www.thedisappearedreport.org/reports.html.

No More Deaths, and La Coalición de Derechos Humanos. "Left to Die: Border Patrol, Search and Rescue, & the Crisis of Disappearance." Tucson: No More Deaths and La Coalición de Derechos Humanos, 2021. http://www.thedisappearedreport.org/.

Nolland, John, and Bruce Manning Metzger. *Luke 9:21 - 18:34*. Edited by David A. Hubbard and Glenn W. Barker. Nachdr. Word Biblical Commentary / [General Ed.: Bruce M. Metzger; David A. Hubbard; Glenn W. Barker. Old Testament Ed.: John D. W. Watts. New Testament Ed.: Ralph P. Martin], Vol. 35,B. Nashville: Nelson, 2008.

Odell, Margaret S. *Ezekiel*. Vol. 16. Smyth & Helwys Bible Commentary. Macon: Smyth & Helwys Publishing, 2005.

O'Donovan, Oliver. *The Ways of Judgment*. Grand Rapids: Eerdmans Publishing Co, 2008.

"Office of Public Affairs | Attorney General Jeff Sessions Announces the Department of Justice's Renewed Commitment to Criminal Immigration Enforcement | United States Department of Justice," April 11, 2017. https://www.justice.gov/opa/pr/attorney-general-jeff-sessions-announces-department-justice-s-renewed-commitment-criminal.

Olyan, Saul M. "'We Are Utterly Cut Off': Some Possible Nuances in Ezek 37:11." *The Catholic Biblical Quarterly* 65 (2003): 43–51.

O'Sullivan, John. "Annexation." *United States Magazine and Democratic Review* 17 (1845): 5–10.

O'Sullivan, John L. "The Great Nation of Futurity." *The United States Democratic Review* 6 (1839): 426–30.

O'Sullivan, John L. "Introduction." *United States Magazine and Democratic Review* 1 (1837): 1–15.

Ovid. *Fasti*. Translated by James George Frazer. New York: G.P. Putnam's Sons, 1931.

Oztaskin, Murat. "'USA v Scott' and the Fight to Prove That Humanitarian Aid Is Not a Crime." *The New Yorker*, July 8, 2020. https://www.newyorker.com/culture/the-new-yorker-documentary/usa-v-scott-and-the-fight-to-prove-that-humanitarian-aid-is-not-a-crime.

Paipais, Vassilios. "Overcoming 'Gnosticism'? Realism as Politial Theology." *Cambridge Review of International Affairs* 29, no. 4 (January 2015): 1603–23.

Pepper, Stephen. "Lawyers' Ethics in the Gap Between Law and Justice." *South Texas Law Review* 40 (1999): 181–207.

Pew Research Center. "What's Happening at the US–Mexico Border in 7 Charts." Accessed July 25, 2023. https://www.pewresearch.org/short-reads/2021/11/09/whats-happening-at-the-u-s-mexico-border-in-7-charts/.

Pfisterer Darr, Kathryn. "The Book of Ezekiel." In *New Interpreters Bible Commentary*, 6:1073–1107. Nashville: Abingdon Press, 1994.

Powery, Emerson. "Under the Gaze of the Empire: Who Is My Neighbor?" *Interpretation* 62 (2008): 134–44.

Proctor, Mark A. "'Who Is My Neighbor?': Recontextualizing Luke's Good Samaritan (Luke 10:25–37)." *Journal of Biblical Literature* 138 (2019): 203–19.

Pummer, Reinhold. *The Samaritans in Flavius Josephus*. Tübingen: Mohr Siebeck, 2009.

Rael, Ronald. *Borderwall as Architecture: A Manifesto for the US–Mexico Boundary*. Oakland: University of California Press, 2017.

Rajendra, Tisha. Justice as Responsibility: Migration, History, and Ethics. Film, December 2, 2021. https://youtu.be/hY-ud1ZXxrI?feature=shared.

Rajendra, Tisha. *Migrants and Citizens: Justice and Responsibility in the Ethics of Migration*. Grand Rapids: William B. Eerdmans Publishing Company, 2017.

Rajendra, Tisha. "The Rational Agent or the Relational Agent: Moving from Freedom to Justice in Migration Systems Ethics." *Ethical Theory and Moral Practice* 18 (2015): 355–69.

Rancière, Jacques. *Dissensus*. Translated by Steven Corcoran. New York: Continuum, 2010.

Rancière, Jacques. *The Politics of Aesthetics: The Distribution of the Sensible*. Translated by Gabriel Rockhill. New York: Continuum, 2004.

Rancière, Jacques. "Ten Theses on Politics." *Theory & Event* 5, no. 3 (2001). https://doi.org/https://doi.org/10.1353/tae.2001.0028.

Rauschenbusch, Walter. *A Theology for the Social Gospel*. Louisville: Westminster John Knox Press, 1945.

Rawls, John. *The Law of Peoples*. Cambridge: Harvard University Press, 1997.

Rawls, John. *Political Liberalism*. New York: Columbia University Press, 1996.

Regan, Margaret. "Tales From the Outskirts: Amado." Tucson Weekly. Accessed October 24, 2023. https://www.tucsonweekly.com/tucson/washed-into-the-land/Content?oid=2096094.

Reinhardt, Karoline. "No Migration in a Realistic Utopia? Rawls' The Law of Peoples and the Topic of Migration." Lucian Blaga University, Sibiu, Romania, 2012.

Renz, Thomas. "Ezekiel and the Ethics of Exile by Andrew Mein." *Journal of Theological Studies* 54 (2003): 180–82.

Rice, Daniel. "Reinhold Niebuhr and Hans Morgenthau: A Friendship with Contrasting Shades of Realism." *Journal of American Studies* 42, no. 2 (2008): 255–91.

Robson, James E. "Forgotten Dimensions of Holiness." *Horizons in Biblical Theology* 33 (2011): 121–46.

Rose, Gillian. *Judaism and Modernity: Philosophical Essays*. New York: Verso, 2017.

Rowe, C. Kavin. *World Upside Down: Reading Acts in the Graeco-Roman Age*. New York: Oxford University Press, 2009.

Saito, Taylor. "The Enduring Effect of the Chinese Exclusion Cases: The 'Plenary Power' Justification for Ongoing Human Rights Abuses." *Asian Law Journal* 10 (2003): 13–36.

Sanchez, Ray, Nicole Chavez, and Priscilla Alvarez. "On a Texas Road Called 'the Mouth of the Wolf,' a Semitruck Packed with Migrants Was Abandoned in the Sweltering Heat." CNN, June 29, 2022. https://www.cnn.com/2022/06/29/us/san-antonio-migrant-truck-deaths/index.html.

Schmiedel, Ulrich. "The Theopolitics of the Migrant: Toward a Coalitional and Comparative Political Theology." In *Christianity and the Law of Migration*, by Kristin Heyer, Raj Nadella, and Silas W. Allard, 212–29. New York: Routledge, 2022.

Schmiedel, Ulrich. "Mourning the Un-Mournable? Political Theology Between Refugees and Religion." *Political Theology* 18, no. 7 (October 3, 2017): 612–27. https://doi.org/10.1080/1462317X.2017.1291399.

Schmiedel, Ulrich, and Rose Cuison Villazor. "'No More Deaths': Religious Liberty as a Defense for Providing Sanctuary for Immigrants." In *Christianity and the Law of Migration*, edited by Silas Allard, Kristin Heyer, and Raj Nadella, 251–75. New York: Routledge, 2021.

Schmitt, Carl. *The Concept of the Political*. Chicago: The University of Chicago Press, 2007.

Sheridan, Thomas E., and Randall H. McGuire. *The Border and Its Bodies: The Embodiment of Risk along the US–México Line*. Tucson: University of Arizona Press, 2022.

Simpson, Brad. "Self-Determination and Decolonization." In *The Oxford Handbook of the Ends of Empire*, edited by Martin Thomas and Andrew S. Thompson, 417–30. New York: Oxford University Press, 2018.

Smith, Ted A. "The Mark of Cain: Sovereign Negation and the Politics of God." *Modern Theology* 36 (2020): 56–73.

Snyder, Susanna. "Walking Wounds, Washing Feet: Pedetic Textures of a Theo-Ethical Response to Migration." *Studies in Christian Ethics* 32, no. 1 (2019): 3–19.

Snyder, Susanna. "The Art of Wounded Hope: Forced Migration, Prophecy, and Aesth/Ethics." *Political Theology* 19, no. 6 (2018): 497–516. https://doi.org/10.1080/14623 17X.2018.1503450.

Snyder, Susanna. "'La Mano Zurda with a Heart in Its Palm': Mystical Activism as a Response to the Trauma of Immigration Detention." In *Post-Traumatic Public Theology*, edited by Shelly Rambo and Stephanie N. Arel, 217–40. New York: Palgrave Macmillan, 2016.

Snyder, Susanna. *Asylum-Seeking, Migration and Church*. Burlington: Ashgate, 2012.

Sontag, Susan. *Regarding the Pain of Others*. New York: Farrar, Straus, and Giroux, 2003.

Sostaita, Barbara. "Making Crosses, Crossing Borders: The Performance of Mourning, the Power of Ghosts, and the Politics of Countermemory in the U.S.-Mexico Borderlands," August 18, 2016. https://mavcor.yale.edu/conversations/mediations/making-crosses-crossing-borders-performance-mourning-power-ghosts-and.

Southern Border Communities Coalition. "Fatal Encounters with CBP Since 2010." SouthernBorder.org, December 22, 2020. https://www.southernborder.org/deaths_by_border_patrol.

Sprinkle, Preston. "Law and Life: Leviticus 18.5 and the Literary Framework of Ezekiel." *Journal for the Study of the Old Testament* 31, no. 3 (2007): 275–93. https://doi.org/10.1177/0309089207076358.

Strahan, Joshua Marshall. "Jesus Teaches Theological Interpretation of the Law: Reading the Good Samaritan in Its Literary Context." *Journal of Theological Interpretation* 10 (2010): 71–86.

Sullivan, Eileen, and Colbi Edmonds. "Biden, the Border, and Why a New Wall Is Going Up." *The New York Times*, October 6, 2023, sec. U.S. https://www.nytimes.com/2023/10/06/us/border-wall-biden.html.

Svenungsson, Jayne. "Law and Liberation: Critical Notes on Agamben's Political Messianism." *European Judaism* 50, no. 1 (2017): 68–77.

Svenungsson, Jayne. *Divining History: Prophetism, Messianism, and the Divining of the Spirit*. Translated by Steven Donovan. New York: Berghahn, 2016.

Taubes, Jacob. *The Political Theology of Paul*. Translated by Dana Hollander. Cultural Memory in the Present. Stanford: Stanford University Press, 2004.

Taylor, Charles. *A Secular Age*. Cambridge: The Belknap Press of Harvard University, 2007.

The White House. "FACT SHEET: President Biden Announces New Actions to Secure the Border." The White House, June 4, 2024. https://www.whitehouse.gov/briefing-room/statements-releases/2024/06/04/fact-sheet-president-biden-announces-new-actions-to-secure-the-border/.

Thomas Aquinas, and Alfred J. Freddoso. *Treatise on Law: The Complete Text*. South Bend, Ind: St. Augustine's Press, 2009.

Time. "Humanitarian Scott Warren Found Not Guilty After Retrial for Helping Migrants at Mexican Border," November 21, 2019. https://time.com/5732485/scott-warren-trial-not-guilty/.

Turner, Victor. "Frame, Flow, and Reflection: Ritual and Drama as Public Liminality." *Japanese Journal of Religious Studies* 6, no. 4 (1979): 465–99. https://doi.org/https://doi.org/10.18874/jjrs.6.4.

Ulibarri, Kristy E. *Visible Borders: Living Death in Latinx Narratives*. Austin: University of Texas Press, 2022.

United States Border Patrol. "United States Border Patrol Fiscal Year Staffing Statistics." Washington, DC: United States Border Patrol, 2020.

United States v. De Jesus Batres, 410 F.3e 154 (5th Circuit 2005).

United States v. Rubio-Gonzalez, 674 F.2d 1067 (5th Circuit 1982).

Urrea, Luis Alberto. *The Devil's Highway: A True Story.* Boston: Little Brown, 2004.

US Customs and Border Protection. "CBP Use of Force Policy." Washington, DC: US Customs and Border Protections, January 2021. https://www.cbp.gov/sites/default/files/assets/documents/2021-Jul/cbp-use-of-force-policy_4500-002A.pdf.

Valle del Sol Inc. v. Whiting, 732 F.3d 1006 (9th Circuit 2013).

Vollmer, Bastian A. "Border: Meanings, Practices and Fields in Academia, Politics, and Public Domains." In *Contested Concepts in Migration Studies*, edited by Ricard Zapata-Barrero, Dirk Jacobs, and Riva Kastoryano, 12–30. New York: Routledge, 2021.

Walton, Steve. "The State They Were in: Luke's View of the Roman Empire." In *Rome in the Bible and the Early Church*, edited by Peter Oaks, 1–41. Grand Rapids: Baker Academic, 2002.

Walzer, Michael. *Spheres of Justice: A Defense of Pluralism and Equality.* New York: Basic Books, 1983.

Warren, Scott D. "Across Papaguería: Copper, Conservation, and Boundary Security in the Arizona-Mexico Borderlands." Arizona State University, May 2015.

Weitz, Eric D. "Self-Determination: How a German Enlightenment Idea Became the Slogan of National Liberation and a Human Right." *American Historical Review* 120 (April 2015): 462–96.

Wharton, William H. "Address of the Honorable Wm H. Wharton, Texas Comissioner." Masonic Hall, New York, April 26, 1836.

White, James Boyd. *The Legal Imagination.* Chicago: The University of Chicago Press, 1985.

Wilbanks, Dana W. *Re-Creating America: The Ethics of US Immigration Policy in a Christian Perspective.* Nashville: Abingdon Press, 1996.

Wilsey, John D. "'Our Country Is Destined to Be the Great Nation of Futurity': John L. O'Sullivan's Manifest Destiny and Christian Nationalism, 1837–1846." *Religions* 68 (2017).

Wilson, Woodrow. "Historical Documents - Office of the Historian." Accessed May 26, 2024. https://history.state.gov/historicaldocuments/frus1918Supp01v01/d59.

Wilson, Woodrow. "President Woodrow Wilson's 14 Points (1918)." National Archives, September 21, 2021. https://www.archives.gov/milestone-documents/president-woodrow-wilsons-14-points.

Yamazaki-Ransom, Kazuhiko. *The Roman Empire in Luke's Narrative.* New York: T&T Clark, 2010.

Index

www.ingramcontent.com/pod-product-compliance
Lightning Source LLC
Chambersburg PA
CBHW071412290326
41932CB00047B/2813